AU PAIR

ZB – To my grandmother
DM – To our au pairs (well, most of them)

AU PAIR

ZUZANA BÚRIKOVÁ AND DANIEL MILLER

polity

First published in 2010 by Polity Press

Polity Press
65 Bridge Street
Cambridge CB2 1UR, UK

Polity Press
350 Main Street
Malden, MA 02148, USA

ISBN-13: 978-0-7456-5011-1
ISBN-13: 978-0-7456-5012-8 (pb)

A catalogue record for this book is available from the British Library.

Typeset in 10.5 on 12 pt Sabon
by Servis Filmsetting Ltd, Stockport, Cheshire
Printed and bound by MPG Books Group, UK

The publisher has used its best endeavours to ensure that the URLs for external websites referred to in this book are correct and active at the time of going to press. However, the publisher has no responsibility for the websites and can make no guarantee that a site will remain live or that the content is or will remain appropriate.

Every effort has been made to trace all copyright holders, but if any have been inadvertently overlooked the publisher will be pleased to include any necessary credits in any subsequent reprint or edition.

For further information on Polity, visit our website: www.politybooks.com

CONTENTS

ACKNOWLEDGEMENTS

We cannot name our informants individually, either au pairs or host families, because that would breach our agreement with them to preserve anonymity. We hope this will not be taken in any way as a sign of our ingratitude. We are both hugely grateful to everyone who provided us with their time and their own insights. The generosity of the au pairs to Zuzana was remarkable. For her, this was never just an experience of collecting information. As in the true sense of participant observation, these are basically the stories of the friends with whom she spent a year, many of whom gave her unqualified trust and companionship. They may not agree with everything we have to say, but we hope that our mutual efforts will lead to better understanding and justice in the institution of the au pair.

We are also very grateful to the Leverhulme Foundation, which provided the essential funding of the project. Zuzana would like to express her gratitude to IWM in Vienna, where she prepared the project as a junior visiting fellow. Grant VEGA 1/0632/08 (*Sociologická a antropologická analýza spotreby produktov a voľnočasových aktivít na Slovensku*) enabled Zuzana to spend a month writing with Danny in London. Since completing fieldwork, she has been employed at the Institute of Ethnology at the Slovak Academy of Sciences and later also in the anthropology section of the Department of Sociology at the Faculty of Social Sciences at Masaryk University in Brno. She worked on this manuscript while employed at these institutions.

We are very indebted to the following people, who provided us with thoughtful comments on sections of the manuscript: Miloslav Bahna, Ivana Bajič-Hajdukovič, Danijela Djuršič, Martin Fotta, Nicky Gregson, Jan Grill, Ľubica Herzánová, Jana Levická, Deirdre

Mckay, Anna Pertierra, Ira Price, Michal Šípoš, Helena Tužinská and anonymous readers from Polity Press. This book was also fed by numerous discussions with colleagues and friends, including Bridget Anderson, Rosie Cox, Mirina Fornayová, Radovan Haluzík and Lenka Nahodilová.

Zuzana would like to thank to Ján Gregor, Jozef Gryga, Milka Pribišová, Helena Tužinská and Elena Želibabková for their friendship and trust during the project. Her sister, Petra Slamová, made her stay in London much more pleasant than it would have been otherwise. She is especially grateful to her granny and to her partner, Peter Sekerák, for all their love, support and encouragement during the years of writing. Without them it would have been much more difficult if not impossible to finish the book. Danny is particuarly indebted to his own family, to his wife, Rickie, and also to his children, Rachel and David, who, in retrospect, now appear as the subjects of his own early participant observation work on this institution. Finally we should like to thank John Thompson and Polity Press for their help and guidance through the process of publication.

PROLOGUE

This is a book about what it is like to be an au pair in a Western European city – not just working for a family, but the whole experience of deciding to become an au pair, seeing oneself as an au pair, and its longer-term consequences. It is based upon spending a year hanging out with au pairs and conducting an ethnography, the standard methodology used by anthropologists. We undertook this work because, as with most forms of domestic labour, we suspected that most people tend to take this institution for granted. They may use au pairs when they need to, but are somewhat embarrassed by their presence and even by the existence of the relationship involved. Yet we would hope that most of us would actually want to have some better sense of what the consequences of such an arrangement are for the people who make this journey and work in the somewhat strange situation of living with a family but not actually being part of that family.

For an academic book this work is quite unusual in containing almost no academic references within the main body of the text. So we are hoping that much of it is a good read, uncluttered with constant external referencing. Nevertheless we certainly also intend it to be viewed as an academic contribution, based on scholarship, original analysis and insight. To achieve this we have tried to experiment with several styles of writing, combining individual stories with more analytical chapters.

There was a second reason why we have left our engagement with the academic literature to an appendix and to differentiate our study from the mainstream academic research on domestic labour. That literature is concerned primarily to reveal the exploitation and inequality found in this form of work, and it is thereby directed to domestic workers largely in their capacity as labourers. In this book, by contrast, our primary commitment to au pairs has been that of ethnographers. Au pairs may be concerned more about relationships with boyfriends or with London than with their host families. Many of the topics that we explore have to do with intimate issues of embarrassment, humiliation, mutual misunderstanding, and uncertainties that are not formally aspects of labour.

One of the strengths of an ethnographic approach is that it provides material to humanize its subjects – to treat them as just ordinary people, with their own foibles and imperfections, and not only as victims or perpetrators of a process. We do examine issues of exploitation, power and prejudice. But we could certainly imagine positions being reversed – how, given the opportunity, the au pairs would have behaved much like their hosts. There was racism, stereotyping and opportunism in exploiting the other on both sides. This is why we are also concerned in our concluding chapters to analyse the institution itself and see how it is often institutional structures that have fostered rather than prevented such exploitation.

In contrast to most forms of domestic labour studied by academics, the institution of the au pair did not arise out of the international division of labour or from a servant culture. It started from a more egalitarian tradition by which German and English middle-class families sent young women to spend time with French and Swiss families, largely to improve their French. This was a much more reciprocal sense of engagement that followed from exchanges of schoolchildren between families, and is mainly a reflection of the dominance of language. The official model is of a pseudo-family arrangement in which the au pair is supposed to be incorporated within the household more as a member than as a labourer.

We restricted ourselves to the study of Slovak au pairs in the London region. Slovaks may well be one of the largest groups of au pairs in London relative to population size. Our research took place at a time when the typical au pair was starting to come from locations such as Slovakia, Turkey or Croatia rather than from Paris or Stockholm and employers were beginning to extend from the first and second zones of the London underground to zones 5 and 6. We were concerned to investigate the degree to which this represented a change in the institution. Au pairs are now coming with different motivations, while families may not see Slovaks within the same egalitarian framework as they do Scandinavians. Our fieldwork also took place shortly after the time when Slovakia joined the EU. This meant that one of the main reasons people might choose to become an au pair

2

– to gain a visa to visit the UK – was no longer valid. Despite this, au pairing seems to have retained its central role for young Slovak women coming to London.

The project consisted of working with fifty au pairs, who, because they sometimes changed families, represented eighty-six host families. Zuzana recorded interviews with all fifty au pairs. But the primary methodology of anthropology consists of participant observation, which seeks the broadest possible engagement with every aspect of the lives of the people whom the anthropologist seeks to understand. In addition, we both work within a particular subdiscipline called material culture studies. So, as well as talking with au pairs and observing their lives, we paid particular attention to details of how exactly they decorate their rooms within the family house and their attitude to things such as cleaning materials, food and clothing.

Zuzana is herself a Slovak, from a region in which it was becoming increasingly common for young women to become au pairs. As an ethnographer she spent nearly every day of her year in London in the direct company of au pairs. Although she was very careful to ensure that the au pairs were aware that she was there in her capacity as academic researcher, generally this hardly constrained the development of friendship and companionship. In many ways these were ideal conditions for participant observation. Most of the au pairs spent the day in isolation looking after children and cleaning houses. Not surprisingly, they welcomed the presence of a fellow Slovak who could also assist in these tasks. Zuzana's study often developed into more general friendships in which she shared a wide variety of experiences and confidences.

Danny, by contrast, comes from a North London, middle-class Jewish milieu, the typical background for a household employing au pairs, and had himself employed sixteen au pairs from a range of different countries in raising his own children. He was well placed, then, to carry out a small complementary research project on those who employed au pairs. In some cases he worked with the same families that Zuzana was seeing from the other side and in others he used his own networks. Although there was a considerable imbalance in the time spent in fieldwork, in every other respect this is an entirely joint project. As well as working with host families, Zuzana introduced Danny to many of the au pairs and the places they frequented. The whole book has been written collaboratively, with each aspect of the material being discussed, much of it while sitting side by side at a computer, supplemented by rewriting exchanged through e-mails between London and Bratislava.

3

All the names that appear in the text are fictitious, and other minor changes have been made in order to ensure that we kept the promise made to all informants, to respect their anonymity. The same name always designates the same person. All descriptions are taken from actual observation or interviews, unless we specify otherwise. But in the interests of anonymity some details are switched between different persons. The chapter that is written as a day in the life of one au pair is built from many different days, and involves several au pairs. All participants were informed by us of our status as researchers who were intending to publish this material under conditions of anonymity.

Each chapter of this book is written in a different style. Chapter 1 consists simply of the story of four individuals, with a brief, more generalized conclusion, while chapter 2 is a more conventionally academic discussion based on material culture analysis of the relationship seen through rooms, cleaning and food. Chapter 3 uses a different genre – a day in the life – describing the work of an au pair, but this is followed by the completely different interpretation of the same relationship by a host mother.

Chapter 4 tackles one of the most difficult aspects of the encounter, which is that of racism, as seen on both sides of this relationship. The next two chapters move out of the house and examine the leisure activities of the au pairs and their relationship with men. Again we flow between more literary methods for conveying the stories of the place and individuals to more generalized academic descriptions. By chapter 7, however, we feel ready to move to a more academic analysis of the time spent in London, using the model of a *rite de passage*. This leads to the conclusion, where we felt we needed to take responsibility for making our own recommendations as to how to improve the current situation – recommendations that we believe would help curb the tendencies towards exploitation which we have uncovered, and thereby help families as well as au pairs. Finally the appendix provides both a brief immersion of our particular study within the larger comparative study of domestic labour and an effective reading list for those who want to learn more about these kinds of relationships.

WHY NOT?

Barbora

As with several other major decisions in her life, Barbora's decision to become an au pair was made while sitting in a shed surrounded by a circle of appreciative pigs. Actually people also appreciate Barbora, who is often seen as the life and soul of social gatherings, radiating warmth from smiles that arise from genuine generosity rather than any desire to be liked. A friend described her as looking like a small bird, though with disproportionally large attentive eyes and a contagious laugh. She is effervescent, though not particularly pretty, and her sparkle is balanced by the feeling of solid stability that speaks to her village background and seems to put people at their ease. Despite this, for Barbora herself, the only place that seemed completely calm and free of the stress that somehow attaches itself to all relationships with people was in her retreat at the pigsty. Pigs also seemed to sense that she is a village girl who has grown up knowing their ways, and were entirely at ease in her company. Yet it was her close relationship with pigs that ironically had become one of the reasons why she now had to escape from stress by becoming an au pair.

Barbora's detailed observations of pigs had led from an impoverished village upbringing to being within a few weeks of completing a PhD on critical factors in pigs relating body weight to reproduction. This was the reason she had visited this particular sty in southern Slovakia nearly every day for the last three years. But today (in early June 2004) she discovered for the third time that the department had failed to purchase the software required for her to complete her analysis. This failure had brought to the surface a truth she had tried to suppress for a very long time – that actually the potential career that would have followed, had she been able to complete this work, had far more to do with her mother's ambition than her own.

The decision was not entirely of the moment. A week earlier, when she was already well aware that the departmental news might not be good, Barbora had been sitting with the pigs and calculating. While there were many things at that point in her life she did not want, her fantasies for the future all seemed to be focused around one thing, giving these pigs a proper home. Admittedly, in this farmstead of the future there was probably an adoring husband and many happy children, but they all seemed to come naturally as accoutrements to accommodation that after three years' research she knew would be absolutely perfect for the pigs. But this vision would cost money. The only way she could think of to raise the capital and at the same time to escape the combined stress of parents and academic frustration was to plan for a year as an au pair. Who knows, maybe this might be followed by an internship at an ecological pig farm she had read about somewhere in the British countryside. Perhaps the reason why in this vision of her future the pigs were in the foreground and a husband in the background was because she had also recently broken up with her boyfriend, who, in contrast, seemed quite clear about his academic ambitions – a single-mindedness that, she had felt, would very likely be to the detriment of whoever turned out to be his partner.

It wasn't really that becoming an au pair was such a positive choice; it was just that it formed in her head as something a bit more concrete when everything else was hazy. Barbora simply had no clear idea of what to do, and every other thought about the future would soon become crowded out by caveats and fears. If you were not sure about the direction of your career or education, where the next man might come from, or indeed whether there would be a next man, then the one great advantage of becoming an au pair was that it was bound to be temporary. It was less a decision and more a putting off of all other decisions. Surely if it seemed impossible to decide at this precise moment what to do next, in a year's time things might have straightened themselves out somewhat. Barbora might then have a better idea of who she was, and that seemed to be a precondition for knowing what she should become. It was impossible to take an equivalent childcare or cleaning job in the capital, Bratislava. Given her education, her parents would have been mortified, and the pay was dreadful. So becoming an au pair seemed more like a gap year. Furthermore, improving her English was the ideal skill to develop when she didn't know what she wanted to do, because it was likely to be useful in practically anything – even watching the television.

Cleaning a house was work, but of a kind that Barbora found relatively relaxing and quite compatible with having lots of time for contemplation about life and her future. Finally there was something about going to Britain. Just looking at a map and knowing there was that little bit of sea between her and her mother seemed an integral part of the plan. So why not go to Britain?

A week later Barbora was in such a state of frustration that she was desperate to get back to the pigsty. Whatever the failures and absurdities of the outside world, there was some kind of rational world and order that she associated with her pigs. By comparison this au pair business, after just one week, seemed like an absolute farce. For somebody who was used to the patient accumulation of knowledge, it seemed that arranging au pair work was based on the principle that nobody should know anything about anybody. This had started from the moment she had decided to prepare her documentation for e-mailing to the agency. Her friends had been horrified that she had intended an accurate self-portrayal, and she was even more horrified at the idea that she would have to falsify photographs and references. After reading six instruction guides from agencies, all of which stressed she had to supply a photo of herself smiling in the company of children, she remarked she had no children, but surely they could make do with one of dozens of photos that she did have of herself surrounded by happy pigs.

What really made this into a farce was the phone call she had just received from the agency. Having decided on this radical change in direction, she had thought she might as well make a complete break and, rather than stay with the countryside and farm life, opt for London itself. So in filling out her form she ignored all the options and boxes provided for her to state her preferences except those that specified that she did not want to be in the countryside and she did not want to be placed with a single father. Unbelievably, the agency just telephoned to report with great delight they had already found her a new home in England which turned out to be with a single father living in a village. As she remarked, it was just as well she had not specified that she did not want to be with a black man, because otherwise he undoubtedly would have been black as well. When she had remonstrated with the woman in the agency, the woman had said there were actually no homes in any town in England that were likely to be available, and that all families living in towns would want someone who could drive. She continued that Barbora was lucky to be working with such an efficient agency and, furthermore, that she herself had worked as an au pair with a single man and found it a fantastic experience. In response Barbora had gently inquired as to just how many single men this woman thought would make for a perfect stay. The irony seemed to be lost on the agency woman. But by this point Barbora somehow felt that she had already surrendered herself to fate and that actually the agency's insistence that, if she did not take up this placement, there was no telling when the next possibility would emerge might actually be the case. The final, but to her essential, communication was the agency's assurance (though how did they know?) that the man in question had a girlfriend.

Barbora was becoming irritated by the medium as well as the message. Typically, the agency was Czech owned, and the woman had that condescending Czech manner which meant the only thing you could be sure of was that she was acting in her own interest – happy to talk and talk, but not actually to give out any of the information you really needed. Yes, this was typical of Czechs, Barbora thought. Finally the agency woman had told her that this single man would phone her on Tuesday afternoon. Barbora made sure she was ready and persuaded a friend with a better command of English to wait with her in order to avoid any misunderstandings. Her English was good enough to read agricultural literature, but the prospect of a phone call with a 'native speaker' whose language was likely to be very different from the usual Slovak high-school standard seemed quite daunting.

On the other hand, she didn't want to go quite as far as her friend Edita a couple of years before. Edita didn't speak a word of English and had persuaded a friend to do all the talking for her. This risked a rather less than favourable outcome when she arrived and the family found out the truth. For a while they thought she might be some kind of criminal; they even phoned the police. But, surprisingly perhaps, once they got over their shock and annoyance they actually paid for her to take a summer language course in Cambridge, and after two months of intensive English tuition she returned to them and stayed for a year. The family was happy they had ended up with an educated au pair, and dined out with many friends on the story of their domestic version of *My Fair Lady* crossed with *Cyrano de Bergerac*. In Barbora's case, however, although she stayed in that afternoon and all evening too, the man did not call. He phoned three days later, when Barbora did not expect it and there was no supportive friend present. She felt she had somehow coped by restricting her responses largely to yes and no. Somehow the two understood each other – at least she hoped so. They ended up having three phone discussions, in each case with the man phoning at some time other than what they had previously agreed. What also seemed entirely unfair to Barbora was that he had all the information he could possibly want about her: her address, mobile phone number and e-mail, plus a smiling picture (with children), while the agency provided her with no information at all about him. Finally he did let her have his e-mail, as it was easier to write than to speak, but even a week before leaving home she still did not have the address where she was supposed to go to in England, so she couldn't even tell her relatives and friends where she would be. Typically the agency couldn't see anything at all untoward about this asymmetry of information.

Having accepted the placement, Barbora had a month to get ready. Actually, even a month was ridiculous: it would be be her first big farewell, as she had never previously left her family and friends for any extended period. Her circle of friends and relatives was enormous, and it was clear that most of her goodbyes would be hurried and entirely out of character for a proper farewell. There were some people she was never going to get round to see at all. It was an odd feeling that the first time she truly appreciated how many people cared for her was the very moment when she was preparing to leave them. But the thoughts about who she was leaving behind were soon crowded out by having to think about what she had to take with her. One soon became as personal as the other. First came her Bible. Barbora was a staunch member of the minority Protestant faith, and her friend Robo presented her with a special travel edition of the New Testament which he had inscribed with the words 'Never forget your friends, your language and your God'. Her supervisor presented her with a blue furry pig and a ruler on behalf of the department. Her best friend took her on one side and pointed to a bear. 'Since time began', she said, 'no Slovak au pair ever left home without a teddy bear. You might think you are no longer a teenager, but, believe me, a teddy bear lying on your bed is a wonderful talisman against bad sex.' Barbora had replied, 'Don't worry, you know I only like cute things, whether it is a teddy bear or a man.'

Having exhausted herself between goodbyes and shopping and the sheer stress of a very awkward parting from her parents, Barbora was just about ready. Then, two days before leaving, she heard from the agency that this single man, whom she had never seen, had had a heart attack and, as he had apparently put it, was now rather more in need of a nurse than an au pair. Oddly enough, the agency that had assured her that alternatives were so few and far between immediately came up with what sounded like an ideal family in a place called Beddlingham somewhere on the outskirts of London. There were two children, perfectly positioned as neither toddlers nor teenagers. Barbora also felt positive on hearing that the family were religious Jews, which for her translated directly as the people of the Bible and therefore a family with whom she would feel comfortable, in a proper moral setting. This was particularly welcome as her friend Irena had just been teasing her with news of another au pair who had reported back that a man in the house where she lived sometimes walked around naked.

Having never flown before and feeling she didn't want too many new experiences at once, Barbora decided to travel by bus. One advantage was that this went through her local town of Liptovský Hrádok, so she wouldn't have to go first to the capital. Another advantage was that coaches had no weight limits for luggage. Before Slovakia joined the EU in 2004 the only option had been more expensive planes from Vienna, not the low-cost flights now available from Bratislava. At that time the au pair agencies used to run their own coaches, and before Christmas some eighty express buses a day would leave London for Slovakia to take au pairs home for the holidays. Barbora's cousin Júlia had told her many stories about these buses, for example the driver who used to start with a 'Welcome, ladies and gentlemen' in English, followed by a 'Hi girls' in Czech, interspersing the journey with supposedly funny short poems taken from TV cartoons. When they approached the English Channel he would tell them that, if any of them were stopped at the border because their invitation letters weren't in order, he would drop them off at the 24-hour supermarket in Calais and pick them up on the way back next day. In the event Barbora rather regretted her choice, since for half the journey she was sitting next to a Hungarian who spoke hardly any Slovak, and who, because she was instantly homesick, cried almost the entire way. Almost as disconcerting was the first question she was asked by the woman at the immigration desk, having sleepily trundled all her luggage there from the coach, which was whether she was coming to England to find a boyfriend. On the other hand, the coach provided a great opportunity to swap telephone numbers with others, and this gave her a sense of security in case no one was at all friendly when she arrived. In the event she never used any of these phone contacts.

Barbora regretted the bus even more when she arrived, as agreed with the Cowans, her new prospective family, at Victoria station. She had no idea that there could be Victoria stations for the train, the underground and, more problematically, something called the Green Line, which is where she was dropped, and which was different from the main coach station. Eventually someone who had better English than herself had phoned on her behalf and managed to explain the mix-up. Still, she was rather more flustered than she had planned when she first met Mr Cowan. The rest of that day seemed like a blur. Everything seemed to happen so fast. Mr Cowan seemed to want to tell her about all the places they were passing, but there were so many of them and he spoke so fast that she simply couldn't take any of it in. The English she had learnt at school now seemed suited to another world, and certainly another accent from this new English she would have to get used to in London.

When Barbora arrived at the Cowans' home it was even more confusing. On the face of it the family seemed very friendly and warm and welcoming. They were constantly smiling at her, loved the presents she had brought, and were enthusiastically showing her not only her own room, but all sorts of things that the children had done to their own room or made at school. But at the same time it seemed very different from her own home. They all seemed somehow distracted, as though they were simultaneously showing her around but also busy with other things and somehow only half paying attention to her. It wasn't the simple patient sitting around together that she would have expected. There wasn't anything particularly lacking, it just seemed to happen too quickly to give her time to acclimatize either to the house or to the people. It was only later that Barbora came to appreciate that, since people usually have au pairs precisely to save rather than to spend time, they expect them to learn things quickly. In particular she found quite bewildering the number of rules she was told concerning what she should and should not do in the kitchen of religious Jews: different colour drying-up cloths for meat and for milk, something to do with blood in eggs – did eggs have blood? – and a real concern about foods that she must absolutely never bring into the house. At this point she was quite glad that the only little pig she had brought with her was blue and furry.

Jarmila

Jarmila managed to combine being an au pair with always looking like she was about to be discovered as a model. With her high-heel boots, skin-tight jeans, bare waist, shiny top, glossy lipstick, and long hair dyed blonde, she just seemed to be waiting to fulfil what was evidently her true vocation. She was one of those au pairs for whom the almost imperceptible differences between six pairs of Nike trainers were of profound significance – not least because none of them were

11

Adidas. The association with sports was for her an aspect of style rather than action. Jarmila did in fact go to the gym quite regularly, but only because it was an excellent excuse to get away from her boredom with the house and housework. Furthermore, the bar there sold her favourite chocolate, and there was something about men who had just finished working out.

While choosing to be an au pair was by now a very well-established option for women of Jarmila's age, it was still considered as one of several alternative forms of migration. One of Jarmila's married sisters, for example, had opted for another scheme which was becoming established through a local agency – that of looking after elderly Austrians. This was based on alternating 24-hour availability for two weeks, followed by two weeks' leisure time back home with her husband and child. It also involved her retired mother looking after the child while she was away. Jarmila's other married sister had tried to establish an ordinary home life but found it increasingly hard to earn a living, and more particularly to save the money required to construct their own family house. So she had eventually gone abroad to work as a nurse, while her husband had left to become a migrant labourer.

Jarmila, with her sense of style and fashion, simply knew that London was the place she had to come to, whatever the opportunities now becoming available in Austria. It wasn't just that English rather than German was going to be increasingly important to her future. It was equally that English was also associated with fashion, her favourite pop music, Lady Di, MTV, and really good accessories. In contrast, what was Germany associated with? Elderly tourists coming for walks in Slovak holiday resorts? Soviet films about Nazis and partisans? Techno? The Austrian countryside was fine for postcards, but London had an air of being in the middle of something and being a capital of cool. Basically Austria sounded disciplined and boring, while London just had to be fun. Jarmila already had heard many stories about clubbing in central London from former au pairs. The most famous Slovak groups played in London: one could really meet everybody from the whole world there. In her imagination of the world, there was this huge circle and right at its centre was London, the ultimate source of clubs and hedonism. Perhaps even more important for Jarmila personally was that she had been present when other au pairs returned with several suitcases of clothes. In Slovakia she could buy either the cheap Chinese imports or the expensive clothes in town, but London seemed to have everything that was in between, genuinely stylish but affordable.

12

It wasn't at all that Jarmila couldn't imagine an entirely different life, a stable life near her own small city of Gelnica. The problem was that she could imagine that only too well. This went to the heart of her decision to become an au pair. The future, far from looking uncertain, looked only too obvious. Both sides to her future, career and partner, were completely assured. Her parents had provided everything that was necessary for her career. Their garage, attached to their house, was converted into a small hair salon when Jarmila had finished her vocational training and she was already practising her craft there. However, the money she would earn as an au pair would certainly allow her to refurbish the room and make it into the kind of glamorous hairdressing suite that she had set her heart on.

Equally secure was her primary relationship. Jarmila didn't need to speculate about potential partners, because there was already Pavol, who was not just a boyfriend, but seemed like the kind of man with whom, for the first time in her life, she could imagine spending the rest of her life. He was twenty-seven, six years older than she was, and he wanted to marry her. And now she realized she wanted this too. So if Jarmila stayed she could so easily imagine that in the next year or two she would marry Pavol; they would settle down, build a house, have children and she would develop her hairdressing and grow her own potatoes in the yard. She liked this image of herself. It seemed comforting and proper. She really wanted to have children with Pavol, which seemed the natural culmination of what she thought of as her life of love, full of romance and companionship. Of course she also wanted a house, just as large as the one her sister's husband was building for his family. But for all these desires there was a caveat: just not immediately. There was something frightening in this stability, as if she was settling down because there was nothing else to do or, worse still, because she was not capable of doing anything else. She was still only twenty-one, and she could already foresee a life of hairdressing, domestic work, the annual cycle of Christmas and birthdays, without anything dramatic ever having happened to her. This future was only bearable if she could show herself and others that actually she was one of those who had the initiative to get out and see something of the world, even if this would be a lesson in dangers and suffering that would make her finally appreciate the peace and stability of her own city.

It was not that she did not love her boyfriend – the act of returning to him after seeing life elsewhere and his waiting for her would be real proof of their love. She had no doubts about this and actually thought it might secure their love. She had the image in her mind of her cousin, who had married her first boyfriend when she was eighteen, having not seen anything of world, and after a few years had discovered that they were both bored and that the relationship was not satisfying, but had not wanted to divorce because they already had two small children. This was the exact scenario Jarmila wanted to avoid, and felt could be avoided, if she and Pavol settled down only after they had had a life.

Pavol did not object when she told him she would leave – anyway, he had lost his job recently, and had, at least for a while, to take up migrant work himself, in the Czech Republic. So they would not have been much together even if she stayed in Slovakia. What was critical was that the engagement should take place before she left, which it did. It was not that Jarmila felt it needed any formal occasion to make clear to the world that going away to London posed no threat to their relationship – or so she thought. But the gesture was still one of reassurance, and she knew there was one matter in which such reassurance was required. This was the matter of sex. Pavol had always been uneasy about the asymmetry in their looks. Like many men he felt ambivalent about the fact that he had ended up with a woman better looking than he was. He saw Jarmila, the young model and hairdresser, as consummately beautiful, compared to which he felt at best ordinary. He therefore felt no difficulty in assuring her about his own sexual fidelity during her absence, but he couldn't but feel uneasy about hers. He knew she was virtuous and loved him and intended to be faithful, but he also thought about the pressures that would be there, just in that state of distance and freedom, and these tormented him. So the engagement was the one thing Jarmila could do to reassure him of her depth of commitment.

Her relationship to Pavol also highlighted another reason Jarmila had for going away, which was to find a female equivalent to the life stages of men. In a way men already had their *rite de passage*. Their time out from living with their parents and proving themselves came through military service, which in many cases these days was followed by a period of migrant labour. For Jarmila, being an au pair was simply the female equivalent (although such military service had ended when Slovakia entered NATO in March 2004). It was also a time when a woman could demonstrate her strength of character, initiative and independence, to show that she could cope with life outside of the village, to be one of those people who had been to the place that elderly villagers called, with some awe, 'the world'. Between their days and Jarmila's time things had changed radically. Even if you lived in a village or, in the case of Jarmila, a small town, you couldn't escape the sense that your life was also tied to the changes in the whole world through the things you used: fashions, technology, media, politics. Everything was happening at a rate dictated by the much faster pace of that world. So you had to find a way of forging some sort of link beyond the village so that, when later on you retreated to this home, you had built up the knowledge and connections that meant you could still somehow keep up, not become a member of just another generation of peasants who are made to feel like living museum pieces. Jarmila never really talked about these things in such terms. When asked, she would always give the economic grounds for migration, the money for the salon. But she argued in a way that people could tell that money was more an excuse for something deeper and more fundamental, the idea that one day she could settle down in Gelnica, because she would be doing so from knowledge and strength and not from ignorance and weakness.

As with many in her situation, there was remarkably little relationship between the contemplation about why Jarmila might become an au pair and her actual decision to become one. The decision itself had been almost entirely spontaneous. It arose from a conversation with a schoolfriend, Aneta, who was working as an au pair. When she came back to Slovakia, it wasn't just to see her family: typically an au pair would also see her dentist or go for any other medical checkups required, but naturally she would also go to see her hairdresser, which in this case was Jarmila. Jarmila confessed that not only was she really bored, but that she simply couldn't see a future that wasn't going to be just as boring. She admitted she had contemplated going abroad, but it all sounded complicated and difficult and she couldn't see where to begin. Aneta simply took her in hand and suggested that it was all really quite simple. As it happened, Aneta was arranging a family for a friend of hers who was supposed to travel to the UK that week, but the friend was now deciding not to go. Was Jarmila interested? Jarmila was, and within a week she found herself in London. This so often seemed to be the way of it: years of thinking about the possibility of being an au pair, but an actual decision that came about in a few hours, from a quite unexpected source.

Having said that, Jarmila managed to cram an awful lot into the few days of frantic preparation for moving to London. There were the obvious issues of farewells and dealing with her family, but the practical issues almost all revolved around shopping. While Jarmila had never actually bought anything specifically to travel, she could not dream of being in London without the clothes that would be good enough to wear in the city. In the past she had only visited neighbouring countries, mostly in order to shop there. Paying for such things was also not straightforward, since as a 21-year-old in her first job she hadn't yet saved much, and the airfare alone was going to take half of her monthly salary. In the end she borrowed the airfare from her parents and used her own savings for the shopping. Most of this was dictated by necessity – a suitable suitcase or two, cosmetics and better clothes of the kind she might not be able to afford at first in London.

Then there was the question of what to pack. Ultimately the priorities for her suitcase turned out to be her favourite denim jeans and some sports clothes already intended as suitable for cleaning work or leisure rather than actual sports. Since she already had a boyfriend she didn't take much by way of clothes for going out, just some disco wear. Aneta gave her a list of things that she wished she had had when she had first arrived. Among these was the suggestion of 'a presentable nightdress', which her own host family had specified in their 'house rules' for au pairs. Actually the idea was pre-empted by Jarmila's grandmother, who had decided to give her, as a suitable going-away present, a nightdress that was pretty and blue and certainly presentable, but was also entirely asexual – buttoned to the neck and with trousers. This was fine by Jarmila, who carefully vetted all her clothes in order to avoid any potential misunderstandings with her new family. She had two stuffed animals: her old friend Maco, her teddy bear from childhood, and her new friend Čertík, given her by Pavol, a wonderful scarlet and black fluffy devil with the most mischievous-looking smile that made her laugh whenever she glanced at it. Her godmother had given her a new cosmetics bag. She had her dictionary and what turned out to be a quite appalling textbook, *English for Autodidacts*. Her mother had given her a guardian angel in porcelain with gold-tipped wings, a skipping rope to keep fit, and an embroidery set to work on in winter evenings. Through these gifts people were not only connected to Jarmila but helped influence the way she would be communicated to her hosts in London. Finally Jarmila had her gifts for the Whitley family: a piece of lace handiwork from a tourist shop, a book of photos of the Tatras – the Slovak mountains popular for hiking and skiing – and a box of chocolates for the children.

Jarmila also brought with her a photo album of *memories*, the very first picture of which had precisely that focus, on the gleaming white church with its terracotta roof backed by green meadows that conformed to her host family's idealized image of her upbringing in a small rural town. The next picture complemented this, being a snapshot taken from the birthday party for her eighty-year-old

16

grandmother, with the large extended family surrounding and sup-porting her. The third showed Jarmila as a three-year-old, when her hair really was blonde, wearing one of those thick cotton babysuits so characteristic of the early 1980s socialist designs, embroidered by her mother with a patchwork heart, both her adoring parents and her two older sisters around her. These three pictures framed her memory of home and were followed by a dozen images ranging from her Young Christians' group visit to Poland to one with friends clearly having fun at the party that marked the end of high school. Finally there were the glamour shots showing her in her best clothes and most painstakingly applied make-up: one from this same end-of-school party, in a long dress with lacy décolletage and with her hair carefully permed (she also took with her the video of that party) and a second that had actually been taken one day when she was at work as a hairdresser, but dressed and posed in a manner that clearly showed her other ambition to be discovered as a model.

This was typical of Jarmila and the way she needed to control her appearance in public. Everything was planned around her making the best possible first impression on her new family. But, in all this concen-tration on herself, somehow she hadn't really faced up to the reality of the change. This meant that the actual trip itself came as something of a shock, leading to a single, really quite dramatic, moment of transition – landing at Stansted airport. Suddenly being there was no longer about her relation to things and people in Slovakia. Her deci-sion had landed her in a place that at one glance was revealed to be astonishingly different. The terminal building seemed huge, and she wasn't sure which type of transport she was supposed to take next. It was the first time she had flown in a plane and she was still nervous from the experience. Suddenly it seemed as though everyone from now on was going to be a complete stranger, and she felt herself to be out of place in a way she couldn't have imagined. Suddenly she real-ized there was no granny to turn to or friends to confide in, that with this new freedom came all sorts of new responsibilities she would have to bear as an adult rather than as a child. She burst into tears and cried constantly through the bureaucratic process of entry. As a result, Jarmila with her perfect hair and her perfect make-up had had to go to the airport toilet and wash her smeared face and meet her family with a look she regarded as plain, unadorned and completely out of character, perhaps fulfilling her new sense that she was really now a stranger even to herself. She had made her choice, but now saw that she hadn't consciously chosen much of what she was about to become.

Darinka

It was only in a pub in Beddlingham that Darinka finally discovered what she was. Sean looked into her eyes drunkenly. At this point he would usually recite Irish poetry, but on this occasion he talked to her directly: 'You're a pixie.' A pixie, he explained, is a relative of an elf:

> You do not actually come from Slovakia at all. Slovak au pairs all wear loads of make-up and are trying to look glamorous. You have no make-up at all and are entirely a creature of nature. You are simply a waif. As soon as men see you they desire you and they want you to stay. But they merely have to blink and you have disappeared, leaving them bewitched and abandoned. In fact you never sit still. Everything about you is continually moving.

This would be her most poetic encounter. Most of the Irish and, indeed, other men she met when they were drunk were more interested in her knickers than her spiritual self. Typically things would begin: 'And where are you from?' or 'Hey, I just had a bet with my friend over there that you're South American', and when Darinka would reply otherwise they would insist on asking, 'Are you sure you're not South American?' or 'Maybe you're a bit South American.' So Sean was very different. He had seen that what he called her elfin quality had a certain flirtatious side to it, but that was not the point at all. It was more that she was in constant movement, in the here and now and somehow simultaneously somewhere else.

On that occasion Darinka thought that Sean's poetry had more to do with his intoxicated state than any profound truth about her, but on reflection it was simply a rather more appealing variant of what many of her friends said about her. It is not something Sean would have noticed, but Darinka was someone whose horror of being fixed was evident even in her clothes. She could never be clothed in just one style. The trainers accompanied the gypsy skirt; the plain top was set off by the romantic hat. Actually that was perhaps the one constant feature. The way she wore her hat at an angle, leaving one winking eye exposed, was inevitably romantic. But it looked very natural on her, not foolish or affected, more beguiling.

For all her strategies intended to ensure a rather more planned life, Darinka had to admit that sometimes the things that had really made her change direction were completely unplanned and spontaneous, and quite often had to do with men. Her home town, Trenčín, was two hours' journey from Bratislava, and it was natural that after she finished school she would spend some time exploring the capital. It was in Bratislava that she met Mustapha, whose mixed parentage, Arab and Slovak, had immediately attracted her. Although they had never developed any proper or formal relationship, somehow Mustapha's journey to London for a study trip had sown the seeds of her own idea that she really ought to go to London too. In her imagination, once she and Mustapha were in London together the relationship would surely blossom. In retrospect she was amazed at the way she must have thought of London then as a place where two Slovaks would naturally keep meeting each other, as if they were in some overgrown village. Although they did meet occasionally, they never did form a relationship. But then Darinka often felt that, even if they are good for nothing else, men could always be a good reason for moving on to somewhere new. Even though she did not stay with Mustapha, he had moved her to London.

One reason things did not work out with Mustapha was that, soon after she had arrived in London, Darinka actually met up with Jano, who was working as a male au pair. Meeting Jano was something of a surprise because it simply hadn't occurred to her that there were now quite a few male Slovak au pairs in London. She was even more surprised that he would be working in this capacity at the age of thirty; she thought she was getting on, even at twenty-four. Age was not the only way he was in advance of her. She was already thinking about using her income to fund some further education in London, but he was way beyond her. As he told the story, he had come to London after starting his PhD in politics in Bratislava, but soon realized that he just wouldn't progress without better English. While the new generation of post-socialist students had a better grounding in the language, much of his training had been during socialism, which gave him fluency in Russian and German but not English. He was also one of the few au pairs who loved travelling for its own sake. What he hadn't told Darinka was that he also came because his then girlfriend had already moved to London as an au pair, and he really missed her.

The problem was that Jano's girlfriend was in North London and his first job was in South London, with a single mother who, as he later came to realize, really exploited him, giving him more and more jobs, which ranged from taking out tree roots to painting the whole house. Fortunately after a few months his girlfriend found him a family he got on with much better. As he put it, they were educated and so they could really communicate. They paid him a decent amount as an au pair, more than his income while at university, which was one of the reasons he had left his PhD. Then their gardener left and he told them he could easily undertake that work; after all, he had been doing this for nothing in his last au pair job. But this family felt morally bound to pay him the rate of the previous gardener, which was much higher than his au pair wage. Then the lady who did the cleaning and ironing died, and these were two more tasks he was entirely capable of undertaking. Unfortunately the family didn't also need a chauffeur! But in any case, given the free board and lodging, he realized that £160 a week was a pretty good income. Indeed, to his surprise, after six months the family gave him a further rise to indicate how happy they were with him. On this basis he calculated he would actually be able to afford to return to his PhD in politics – but not in Bratislava. He had just received an acceptance from the London School of Economics. The downside was that his girlfriend had left him, seeing that he was not going to return to Slovakia at any time in the next few years. On the other hand this represented an opportunity for Darinka, who thought that, compared with Mustapha, Jano had some very concrete qualities that appealed to her immensely. In him she could see the kind of future to which she herself aspired. It was important to her because she soon recognized that, while many au pairs said they wanted to do some kind of study, she knew either they never would or they would take some obscure, probably quite unproductive course at an institution local people would have known to avoid. But Jano represented her way of differentiating herself from those au pairs and establishing her identification with those who really were quite serious about their intentions to study.

It wasn't just a potential future she recognized; it was just as much an actual past. They were both *panelák* children. Almost all Slovak au pairs either come from a rather small *panelák* flat or a rather big family house. Actually a third of all Slovak families today live in a *panelák*. As is the case with so much Soviet-inspired modernism, these basically concrete high-rise blocks that constituted the suburbs of most towns and cities are quite remarkably ugly from the outside. But on the inside they could actually be made quite pretty with extensive refurbishment, almost as though people were trying systematically to repudiate the exterior by their devotion to personalizing the interior, replete with pictures and flowers and sometime huge house plants that dominated a whole room. Although cheaply constructed, the flats were hygienic and had strict controls over central heating. Darinka was really shocked when she saw some of the accommodation in London, since for her certain basic standards and conditions were seen as things everyone should be able to take for granted.

Not everything was pretty on the inside of these blocks. One of the less attractive aspects of being *panelák* children in the era of late socialism was the high divorce rate compared to that among village families, and the problems that ensued. Like many children of the time, Darinka could remember when she used to have her house key strung on a ribbon around her neck, so that she could let herself back into the apartment after school. Her parents' divorce was not sudden, but took years of a gradually deteriorating relationship. This meant that they tended to remain focused on each other, and Darinka became something of a pawn in the intimate power politics within the home. She mostly took refuge with her friends who played outside. Contrary to the stereotypes of people she knew from rural areas, she recalled the street life of her childhood as very full, friendly and safe, even in these heavily built-up areas.

So when Darinka came to London she had two images of education. One was the ideal of more formal education that was closer to what she could see Jano might now achieve; for that being an au pair was only a source of income. But for Darinka there was another kind of education, for which being an au pair was probably the ideal means of obtaining the knowledge that she required. This was the knowledge of how to be a good parent. There were some things she knew her mother had simply got wrong. The order and discipline of her upbringing were right but should have been leavened with humour and at least some encouragement of the freedoms that give one the experience to cope with life. She used to say that parents should provide order and morality, but they should also help their children to grow wings. She was determined that, when she became a mother, she would know just how to achieve this aim.

The very anonymity of being an au pair, however, reinforced another way in which Darinka had become determined to repudiate the legacy of her parents. It added to her memory of a family that never seemed to see people as individuals. This may well have led her somewhat consciously to embark upon a strategy of making herself into this slightly quirky, even perhaps slightly eccentric, character that people saw today. She knew, for example, that her mother would find completely incomprehensible the fact that she had seven pairs of summer shoes and wore them all. So in the end perhaps it was her parents who, unbeknown to themselves, had prompted the birth of this pixie that so enchanted Sean.

So, having learnt from her mother a good deal about what not to do, Darinka was sure that being an au pair, in a position to observe closely the intimacy of other families, would tell her everything about parenting that was never discussed at school. This was not to be, however. At least in the first year she simply learnt that there was much more variety to getting things wrong than she would ever have guessed. As an au pair Darinka was fascinated by the different attitudes to childcare. English mothers were constantly talking about quality time and feeling guilty if they were not actually reading to or directly playing with their children. Yet in most cases it was pretty clear they really did mean quality time as opposed to quantity time, given that it occupied such a short part of the day. This intense but short period of parenting was supplemented by the children spending much longer periods with a stranger, typically a foreign girl with a limited command of the language and who, as Darinka was perfectly well aware, knew next to nothing about children and did not necessary care for them at all. So her repudiation of her parents had not been accompanied by any clear exposure to some better form of parenting.

Still Darinka could see a positive side. She always felt that this was the most interesting thing about other places. Normally you never get to know how other families look from the inside, either in your own country or when talking generally about those abroad. Being an au pair was a unique insight into the truths of family life, otherwise carefully hidden from view. Darinka's idea of a tourist trip to London was not about finding this thing called English culture in dead monuments (she has totally ignored them) but about discovering the nuances and intimacies of English home life. Most au pairs simply ended up knowing more than anyone could ever want to know about doing housework. For Darinka, the secret, and the way never to get bored, was that, once you have a good sense of what you can learn from one family, you just move on to another.

Actually this current stay was Darinka's postgraduate degree in au pairing. Slovak au pairs are perhaps unusual in the number of times which they return to Britain. She had already been in England for a year, during which she stayed with five different families. But she decided after a year at home that there was still lots more to learn. This decision was more complex than it might have appeared. Darinka at one level was using this experience in order not to have to face up to a basic problem. Back in Slovakia it had been clear to her that any job that was remotely satisfying required a university degree. But at the same time she could not see any prospect of either her parents or herself being able to fund her living expenses during such a degree. Although there were no tuition fees, there were no scholarships either, and it was impossible to work for long

22

enough to earn a living and study at the same time. Perhaps it was this inability to pursue a real university degree that led Darinka to persuade herself that au pairing was a kind of education. In any case it was also the only practical means to try and save money and then perhaps eventually start a college course in London. She had already picked a particular course: teaching English as a foreign language together with development studies, at the University of East London. Her ideal career included plenty of travel and genuine commitment to development. Perhaps teaching English as a foreign language in a school in the Middle East? Her first year in London had reinforced her impression from Mustapha about how attractive some Arab men could be.

Now on her second visit, Darinka felt sure that she had grown out of many of the limitations she associated with new au pairs. On this trip she would be in charge. The whole thing was planned ahead in three stages. As she said to a friend on her arrival:

> What I need right now is free accommodation, free food and free time. The second stage will be to find a position associated with a decent language school and a bearable, well-paying family. Finally, once I have finished with all the family stuff, I will be on to some other job. Then on the spot I will just tell them, 'Bye bye families', 'Bye bye children', and it will be 'welcome pastures new'.

She also felt that what she had learnt from her first trip could help her to think strategically in other ways. After an initial bout of glorious shopping for the cheap clothing that had also drawn her inexorably back to London, she was now carefully saving the money that she earned from her multiple cleaning and babysitting jobs – manageable, once she had located a family that needed her for relatively little time. But there was still that pixie in her. On this trip it had taken stints with eight families to get things right, and even now, although there was not much to complain about, she found herself getting restless.

Ivana

In most cases the actual stories of au pairs differ markedly from the stereotypical tales of Eastern Europeans looking for economic improvement based on circular migration. Nor is becoming an au pair some form of cultural tourism: most au pairs don't have the money to be effective cultural tourists even if they wanted. If there is one factor that dominates the reasons people become au pairs it is the one that tends to be ignored in the academic literature but is blindingly obvious if one reflects on why most people make other key decisions in their lives – that is, the state of their personal relationships. It is much more common that young women go abroad to escape from the consequences of breaking up with their boyfriends or in order to obtain a critical distance from their parents. Of course, such reasons for leaving might frequently be mixed up with the popular representations – such as 'There are no jobs here' or 'If I want to achieve something I have to go abroad.' Having said that, there are at least some au pairs for whom this is not true, who do fit the generalizations that reduce the personal to the categories of migrant labour. And one such au pair was Ivana. In her case there is no deep complexity that requires unravelling. The term 'why not?' can become just as superficial as it sounds.

Ivana had just finished high school, so-called girls' school, which is an average kind of general education not intended to prepare their students for college but for lower jobs in administration or business. Ivana lived with her parents and her eleven-year-old sister in a house in a large village on the outskirts of the city of Žilina in central Slovakia. After three months the employment office found her a job subsidized by the state as an assistant in a small company. She was horrified when she found out that, after paying for transport and the lunches she had during work days, she basically had nothing left from her salary. Not only could she not help her parents by sharing household expenses and at least pay something towards the rent, as she had hoped; it actually meant that her mother was continuing to give her pocket money so that she would not be totally broke.

Ivana felt guilty about this continued dependence, even though her parents never said anything to make her uncomfortable. She did not mind at all the fact that she was living with her parents, which was normal among unmarried Slovaks of her age; she had just assumed that, once she had finished her education, she could graduate from being an economically dependent child to become a more equal and supportive part of the household. But despite looking for other jobs she could not find anything. Her education was just not good enough. She couldn't hope to compete with those her age who had graduated from high schools with some specialization, such as secretarial qualifications. On the other hand she did not consider the option of manual labour, as she had qualifications equivalent to English A-levels. The jobs that remained open to her, such as being a waitress or shop assistant, were precisely those that were open to a mass of women in similar circumstances, and this made them very difficult to obtain. Some people were finding work though their parents' connections, but Ivana's father's employment did not come with the kinds of contacts that seemed to be necessary for getting such a job.

It was her mother's suggestion that Ivana might become an au pair. Her mother liked the idea of Ivana going out into the world. It was not that she wanted her to leave or that she saw her as a burden; she simply thought it would give her a different life and perhaps more opportunities. Ivana's mother had married soon after finishing high school and, while she was happy with her marriage and comfortable with her work and motherhood, she thought her daughters could do better. She herself had never travelled or had much choice over her employment. She had had her children too early to pursue any dreams that might take her far from her home base, and she was convinced that, through being an au pair, Ivana could become all that she had been unable to be.

Ivana had no difficulty sharing these views. A group of her high-school friends had already been to London to work as au pairs; five of them were actually staying in one neighbourhood. Although she heard that in London the money they were given was considered pocket money, Ivana realized that their monthly income was more than twice her full-time salary. If one took into account that further work could be taken on as an au pair for other families, then this sounded much more like the kind of income she was hoping for. So after a couple of weeks she thought: why not? She wrote an e-mail to a friend staying in Beddlingham, and her friend contacted the local agency on her behalf.

The only problem seemed to be her father, who was much less comfortable with the idea of Ivana becoming an au pair. He thought it was not safe. What kind of family would she be in? Would they treat her well? Also, he had a strong aversion to the idea that his girl might become a servant. He saw in au pairing a repetition of nineteenth-century history, when poor Slovak girls who could not make a living at home worked as servants in Budapest, Bratislava or Vienna. He felt some pride in the fact that his family had never been poor enough to be forced to work in service. Also there was some nationalism in this: Why should Slovak girls clean foreign houses? Was Ivana unhappy? Did she not like staying with her parents? He was perfectly able to feed his family; she did not have to go. So there were several weeks of discussion in the household, but after a while it was clear that Ivana's father was outnumbered by the two women and Ivana followed her high-school friends.

Ivana probably had more of an idea of where she was going than her host family, the Humphreys, had of where she was coming from. Their first impression was that Ivana was a descendent of Heidi come to seek new urban pastures. The photos she had sent in advance showed off her long flaxen hair and the view taken of the countryside around her village. The backdrop chosen for a family snapshot showed bright green meadows topped by copses of conifer and backed by mountains interlaced with seams of winter snow. Although the family would have used a less derogatory expression in her company, they were quite comfortable with the idea that Ivana came from peasant stock, which for them implied a background in bucolic villages and valleys that spoke of a hard-working self-sufficiency – people who made their own cheese with milk from their own cow. They imagined a genuine care and experience in looking after children and pets and a wanderlust that was derived from living in a sufficiently remote region that would be largely satisfied by the urban delights represented by Beddlingham, rather than central London.

The word 'peasant' conjures up certain elements of Ivana's background, some of which she would have been comfortable with, others not. Certainly her family had strong roots in this particular village, strengthened by a tradition of marrying within the community. And in the past most villagers would have been closely associated with working the land in small inherited plots. Her own family, as with most of those around her, remained impressively industrious in their growing and processing of much of the food they consumed. Although they no longer have access to farmland as such, they have a large yard and a small plot some distance away. The house is surrounded by intensive cultivation. The Humphreys might well have wondered at the large bed of poppies unless they had reflected on the considerable use of poppy seed in Eastern European cooking. Actually at least they knew what a poppy looked like. If truth be told, they couldn't even recognize the larger bed of potatoes, let alone the kohlrabi grown next to it.

They would have been impressed by the abundance of flowers. Although the Humphreys had just started learning how to make a few preserves from the fruit in their own garden, influenced by the latest cookery books, they could never have competed with Ivana's family, who seemed constantly to be engaged in the processing of fruit and dairy produce. In their home one could find everything from pickles and cheese to their own jars of beans and wild raspberries. Ivana's knitted jerseys and a couple of her dresses were made by her

26

mother, who had cultivated any means of making clothing that stood out from socialist homogeneity and had created a collection of pretty clothing, which was important given she had two daughters and limited financial resources. Ivana herself had so far inherited no such skills, or so she thought. The fact that she could change a zip or let out a skirt would prove rather more valuable than she anticipated.

Ivana slept in a room most of whose contents would also have fitted the image being prepared of her in Beddlingham. On the floor of her room was a style of woven carpet found throughout this region. Her aunt had made it from brightly coloured strips of cloth, several of which Ivana had helped shred from her no longer wearable clothes, which the aunt had then sewn into a cotton base. There was not just one image of the Virgin Mary but several, and the little collection of stuffed animals and framed embroideries she had also made spoke of her strong Catholic upbringing and domesticity. This was also a family where young children basked in the love and attention not only of their parents but of quite a few aunts and uncles, neighbours and friends. Ivana, in turn, had already begun her own process of identifying with the children whose photos she had received from Beddlingham, and couldn't think but that they would get on brilliantly.

As with many au pairs, Ivana had pretty much made her résumé fit with what she had been told was required by both the agency and others in her village who had previously worked as au pairs. For example, there had been no institution as formal as babysitting in her village; it was simply that she frequently cared for children of both relatives and neighbours. But in her résumé she had been told to call this babysitting. So while the claims she made were perfectly true it just wasn't something one would normally write about. Much of the content of her résumé was pretty much dictated by agreed formulas, such as 'loves sports and outdoor activities', and it included two faked reference letters translated by a university student who lived in the neighbourhood.

But if some of the new family's assumptions were well founded, stepping out of the frame of the carefully selected photographs she had sent them to see the wider context from which Ivana hailed would have revealed all sorts of unexpected juxtapositions that the family would have found surprising if not incomprehensible. For one thing, for people in Beddlingham the word 'village' meant not just a small settlement but one directly opposed to the heavy industry of urban conurbations. In Slovakia, however, much industry, even heavy industry, lies dotted around the countryside, often in villages

similar to Ivana's. Had she chosen to point her camera in the opposite direction to the fields, Ivana would have revealed at the heart
of her village an extensive Soviet-built factory that had produced
tractors. Before it had closed down with the end of socialism, this
had provided employment for almost all her own and several other
nearby villages. It was now occupied by a dozen small light industrial
firms supported by foreign, largely Korean, investment. Her parents'
industriousness related not only to their domestic labour but the fact
that her mother had to be up at 5 o'clock on weekdays in order to
sell goods to the workers before they started their day's labour in the
factory compound.

Near to the factory were those typical *paneláks* housing many of
the teenagers who had been to school with Ivana and were considered just as much part of the village as those who lived in their own
houses. The houses themselves would have been another source of
surprise. The Beddlingham model of the au pair exchange was of girls
from relatively small homes coming and being suitably impressed
by the extensive suburban accommodation of London. So even if
they were given the smallest room in the house it was assumed that
this would represent a step up from what the hosts imagined were
crowded rooms shared by several siblings. Actually most rural houses
in this area of central Slovakia are impressively large, with several
extensions, and most au pairs found on their arrival in London that
they were in fact migrating from larger to smaller homes. The rooms
they were allocated seemed, as one of Ivana's friends put it, more
like dormitory rooms compared to the bedrooms in which they had
grown up.

The closer the inspection, the more complex the image. Along with
the religious images and fluffy animals were CDs of rock music, and
DVDs ranging from *Dirty Dancing* to action films with Tom Cruise.
Open her wardrobe and one would be faced by a very different icon:
Christina Aguilera in the sort of pose that, as Ivana had once put it,
'anyone would want to fuck'. So some of Ivana's interest and character related to the long-term history of a peasant community, but she
was just as much a product of a very particular mixture of recently
elapsed socialism, Slovak nationalism and global hip-hop cosmopolitanism. For Ivana herself, these were all equally authentic and taken
for granted elements of her background.

Ivana was fond of her homeland and the possibilities of a newly
independent Slovakia which has struggled through the centuries to
survive the incursions of more powerful neighbours and now, for all
the failings of local politicians, seems to have a great deal to offer in

its new independence and participation in the forging of local identification. She was also aware that several of her older friends with very similar feelings left to become au pairs and did not return, but moved on to other occupations in London and in some cases settled with men from countries such as Morocco and Kosovo – men whom she considered were on the dark side if not black, something that seemed to her incomprehensible. It would have been fine if, like her distant cousin, they had hooked a genuine English man, when all his relatives came over for a fancy wedding in the village. But who would want to come home like Hela, who returned three years ago with a dark baby by some Middle Eastern man, who of course had left her as soon as he had had enough of her? Mind you, in the end Hela was happily married to a fellow villager.

So Ivana, Ivana's mother and the Humphreys all had their own ideas about what this process of becoming an au pair was all about. In the case of the Humphreys there would never be a reason to confront their image of Slovakia. They never travelled there. But in the case of Ivana, the grounds for coming to London were largely its economic muscle and her mother's thwarted life. So it was not some specific knowledge about London itself; it was much more a sense of 'why not?' What was there to keep her in Slovakia, given the lack of local opportunities? But in addition there was something else. Ivana was aware that, one by one, a whole group of her schoolfriends had already come over to London as au pairs. So the final attraction that tipped the scales in favour of leaving was that in one sense she wasn't really leaving at all. It was more that she was rejoining the friends she had already known. A couple of these friends were in Beddlingham, but the major reunion took place two weeks after her arrival. The local au pairs in Beddlingham took her down to the Czechoslovak monthly dance night at Camden Town Hall. It was ridiculous: first she spied Miša, the short sweet girl who occupied the desk behind her in class; then, as she might have guessed, Zdenka was dancing rather too close to some well-built man and, just as in class, there were Lenka and Vierka gossiping away with a drink in the corner. Ivana had gone abroad, but at this point she also felt as if she had just come home.

We can easily characterize the fifty au pairs we worked with in 2004 and 2005 in standard terms. They came to London for a period of six months to four years, usually through specialist au pair agencies. They were from eighteen to thirty-one years old. Only five of them were men. Approximately half came from rural and half from urban areas, though most of these towns have fewer than 50,000 inhabitants. Thirteen participating au pairs were university gradu-ates, of whom five had embarked on PhD studies. Others had just finished secondary education. More tended to be from working-class than from middle-class backgrounds. But in this introductory chapter we are concerned more to convey the fact that every au pair who comes from Slovakia to London represents a story. Their stories need to be borne in mind before the individuals are reduced down to the usual academic generalities about labour patterns and economic migration. This is not simply to humanize the people concerned, but because their stories, when examined in detail, lead to somewhat dif-ferent academic conclusions from those normally given, starting with the issue of why each person comes. It is not that such stories are entirely incompatible with more conventional accounts. Individuals decide to come often for personal reasons and sometimes even on a whim. But in aggregate there are still general trends. Economic aspects are important, such as the fact that an au pair in London at the time of our research could earn more in pocket money than a full-time wage in Slovakia. So too is the general feeling that there are fewer opportunities today in Slovakia and that London may repre-sent an opening up of possibilities. But both these factors have to be set against our evidence that the actual reason individuals decide to become au pairs is more often initially to do with their personal rela-tions. After perhaps breaking up with a boyfriend or needing to find distance from their parents, London seems to provide the requisite distance.

The stories also start to introduce the sense of being an au pair as a time in life that, like a gap year, is more a transition between two more established stages. This is something we will explore in much more detail towards the end of this book. But already one can see that deciding to become an au pair can be as much a deferment of decision-making as a decision – a point evident in giving this chapter its title. It can also be seen as a temporary solution to or an alternative way around personal problems, not just for those who leave but also for their friends and family who may participate in this decision. In practice, of course, as implied even by the four cases recounted here, there are actually many factors that combine together to account for this phenomenon, so that the deeper history of Slovak relations with Eastern and Western Europe become implicated in the specifics of a young woman's relations with her family and friends. Our conclusion is that neither these immediate and personal reasons nor the larger political and economic factors can be understood except in relation to each other.

Snippet

The following is taken from the introduction on the web page of the Student Agency, www.studentagency.cz/?SET_jazyk=slovak:

Every year most Czech and Slovak au pairs leave for Great Britain. Why do they choose Britain exactly? The au pair programme is so widespread that there is no problem getting a placement wherever they wish for. There are so many host families available that for sure we will choose the right one for you. The programme is so flexible that you can choose the length of your stay for yourself (anything from three months). The maximum length of stay is unlimited. And, last but not least, Great Britain is the country where you will learn the real, pure, so British English!

— 2 —

AN EMBARRASSING PRESENCE

The pseudo-family relationship

Au pairing combines paid domestic work undertaken by temporary migrants with an ideal of cultural exchange based on cohabitation. According to the *European Agreement on 'Au Pair' Placement* (Council of Europe 1969), the UK Border Agency's *Immigration Directorate Instructions* (2003) and the *Points Based System Tier 5 (Youth Mobility Scheme)* (Home Office 2009), au pairs are young foreigners who stay for up to two years with families in order to learn English and acquire a better knowledge of the country. They must live 'as part of a family' and receive food, accommodation and 'pocket money' (i.e. not a wage) in return for childcare and/or housework. During the time of our research (2004–5) the minimum pocket money was £55. Au pairs are not supposed to spend more than five hours per day helping families, with up to two additional evenings babysitting. They should have two rest days per week. In the United Kingdom they had to be between seventeen and twenty-seven years old (this was changed to between eighteen and thirty in November 2008), unmarried, without dependants, and originate from a specified group of largely European countries. Families are bound to treat au pairs as equal (*Immigration Directorate Instructions* 2003, chap. 4, section 1, paragraph 1) and as family members, a point stressed by au pair agencies, who often mediate this relationship. Equality is anchored in the very name of the institution, since *'au pair'* in French means on a par, or on equal terms As the legal conditions are defined only vaguely and there is no institutional control of particular arrangements, conditions and relationships depend on individuals. The result varies from conditions approximating a pseudo-family to those more like contract labour, and from generous provisions to (more commonly) exploitation, which betrays the intent of the regulations.

At the heart of this arrangement is the concept of a pseudo-family relationship. The au pair is separated out from normal forms of employment. The remuneration bears no relationship to any minimum wage, and neither family nor au pair pays taxes. Nor do au pairs have employee rights. All this is based on the assumption that they will be incorporated into the family (which seems to take a rather benign view of families as institutions). It is highly unlikely that many au pairs or host families have ever read these regulations. But almost everyone, on both sides, is fully aware of the pseudo-family as the idiom through which the relationship is described. The initial correspondence from the au pair almost invariably contains friendly pictures that portray her as a happy member of a household, and is reciprocated by a welcoming response designed to reassure her that this is really a lovely family to spend some time with.

In practice, however, most host families are quite ready to acknowledge that they choose an au pair, over other forms of child-care and house cleaning, largely because it is what they can afford. It is most commonly a means by which they can continue in full-time or part-time employment, providing more flexibility and control over childcare than childminding, while being cheaper than employing a nanny. In either case, the basis of the choice is finance and convenience. The children can remain within their own home; the parents do not have to pick them up at defined times. There is additional help with cleaning and often lower overall costs. The fact that families commonly stress that an au pair was preferable to a childminder because it didn't matter so much if one was late returning from work flatly contradicts the equally common claim that they respected the agreed hours of au pair work.

So the initial decision to have an au pair is very rarely going to be a positive choice based on some value or ideal, let alone that of the pseudo-family. It almost always emerges from a discussion of the problems that follow from some alternative form of childcare, generally quite open and pragmatic debates about cost, issues of privacy and the number of rooms available. The general assumption is that one would not have such a person living in one's own house if one didn't need to do so. Even if people end up feeling quite positive about the arrangement, the starting point is usually that it is the least bad option. This negative sentiment is compounded where a mother sees part-time or full-time work as a necessity, and the presence of the au pair reflects her lack of choice and options. Typically this arose when the reason for employing an au pair was that, following a divorce, a mother found herself house rich and money poor. Either she or others regarded her 'natural' place as being in the home, looking after her own children, but the divorce settlement left her having to go out to work.

There are variants on this theme. Some of the host families hire au pairs while the host mother remains at home, which then creates a position that is closer to the older tradition of domestic service. The situation is also different when the au pair is viewed more in relation to house cleaning than childcare. For example, a mother with older children can reason that having an au pair look after the house gives her more time to be with the children after work, whether or not that is actually how she uses that time. There are also mothers who always wanted to work full-time rather than staying at home to look after children, though they rarely escape at least some social censure for their unwillingness to view themselves as the natural primary childcarer. Not surprisingly, this censure can easily be deflected into a constant critique of the au pair, who can never do as good a job of looking after the children, or of cleaning the house, as the mother would have done if she had had the time. Most mothers therefore project onto the au pair at least some of the ambivalence in contemporary British society about a woman both having a career and being a mother.

Not only does the pseudo-family idiom bear no relation to the reason families employ au pairs, there may also be some specific resistance to this model. Having a live-in au pair runs contrary to a powerful English concern with domestic privacy. This is especially strong among working-class households, where traditionally not even neighbours would be invited within the private home, only kin. It also runs contrary to an upper-class upstairs/downstairs tradition of separate domestic service within a house large enough to accommodate such divisions. Therefore many host families try to limit their interaction with the au pair to a polite minimum. Our interviews revealed that most host families had hardly any knowledge of their au pair's background, their place of origin or their lives in London outside of the home.

By the same token, it should be evident from the last chapter that few au pairs ever decide to come to London specifically in order to experience this pseudo-family integration. Quite often they are coming to work as an au pair precisely because they have reasons for wanting to leave their own family, and the last thing they would want is to replace one set of problematic family relationships with another.

Being an au pair is partly a means to get away, and more positively a means to come to London, to spend some time in this exciting metropolitan environment that they have heard so much about. Slovaks are not coming to London because they particularly want to be cleaning anyone's house or looking after their children, although the latter is something for which they may feel they have a natural affinity. More importantly, they are aware that the cost of rented accommodation is astronomical, and being within a family sounds like a more secure environment than being on one's own. So in many respects the au pair's perspective is the mirror of that of the host family. Becoming an au pair is also the least bad option if your intention is to get away from Slovakia and spend some time in London.

Although neither side therefore really enters into this arrangement in order to experience a pseudo-family relationship, most au pairs clearly expect a degree of family-like integration. This is based on their prior experience of helping with domestic work within their parental households – a context of reciprocal care and acknowledgement. Some, by contrast, never expect or intend to establish family-like relationships within what they view largely as a transient situation. But once the au pair is actually living with a family, either side (or both sides) may start to be drawn to this idiom. Influential factors might include the area in which they are living, the age of the children, whether the au pair has a boyfriend, and the number of au pairs that the family has already had. As with so much of their experience, much depends on the chance factor as to whether a particular au pair and a particular family happen to share a similar perspective on the type of relationship it should be. They may both be entirely happy with a largely distant and cold relationship or they may both have a commitment to constructing a very close and warm relationship. The problems come when there is a marked discrepancy between their respective desires and expectations.

The ideal of a pseudo-family relationship may also have very different meanings for individuals. For some, the analogy is rather negative, because frankly the family represents a series of obligatory ties, dreaded visits and unwelcome duties. Perhaps the most common description used by host mothers came in their complaints that they now had yet one more irresponsible and moody teenager to look after, often claiming that this foreign teenager was less mature and more demanding than their own. Less common were more positive models. For example, a woman who had a sister ten years younger than herself saw the au pair as another younger sibling whom she valued.

One benign interpretation of these relationships was to see the au pair as occupying a very useful position mid-way between parents and children – old enough to be the parents' confidant in talking about the children and young enough to be the children's confidant in talking about the parents. Their ability to bridge and negotiate the often difficult relationship between children and parents meant they could make a major contribution to avoiding family conflict. In at least one case the presence of the au pair was seen as the primary reason why the parents had never had to contend with a stage of teenage rebellion. Au pairs may relish such a role, but more often find it highly problematic. They may see this as an example of the parents shunting difficult issues of authority and discipline onto them, such that, for example, they become the ones who have to make the children eat their vegetables. They feel this will inevitably lead to tense relationships between them and both children and parents.

There was constant ambiguity about what was implied by the use of this pseudo-family idiom. As one mother noted: 'The pretence is that they are members of the family, but the truth is they can hear your rows but they can't join in!' Host families could also feel insecure as to their responsibilities *in loco parentis* over the au pair. One mother was faced with such a dilemma when her au pair asked her if she could have a stud in her tongue. The only response the mother felt she could reasonably make was to ask what the au pair's own mother would have said. On the other hand, it can be the host family which decides to interfere in, for example, stopping the au pair from displaying such piercings or from smoking. The au pair may then regard this as an unwarranted presumption of parental-like authority. The relationship may take on a more pseudo-family form when au pairs look to mothers to sympathize with their difficult relationships with boyfriends. Au pairs differ in how much they talk and mothers in how much they listen, but at least in some cases this becomes an almost pseudo-parental role for the mothers. In one case it was a male au pair who often cried and become very emotional in discussing his girlfriends. These ambiguities shade into a less common, but sometimes prominent, idiom: the pseudo-friend relationship. Some more lonely or isolated parents felt personally rebuffed when it soon became clear that the au pair would much rather spend time with their own peers than with the host parent. A single mother became quite upset, since she initially established a close relationship with her au pair, and they would watch TV together and chat. Then the au pair found a boyfriend and wanted to spend her free time with him. One au pair left her family because of this pressure to be a friend. In another case the family was so upset at how little of her leisure time the au pair was spending at home that they packed her suitcase and put her out.

There can also be many misunderstandings about what is required of a pseudo-family relationship. One of the most common concerns gift-buying. Both sides could become quite upset if gifts were not bought when expected, especially when au pairs failed to buy birthday presents for the children they were looking after. This was taken by many English families as a kind of minimal unit of family identification, which they assumed would be obvious to the au pair. One au pair was immediately dismissed when she failed to buy such a present. Au pairs are often uncertain about what they should do, and worried that anything they can afford will look insufficient. One refused to buy gifts on the principle that this was a relationship of work and not of choice.

One of the most important factors determining families' treatment of au pairs was simply how many au pairs they happened to have employed. Almost all families would admit to treating their first and second au pair very differently from the tenth or fifteenth. Early au pairs were generally treated with far greater individual attention and concern and were much more likely to be viewed in pseudo-family terms. The host families showed concern that they were eating well and were keeping in touch with their own families back at home. They would also show more interest in the family, background and personality of the au pair. By contrast, the twelfth au pair was much more likely to experience a family that seemed essentially cold and indifferent and, after one day's initiation, to find herself left more or less to her own devices. Some au pairs are happy to reciprocate this lack of interest. In such cases the au pair often goes out within a few minutes of the mother returning from work, and the two in effect become shift workers, spending virtually no time together. In such cases the relationship becomes reduced to a reciprocal exploitation of mutual interest that pays no regard to the idiom of family. This is one of the main reasons why au pairs return with such a diversity of experiences.

The trajectory is not, however, always a simple movement from good treatment to bad, or from concern to indifference. Sometimes the arrangement benefited from the previous experience of the families. Some families had an effective routine of establishing their au pair with a good English school, registration at the doctor, and realistic expectations based on past employees. Some au pairs suggested that it could be quite difficult being the family's first au pair, since the hosts simply didn't know how to deal with this unprecedented relationship. But then there are also stories of the second or subsequent au pair feeling a bit like a character from Du Maurier's novel *Rebecca* – always living in the shadow of some previous, apparently perfect, au pair who could never be equalled. The family is always saying, 'But Martina did it this way' or 'Martina did it that way'.

More subtle, and perhaps more important, was the way in which the families learnt from the sheer variety of their previous au pairs. After a while both families who had had several au pairs and au pairs who had worked with several families might start to appreciate that the determining issue was not necessarily that the people concerned were good or bad, but rather the overall 'fit' between the expectations of each. An au pair who wanted more independence and distance from the family might not suit the position of being the first au pair of a family who expected a closer relationship. She might be happier with the greater autonomy of a typical late au pair role. Families who have experienced a diversity of au pairs may then make clear to each new au pair that they are actually quite comfortable with a broad range of potential relationships. By allowing the au pair to make clear their own preferences with respect to inclusion and autonomy, some of these latter stage relationships were the most successful that we encountered. Much of this fit was credited to the individuality of the au pairs and the families. One quite charming scenario was a household of two doctors. Despite their professions, they were both rather neglectful of their own health, while their au pair was training to be a gym instructor and was knowledgeable about aerobics and such like. As the family reported, the au pair soon realized that they neglected their own health. She therefore developed the habit of dragging the doctors out to go jogging in the early morning or for a session at the gym: 'She felt I should go for my blood pressure since I am not very health conscious.'

Ultimately, though, it is the pseudo-family idiom that becomes almost the principal form by which the au pairs come to feel exploited. The reason lies in the fundamental asymmetry of the relationship. It is the host family that determines when and whether the idiom will be used and which conversations will be couched in such terms. As a result, after a while, the au pairs come to feel that the manner in which these requests are made – every time the parents say they are going to be late for work and would Helena just stay on a little bit longer, every time they ask an au pair to cancel an evening engagement because little Tommy has a cold.– is clearly intended to ensure that they feel they are simply being asked to make the kind of sacrifice that one family member would expect of another. A labourer can expect overtime, but a family member just puts up with things for the sake of the family, without expectation of monetary reward. By contrast, on those occasions when the au pair wants to make a request from the family – an unexpected party, a visit from a friend – she is made to feel that she is breaking a semi-formal contract of employment between herself and the family. These are not isolated instances, but a constant refrain. Only one side of this equation has genuine control over the use made of the pseudo-family idiom. In the end, far more au pairs will curse the model of the pseudo-family than claim to have benefited from it. In many cases it is the same au pairs who have invested in the discourse of the pseudo-family who come to feel most betrayed by it.

Making room for the au pair

The pseudo-family is a discourse. It is something that is explicitly claimed about the institution of the au pair, and as such is partly responsible for the ambivalence that pervades many encounters between host families and au pairs. But to understand the wider experience we have to examine not only this discourse but also everyday actions. Often the anxieties of au pairs are clearest in their uncertainty about such trivial issues as clothes on the floor, food in the fridge and sitting in the living room. The initial premise for this claim to a pseudo-family relationship is that the au pair, unlike most paid employees, does in fact live with a family. So, if she is not a member of the family, then she is certainly a member of the household. This may explain why, almost inevitably, the key feeling that afflicts both the au pair and the family turns out to be mutual embarrassment – the embarrassment of strangers finding themselves sharing the private space of a home. It is not the separate upstairs–downstairs of traditional servant relationships, but, for the au pair, the experience of having a bedroom next to that of family members, and quite often sharing a bathroom too. The one possible refuge should be the au pair's own room. An approach from a material culture perspective to this room reveals why this doesn't turn out to be the case.

When it came to furnishing the au pair's room, Mr and Mrs Wakeford didn't have to think twice about it. Without any discussion they simply needed to agree a time when they could set off for IKEA. Once there, they again simply assumed that it was not the store in general from which they needed to select, but one particular style of furniture. Item by item, they chose plain white melamine: first the bed, then the desk and then, to match both, the various accoutrements. Even the mirror was framed in white melamine. The only exception was the faux Henry Moore/Barbara Hepworth table light, with a hole in the middle, which IKEA usually has on sale for around £10. In advance of receiving this furniture the Wakefords had prepared the room in a similar spirit of purity and neutrality. Every inch of the room bar the window panes was painted white; even the carpet was off-white. In the interest of efficient storage, the bed had drawers underneath for the au pair's 'things'. The desk was particularly plain: a rectangle of white melamine-faced chipboard resting on four white cylindrical legs, on which was placed the au pair's television and CD system. The white melamine mirror was placed on the white four-drawer chest without handles, such that one could barely discern the drawers from the carcass.

In this the Wakefords were in no way unusual. Perhaps half the furnishing that is selected with au pairs in mind in the London area comes from IKEA, and that half is dominated by white melamine. It seems that IKEA represented the perfect source of au pair style, which is hardly surprising given that, just like the au pair herself, IKEA is generally seen as inexpensive, generically European, modern, and characterized essentially by cleanliness, functionality and efficiency. Like the au pair, it is hopefully going to be reasonably long lasting, and in any case it is quite easy to replace. When there is a change of au pair, the slate is wiped clean and one can begin again with a blank white surface, the impression of the previous occupant removed more or less instantly.

When Iveta, the Wakeford's new au pair, arrived she was perfectly happy with the result: 'And the room furniture is great, it is all IKEA!', she wrote to her sister in an e-mail. No Slovak au pair is ever offended by an IKEA room, so their expectations dovetail quite neatly here with those of their hosts. Such rooms are clean, easy to tidy, functional, modern and bright. Iveta considered IKEA somewhat upmarket. Somewhat bizarrely for a firm based in Sweden but much of whose furniture is actually produced in Eastern Europe, many of the items in her room cost more in the Slovak IKEA than the one on the North Circular Road in London. At this point Iveta thought she understood the symbolic implication of this neutral aesthetic, which seemed to invite a degree of personalization through decoration. It was as though her hosts had thoughtfully presented her with an entirely blank canvas upon which she was invited to paint her own portrait.

The Wakefords provided one of the few cases that fitted most preconceptions about an au pair's host family. Their new house is an upmarket detached property with impressive gates to the front and a swimming pool at the back. Being more central London than suburbia, there is no doubt about the amount of money it represents – an impression reinforced by the number, type and number plates of the several cars parked on its ample frontage. Iveta was quite happy both that her room was an adequate size and with the impressive nature of the house. This was a family that seemed to occupy a highly respectable, upper-middle-class niche where she could feel comfortable keeping up to a certain standard. She would enjoy the vicarious status of living and working in such a house. She saw this period of work as giving her the experience, the routines, the knowledge and above all the aesthetic that she would come to associate with and that one day would represent her own position in the world.

There was no sense of deference accompanying Iveta's respect for the Wakefords; she was, after all, a child of Slovak socialism. It was more that they were simply ahead of her, as one would expect, given that they lived in London and were older and established. She felt that, given time, she could just as naturally assume this mantle of respectability, and that they surely would recognize this basic equality in her. Satisfied with her prospects, she assumed that there was going to be an entirely comfortable fit between host and guest that wouldn't need spelling out, since soon both would just relax into mutual respect. It didn't take too long, however, unfortunately for Iveta, to sense something else in the atmosphere she had now entered – a growing realization that IKEA furniture didn't mean quite the same thing to the Wakefords as it did to her.

Although most host families think that they are acting in accordance with their responsibilities to the au pair – indeed most report that, if anything, they were remarkably accommodating – actually there are many ways in which a fundamental ambivalence soon starts to be communicated. For their part the au pairs are extremely sensitive to any signs of such ambivalence precisely because these mirror their own mixed feelings. While IKEA white melamine may be functional, no one would see it as exactly warm, and there is often a distinct coldness to the reception of au pairs in the London area that is quickly evident. This is often literal, as the au pair soon recognizes that she has ended up in the smallest room in the house with the least heating as well. Often the result of a conversion of a garage or loft, it is also frequently the most distant room from the main area of the house.

Au pairs soon detect other clues to this general atmosphere of disregard – perhaps furniture that had clearly been bought and sized with children in mind who have now outgrown it, and yet which is somehow seen as suitable for the au pair. In other cases it is clear that the family continues to see an au pair's room as a temporary storage area for their own overflowing possessions. In one instance the au pair was startled and upset to find that her room has actually been used to store, among other things, books of photographs, Czech glass, and other obviously unwanted gifts – the legacy of a string of previous au pairs. She could see just those sorts of gifts recommended by the leaflets of the au pair agencies: small toys for children and souvenirs of Slovak origin for adults. She felt the family couldn't possibly have appreciated that such gifts had been quite pricey from the point of view of the au pairs, and was shocked by the insensitivity shown in using her room as storage space for them.

There are other families who are very thoughtful and try to help their newly arrived au pairs to make their rooms their own, and who recognize that the blank melamine is actually a sign of the au pair's freedom to personalize her new environment. They also fully understand that the placement on their walls of the children's photographs, or pictures done by the children at school, is intended to help build a positive relationship between the au pair and the child. Mind you, even with those families there was no expectation that au pair's own photographs could migrate to the children's rooms or communal spaces such as living rooms. This may seem trivial, but it was once the criterion used in a court case about minimum wages. The evidence that an employing family did not treat the plaintiff as a family member was deemed to be the lack of integration of such photographs. But such families are quite unaware of asymmetries of this nature. They spend much time thinking about what would create a warm environment. There is usually a 'welcome' notice in the au pair's room with her name in bright crayon sketches. Such families will also ask the au pairs if they have any particular needs. For instance, one family took each of their new au pairs in turn to Brent Cross shopping centre and asked them to choose a small ornament or poster in recognition this could help them to individualize their rooms and feel comfortable in their new environment. Similarly, when Barbora asked Mrs Cowan where she could listen to music, explaining that she never watched TV, which had been provided for her in her room, the Cowans bought her an additional CD player. Even the clashes may not necessarily be the result of any particular insensitivity. One family asked the au pair to choose the colour in which they would repaint the room and a poster to decorate the wall. The problem was that the next au pair couldn't

42

stand the bright pink and detested the poster of a leather-jacketed rocker on a motorbike.

While au pairs are generally happier with an IKEA scheme as opposed to a room filled with family materials, they often assume they will then be granted sufficient autonomy to personalize and decorate the room in question. This was Iveta's understanding of the implications of the Wakefords' choice. The problem is that they will be told either explicitly that this process is subject to restriction, as in 'Please don't put anything on the walls', or the hosts will say something not intended to be particularly restrictive, such as 'Please use only Blu Tack when attaching posters to the walls', but which is experienced by the au pair, during this period of extreme sensitivity, as amounting to the same thing. As a result most au pairs find themselves doing much less room decoration and personalization than they had expected.

The story of how she accommodated to her new room takes up a substantial part of Martina's diary. Martina was not comfortable with the placement of the furniture as she found it, and she spent three days pacing the room thinking about how to reposition things. She decided to move the bed further from the door to avoid overhearing noises from the rest of the house and to reposition the wardrobes and a writing desk. She then asked Mrs Randall (her host mother) about the possibility of moving the furniture around. She asked this as a purely rhetorical question, considering the room as an equivalent of a room in Slovak student accommodation – that is, as a place one does not really own, but is free to appropriate and decorate, to put anything on the walls (even repaint them) or move furniture around. Hence she was completely taken aback to find out that, though she was permitted to move her bed away from the door, she was not allowed to move the wardrobes without Mr Randall's agreement and supervision. Actually Mrs Randall was afraid that her old wardrobes might fall to pieces when moved. But, as Mr Randall could never find the time to inspect the wardrobes and determine whether moving them was possible, Martina concluded they he really didn't want her to make such alterations. This was reinforced when Mrs Randall looked obviously appalled at Martina having put up her pictures and posters on the wall without using Blu Tack. Martina was asked to remove them and was provided instead with an IKEA cork board to put her posters on.

Actually in the main this was a generous rather than an inconsiderate family. For example, they added a vegetarian cookery book to their collection when they realized that Martina was a vegetarian.

The problem was rather that Martina had been constrained from doing something she considered her natural right: to decorate what she saw as her own space in whatever way she wished. Equally, au pairs, who feel particular fragile when they first arrive and are almost looking out for signs of rejection, are prone to the most negative interpretations of such misunderstandings. As a result Martina decided she could never fully feel at home in the Randall's house. Although originally it was only the limits on luggage that had prevented her from bringing her beloved house plants to London, since then she has never brought a flower or a plant into her room. As a result Martina considers her room as bare as a desert. Without plants it is more like a store room than a real room. Although she could easily have afforded one of the cheap fuchsias or azaleas she could see in the florist, or even in the supermarket, she preferred to claim that they were too expensive and retain the room as a testimony to her growing litany of complaints and resentments against the family. Knowing that some families use the personalization of their rooms as evidence of their fair treatment and care for their au pairs, she was using the room as her silent evidence to the contrary.

More common, though, was simple indifference and a sense of just not being bothered. After a short time many au pairs become much more interested in their leisure activities and the friendships and quarrels that go on outside of the house. Within the house, even time that is supposed to be leisure ends up being spent with the children and is experienced as 'work', or at least the boredom associated with not having found a good reason to get out of the house. Having come to regard their stay as transient and their relationship with their hosts as tightly constrained, they no longer feel it is worth investing their time, things, money and emotions in decorations. They put a picture of their boyfriend on the wardrobe, have their teddy bear on the bed, and that's it. In such cases the possessions they brought with them from Slovakia have the opposite effect of that intended. The very act of putting out on window sills photographs of their family, the boyfriends they left behind, pictures of friends from when they were on camp together in the Slovak mountains, and paraphernalia from their own childhood all serves to distance them from this new space rather than to help appropriate the room as theirs.

Alternatively, Silvia made her room 'her castle' precisely through decorating and distancing it from the rest of the house. She certainly did not feel at home in the house of a family which appeared to be 'treating her just like a servant'. By contrast she 'felt fully at home in her room, because she had all her things from Slovakia there'. Silvia put on display all her postcards, items cut out from magazines, and inspiring quotations from her favourite novels and poems. She took her jewellery out of its box and hung it over the mirror and brought dry autumn leaves from the neighbourhood park and arranged them into the small vase she had bought in a charity shop. The only missing ingredient in her decoration was pictures of her family and boyfriend. She considered these as part of her private life and thought there was something vulgar or exhibitionist in displaying pictures of her loved ones. So her photo album stayed in her drawer, though she took it out frequently to look at it herself. She felt her life and the host family's lives overlapped too much already – they ate together, and her schedule was entirely dependent on the dynamics of their household. She knew what they ate, how they spent their times together and when they quarrelled. It seemed important therefore to keep some things just for herself.

There are several other possible responses to the au pairs' problem of accommodating to their rooms. One is simply to see their room, in opposition to their role as cleaner in the rest of the house, as a place of mess, to which end they cover surfaces with clothes, with the contents of their handbags and with other things that bring disorder, thus asserting a separate identity from the rest of the house. For instance, Eva had enjoyed the four months she had lived with a family in Ilford. But she had moved there after three months in a rather more isolated area, and was prepared to move again if she found a better-paying family in the same neighbourhood. This created a clear feeling of transience in relation to her current residence. Without altering the room much from how she had found it, she started leaving stuff all over the place. Her bras were lying about on the floor, a mass of her clothes were placed on top of her suitcase, and piles of CDs and English textbooks were in sort of lines along the floor. Her cosmetics and toiletries were displayed on her chest of drawers. This mess became for her a more effective appropriation of the space than simply putting up a few ornaments. Her sense was that this was really more like a hotel room than her home.

Petra's room contains no decorative items at all: no posters, no photographs, no calendars, no pictures by the children. One reason is that the room she had been allocated was still full of personal things belonging to her host family. Almost a whole wall was taken up by shelves of books and another with framed paintings, including a portrait of the host mother. This deeply offended Petra, who took an instant dislike to the room. It didn't help that the walls were a dark green. She couldn't imagine anything more depressing, and it certainly didn't seem to go with the turquoise furniture. She had simply no idea why anyone would choose such a style for themselves. Her response was to fall back on the one object she really did enjoy decorating – herself. Having just finished her college course in hairdressing, she felt quite at ease in selecting from a wide range of cosmetics and hair treatments, as well as clothing. It was these items that could be seen liberally distributed around the room – covering the window sill, competing with books on the shelves (Petra was certainly no reader of books) and littered over the desk.

The embarrassment of co-presence

At least with regard to their own rooms the au pairs have a certain degree of autonomy as to whether to decorate or not, or just to create a mess. The situation is rather more complex with regard to the rest of the house, which becomes the domain of what is best described as an embarrassment of co-presence. The term 'co-presence' implies that, while this could be shared space, in practice there is often no more than the mutual tolerance of two distinct entities who simply find themselves in much greater proximity than they would like. In contrast to the equality of shared houses, where most Slovaks in London live, the au pair rarely feels she belongs within what is clearly someone else's property. The more intimate the proximity, the greater the sense of embarrassment. The issue makes manifest the prior ambiguity of the pseudo-family ideal which legitimates her presence there.

For many au pairs the problem starts from their feeling that they just don't understand the house – its rhythms, norms and expectations, whether they should respond to the calls of children when they are off-duty, which meals are for them, whether it is appropriate to watch television with the family or to discuss their personal relationships with them. Being self-conscious about their own presence, au pairs become acutely aware of the noise they might make and whether they are in the wrong place at the wrong time. They do not want to be heard while using the toilet or bathroom or seen when leaving the bathroom after taking a shower. At the same time, they do not feel comfortable hearing others using these facilities. Any encounter with bodily functions could be embarrassing.

Least of all do they want to hear the families' sex life, though there are exceptions. For one au pair, the fact that her bedroom was next to that of the parents meant she could hear very well not only how often they had sex, but how long they had sex for and just occasionally what kind of sex they were having. This was simply great material for gossiping with other au pairs over a drink and making herself the centre of voyeuristic interest. A more widespread problem was the deep embarrassment of co-presence that au pairs such as Paula felt when she regularly found tissues covered with semen on the bed and floor in the master bedroom, when it was apparent that it was she who was supposed to clean them up. She had to touch them simply to make way for more acceptable tasks such as vacuuming or making beds. She was shocked and disgusted and, while she threw away the tissues without complaining to the family, she commented to Zuzana that 'these people have no shame and behave as swines'.

Issues related to sex did not just provoke embarrassment, they revealed deeper inequality in the au pair institution. Mirka was working for a single mother with a rather active social and sexual life, and would regularly find piles of erotic lingerie, condoms and sex toys scattered in her host mother's bedroom. She tidied them with a mixture of embarrassment, amusement, and a bit of voyeurism. But what really appalled her was the sheer discrepancy in the enforcement of shared intimacy. While she was daily confronted with the particularity of the sexual life of her host, the latter ensured that she did not ever have to contemplate the sexuality of her au pair and, as in most host families, anticipated any embarrassment over seeing or hearing anything to do with such matters through a series of clear regulations. Mirka was simply not allowed to have male visitors in her room. Even her female friends had to be agreed upon by her host. Mirka considered herself to be very attractive and thought that London could offer many interesting encounters with men. What particularly infuriated her was the constant babysitting that was required in order to give her host the freedom to entertain men, which was precisely why she was unable to go out and meet men herself, and she felt her host enjoyed men and life at her expense. So the fact that she had to tidy away the debris of sexual activity from someone who seemed to be systematically preventing her from having sex seemed ironic evidence for the larger asymmetry and injustice in the au pair institution.

Au pairs often felt such issues acutely when they had to meet the family in the mornings without the sorts of distance they found comfortable. Still, in most cases, the encounter with sex or with dirt was actually less central to the overall sense of embarrassment than the times when they had to remind the family that they had not been paid. This was probably the single most difficult situation that au pairs felt they had to face – the one that for many seems to have been the critical moment that led to their feeling estranged. Similarly, everyday issues about food and eating would often be more consequential, since they were much more common than issues concerning sex.

Au pairs based in Asian and African families become sensitive to the difference in smell and were concerned with how they themselves must smell to their hosts. They would also be disgusted by the need of Hindu families to start the day evacuating orifices, especially through noisy hawking of phlegm. At least in such cases it was possible to make a judgement as to whether the issue was cultural or personal. In other cases this distinction was unclear. One au pair was terrified that her room would be used in her absence by guests after she felt she had 'polluted' it through farting. Another realized that the comments being made by the family about unfamiliar smells actually referred to her frequent use of garlic, which was not eaten by that family. Although it is hard to generalize, often the embarrassment of co-presence seems to develop as a continually reinforced spiral of anxiety. This often starts even before the two parties meet. The literature sent to prospective au pairs within Slovakia includes highly patronizing statements about the need to shower daily and to use anti-perspirants, together with instructions about asking for permission to avail themselves of the bathroom if, for example, the family needed to have priority before going to work – although one au pair left her family when she found that they actually did expect her to ask before using the shower. Au pairs almost invariably respond to these anxieties by increased eating and putting on weight, which usually adds an element of self-disgust.

Most au pairs reported that their arrival was accompanied by a powerful self-consciousness beyond anything they had anticipated. The simple fact of not knowing when and where it was appropriate for them to be within this new house led to considerable anxiety. Barbora found she was becoming more and more upset because she so wanted to do the right thing but couldn't establish how. One of the worst moments was dinner. She would hear noises in the kitchen. She didn't want to come down too early and be in the way when Mrs Cowan was cooking, but it was horrible to arrive downstairs when the others were already sitting and half way through their meal. The problem was that sometimes they called her and sometimes they didn't, and this wasn't always a sign of whether they seemed to expect her. Also the family seemed somehow just to know that one day dinner might be at six and another day at eight, but there was no simple way of communicating this to her. Sometimes she felt that they were telling her how welcome she was to join them for a meal and yet there were little hints that perhaps it would be better if she ate on her own. It was just as bad when she actually joined them for the meal. Even if they wanted to engage her in discussion, it took her ages to find suitable English phrases, so finally she would just find herself dully sitting there, nodding and smiling, feeling like an idiot, not being able to express herself in any more developed way. She had that horrible feeling that the others must be seeing her as stupid.

The irony was that, if she hadn't cared so much about managing well and being sensitive, she wouldn't have felt so bad about getting these things right. It often involved such trivial things. Why couldn't they just have said that they like to keep the ketchup in this cupboard and not that one, rather than brusquely moving it in front of her without saying anything? Overall it seemed simply as though she irritated them, that they expected her just to know things she couldn't possibly know. As a result she became more and more self-conscious about every single thing. She would stand there and think to herself, Do they turn their washed-up mugs upwards or downwards? Have they done it this way in order to accommodate me, or to remind me to accommodate them? She knew one of them was right and one of them was wrong, of course, but which? The other night she actually asked Mrs Cowan for more detail about how she liked her carrots to be sliced, formulating the question in inches to be polite. Mrs Cowan had just looked at her as though she was mad. Much of the time she just couldn't decide if Mrs Cowan was arrogant or just shy. Was it some kind of British way of behaving (which would be sort of all right), or was she really unpleasant or expressing some disapproval of Barbora? If this had taken place in Slovakia she would have known. Here she didn't. She just couldn't read the subtle signs of etiquette that might imply inclusion – but equally disdain. This mattered a great deal, because Barbora needed to feel she could judge the people she was living with.

Breakfast was just as bad as dinner. Barbora considered herself very healthy. She loved sports; she would run, cycle and generally keep active. For her this was nothing artificial, involving no sense of keeping in shape. It was simply that she came from a household where everyone was involved in physical work. Even if it wasn't part of their employment, they would be busy with the allotment, pulling up potatoes, preparing the soil. Barbora was very well built, with the muscles to show for it. Part of keeping healthy was to eat properly, which for her started with a substantial breakfast full of good natural foods. The trouble was that the Cowans' ideas of nature and good food bore absolutely no relation to anything she had previously encountered.

Barbora expected plenty of full-cream milk and butter. The Cowans supplied her with skimmed milk and a sort of yellow substance that had no fat and no taste either. There was no meat, there was nothing fried, but worst of all there was no quantity. She expected four thick slices of real bread, but what she got was something more like sheets of paper. While she thought in terms of eggs, they would talk about one egg.

It was even worse when one day this was discussed. Barbora had trained in agricultural college. She wanted to explain to the Cowans that they needed these foods, that the fat in butter provided essential amino acids and that full-cream milk contributed in various ways to their health. But she had hardly started when it turned into the Cowans explaining things to her, as though she was simply ignorant. She had to listen to them say how important it was to avoid fats and to keep a decent weight and especially not, by implication, to set a bad example to the children, because a poor diet could lead eventually to heart disease. Barbora was horrified. She realized that the Cowans had simply no understanding of food and nutrition and that in matters of heath they were convinced by complete rubbish, such as echinacea and homeopathy, that any schoolchild could have seen through as a fraudulent scam for selling an expensive quack remedy. She became increasingly aware that perhaps it was they who were stupid, or at least ignorant. Although she was far more muscular than either the males or females of the family, she almost certainly had less fat than any of them. Worst of all were the consequences she observed in the parent–child relationship. She had to watch when Mrs Cowan refused to give her son just one small extra piece of cake to follow the miserly bit that he had been given, thereby denying him what Barbora saw more as a token of love than the hazardous substance from which Mrs Cowan seemed to think she was protecting her offspring.

Within a short time Barbora realized that she seemed to be consuming for breakfast more than the rest of the family put together. She would have hoped this would pass without comment, but the Cowans' children thought this was an entirely fascinating topic for discussion. 'Look, mummy', they would say, 'look at how thick Barbora has spread the butter. Look, mummy, she is eating another one!' They were not criticizing her; on the contrary, they were quite enthusiastic about her apparent appetite. But it made Barbora feel like a freak. When Mrs Cowan responded by asking her if she would like something bought specially for her and Barbora asked for some full-cream milk, she returned with one tiny plastic bottle that would hardly fill a couple of glasses. When Barbora then started buying milk for herself, there was further embarrassment about Mrs Cowan wanting to reimburse her.

While in Barbora's case she found her eating restricted, more au pairs found themselves, like Elena, in a situation where issues of power and hospitality pushed them to eat more than they would like. Elena was horrified when she realized that huge and late dinners, to which she was not accustomed, had led to her putting on 5 kilos in a couple of months. However, she did not feel able to tell her host mother that she would prefer not to eat with them and go on a diet:

> You know, it is impolite. She cooks the food, and it is a nice food. She makes all these special Nigerian things such as apples with beef, and plantains, and it would not be polite to tell her that I will not eat. I can't be really picky here. I am not at home here, it is their home. When you are visiting, you do not tell: I do not eat this or I want that. And here, it is not even a real visit, I am not even a guest, so I can not tell her.

How not to make an impression

Although au pairs commonly discuss conflicts over food – whether too little for Barbora or too much for Elena – behind this was a much deeper issue about self-consciousness and visibility. Host families often reported bewilderment in that, as far as they could tell, the au pairs eat 'nothing'. Not only did their au pairs not eat with them, but day after day they would come home to no evidence that they had eaten at all. In fact, from close observation, it appears that au pairs most commonly do eat from the fridge, but never want actually to finish a product which would make that act of consumption evident. They would drink from a bottle, but not so much that the level went down drastically. They even preferred cartons for that reason. Once Iveta actually finished a carton and was so upset that she found another carton and partly refilled the first in order for this not to be evident. On other days she would take a piece from a half-eaten cheese, but was careful not to finish it off.

This anxiety which led au pairs to take food only in this imperceptible fashion led in turn to anxiety among the host families, who could become very worried about such apparent asceticism and start thinking in terms of anorexia. They quite ignored the fact that most Slovak au pairs actually put on weight during their stay in London. In one case the family even invited a neighbouring Slovak au pair, staying with a family they knew well, to speak with their own au pair about food, as they were worried that Janka did not seem to eat at all. The family were concerned that either she did not like their food or was anorexic or had another health problem. Actually, as she later told Zuzana, smiling, Janka really ate quite a lot and made sure she tried every type of food in the fridge. Not only that, but she had been through every single open bottle of alcohol in the living room, trying out the different tastes individually and in combination, imagining names for her new 'cocktails'. But she did this when no one could see her, carefully hiding the traces of her presence. Her sips from the bottles were very small because, to her intense frustration, the family drank so little themselves that any more would have been evident. Another au pair never felt comfortable eating from the family fridge, especially after her host mother reprimanded her when she took more pieces of ham than she thought was appropriate or drank orange juice not only for breakfast, but also during the day, without even mixing it with water. The au pair's response was to eat in the house as little as possible, leaving every evening to visit her boyfriend, because, as she told us, she was 'at home there', and ate as much as she wished without feeling inhibited.

Where does this consistent pattern of imperceptible eating come from? It must be arrived at independently as an individual strategy, since there is no evidence that any au pair mentioned this behaviour to others. That this emerges as a norm speaks of something profound in the relationship. Our evidence suggests that this strategy of invisible eating and drinking is part of a much wider pattern of masking their actions by many of the au pairs. There is an overall desire never to leave any impression and to hide the signs of their personal presence from the house and the family with whom they live. This often starts with the increasing withdrawal of any signs of their existence from the common areas and may be combined with the already noted strategy of not even leaving any impression upon their own rooms. When au pairs talk about this minimal use of their room they sometimes phrase it in terms of a fear that they will end up having to pay for some damage they might cause. But in many cases it turns into a desire to leave no mark that could be a lasting sign of their presence. Iveta was aghast when once a pair of blue denim jeans left a stain on the white carpet. For a couple of weeks she would phone Zuzana to consult her about different kinds of carpet cleaner, cleaners that she feared would themselves leave a still more indelible stain. She became quite obsessive about this issue, spending considerable sums on possible solutions. Iveta usually sat on the floor while watching TV or making embroidery for her mother, but from then on she always made absolutely sure there was a towel between the carpet and her jeans. It seemed as though even the transient impression made by her body felt like too much of a personal imposition, inappropriate for this impersonal room.

Commonly au pairs do not store their toiletries and cosmetics in shared bathrooms, preferring to keep them in their own room. Especially at the beginning of her stay Iveta found that such an ordinary activity as taking a shower could be a delicate business. She did not have time to take a shower in the morning, as she was busy seeing off the family's daughter to school. However, the Wakefords left their and their son's bedroom door open at night, in order to hear their four-year-old if he cried. She did not want to wake them up or to be overheard. She especially didn't want to be seen in her short nightdress or with her wet hair covered by a towel when passing their door. So she could only shower at midday when the Wakefords were at work and the children at school. For another au pair the problem was that, whenever she wanted to take a shower after she had finishing cleaning, the two toddlers she was looking after couldn't think of anything better to do than claim they needed the bathroom for themselves, knocking on the door and calling for her, or asking her what she was doing there. It became a moment of absolute dread. For this reason having one's own bathroom was viewed as a very welcome luxury. Barbora was extremely happy she had a sink in her room, as at least part of her personal hygiene could be dealt with without having to go upstairs to the children's bathroom.

Hana always left the living room when her host parents were present watching TV, even though she liked them both and did not mind staying there when only one was present. She simply felt they should be allowed their own time for each other. Ultimately the desire to erase their presence meant that some au pairs chose to spend as little leisure time within the home as possible. For this reason some au pairs tried not to be in the house during weekends, and instead would hang around London, eating out in cheap Chinese fast-food outlets, Burger Kings or pizzerias and coming back only in the evenings. They thought their very presence was something that detracted from the ideal of the nuclear family.

So the evidence concerning rooms and food combines as a strategy of self-eradiction. This arose not just from the embarrassment of co-presence but also from other misunderstandings that led to confusion and anxiety among au pairs. For example, the ambiguity over the potential categorization of their presence as guests with hosts emphasized the difference from the Slovak understanding of hospitality. For Slovaks this meant that hosts were expected to ask guests whether they were hungry and offer them food on a regular basis. Au pairs expected that they would be politely asked if they were hungry, even when it was perfectly evident that they were not. Without this, they felt they were neither integrated within the home as an additional host nor treated as a guest, and there was no alternative category with which they could associate themselves. This clearly mattered when as a result they felt insecure about their access to basic food during the day. As Barbora put it: 'Here you should be like at home, and yet you feel you can not even eat normally. This is not even civilized.'

One defence against this ambiguity was to take refuge in the formal arrangements or contract that defines their presence. For instance, Ivana did not like eating in the household during weekends because she thought that, as she was not working there during weekends, and since food is part of an au pair's wages, it wasn't right for her to take food from the house at that time. She also did not like eating in the kitchen when the family were hanging around, possibly watching what she took and how she cooked. This way there would be no sense of debt or obligation, no chance of being accused of greed. The ideal was to be someone who added to the family and to the house, and never be seen as a person who took something away from it.

However, often au pairs found that their sense of thrift proved to be yet another area of embarrassing differences in expectations. For example, Juliana packed a chocolate bar, a banana and a small bottle of water as her lunch when she went out for a day trip to Central London, assuming that it was the responsibility of the family to provide basic food for her free days. She was aghast when her host mother looked at her as though she was stealing, asked her not to take such things, and suggested that she buy food from her own pocket money when she was out. Silvia was similarly appalled when her host mother forbade her to make cooked lunches for herself and ordered her to eat just a sandwich, which Silvia did not consider as 'food' at all. This was despite her being expected to clean the house thoroughly on a daily basis, often working three hours more than had been formally agreed and without any overtime pay. As she put it, 'But I just thought, you know, you cow, I am saving your arse here, and you will tell me not to eat? And I just continued to cook for myself every day. I got extremely clever about that. I was able to cook and eat soup or something in twenty minutes and hide all the traces.' She felt that this was the first time in her life that she had had to prac-tise dishonesty. Several au pairs found themselves taking more food and actually overeating as a form of compensation when the families did not pay their overtime, but again surreptitiously. They felt they had a right to get something for their work, and, when they were not paid, food seemed the appropriate supplement.

There was less evidence for a symmetrical reaction or change in behaviour by host families as a result of being embarrassed by the presence of the au pair. But this may be largely because it is the au pairs who feel they have to take on the burden of that embarrassment. There was remarkably little sense of awkwardness at the behaviour of the au pairs themselves – for example, there were very few stories of a drunk au pair, and relationships with men were generally seen as best kept well away from the family.

Most host families had not the least idea that the au pairs were so obsessed by the impression they might make, let alone these strategies in relation to food and their rooms. Where they were aware, they simply saw them as typical of behaviour common to teenagers and young women pretty much anywhere. They had no way of knowing that it was very rare among women of this age in Slovakia. If anything, their concern was much more with what the au pairs might think about the family than the other way around. If they had been reticent about having an au pair in the first place it was because of their fear for their own privacy, that their own intimate life would become evident to this stranger. As one mother put it, 'If there is any tension going on in the house, they know. So I hated the fact that we have less privacy, but we don't have any choice. If I shout, she knows. If I cry, they come and ask "Why are you crying?"' Some Jewish families wondered what on earth the au pairs made of households where screaming and shouting were signs not that the family were having problems, but rather, as they put it, that they were entirely normal within their own cultural conventions.

Some families are also embarrassed by the screaming and petulance of their children. There was a general awareness that the au pairs would consider middle-class London children as 'spoilt' and relatively badly behaved compared with those from their own backgrounds – which is exactly what most au pairs did feel about these children. However, they found it quite surprising that parents could become so embarrassed about their children, knowing that the au pairs were looking after them all day. For example, one family tried to hide from the au pair the fact that their daughter had done badly in her exams, and even did not want their au pair to eat with them while exams were being discussed as an issue. Consequently, as it was she who had to eat in solitude, the au pair felt punished instead of the daughter. In another case, of a ten-year-old boy who occasionally wet his bed, the mother tried to pretend that it was just that he spilt his tea. The au pair regarded such avoidance as hypocrisy. Rather more difficult were issues concerning the rudeness of children to au pairs. This could be relatively mild, as in being slightly charmed by the way male au pairs would be ordered by lazy schoolkids to bring drinks. But sometimes there was a more problematic exposure by the children of the basic power relationships between the au pair and the family, especially when the children simply told the au pair that she was just a servant and should do whatever they wanted her to do. Often the problem for the au pairs was not that the parents were embarrassed by their children's behaviour, but that they weren't.

Such discussions were not uncommon, and one mother was constantly reprimanding her children for saying things such as 'You are only the au pair and we don't have to do what you say.' Some teenage children can develop an active dislike of the au pair. Most commonly, that just meant ignoring her, and parents acknowledged the upset this caused and were embarrassed by the way the sulky and surly character of the teenager could be taken as offensive rejection. Much more problematic were families where the au pair was effectively caught in the crossfire between divorcees. For example, one ex-husband tried to poison his daughter's relationship with the au pair. As the wife noted, 'My ex-husband really didn't help, since he would tell my daughter he was paying me to be at home to look after them, and my daughter therefore resented the fact that I was working, and then resented Júlia. Her feeling about Júlia was – if I can get rid of you I will have mum back.' Another au pair was asked to leave the house whenever the ex-husband was there, as he hated au pairs around the house. Such family battles are complex, especially when single parents use au pairs as weapons against their ex-partners. One au pair was absolutely appalled when she discovered evidence that an ex-wife was obtaining more money from her ex-husband than she was actually passing on, for example, for babysitting, and just pocketing the difference.

All such embarrassments and misunderstandings provide further context for understanding the au pairs' own strategies of self-effacement. On entering Iveta's room, one could at first see only her jacket hanging over the chair. Almost all her other possessions were hidden in drawers. For the first couple of months the only decoration present was the picture of her younger sister placed on the mirror, a postcard depicting her native town and, on the curtain, a small red plastic heart, a talisman given her by a schoolfriend in order to comfort her during the flight. Everything was kept in a state such that she could gather her things and leave in ten minutes, and the room would have no memory, no impression of the time she had spent there.

Sometimes even this erasure of the signs of one's presence is insufficient, and eventually the embarrassment of co-presence becomes overwhelming. From the first of December Iveta felt an ever increasing homesickness. Browsing in a pound shop for some additional Christmas presents, she discovered an advent calendar. Iveta bought it, as well as some cheap sweets she intended to put behind the doors provided for each day. She thought that this would make the counting down of the days before she returned home for Christmas a bit more agreeable. She was just afraid that either the parents would discover it and mock her for this childishness, or that the children would discover it and eat her sweets. When eating the sweets Iveta thought of herself as a soldier, and of being an au pair as a kind of military service. Her use of the advent calendar was reminiscent of the way young conscripts would use a tailor's tape measure, cutting off a piece each day as a way of counting down to the end of their military service.

Au pairs' understanding of this period as a *rite de passage* analogous to military service is important in explaining why more of them do not just leave their host families when they are exploited or just unhappy. It is the reason why Iveta did not leave the Wakefords after the first few weeks. She thought she had to behave as a grown-up. Anyway, nothing really horrible had happened to her. She would never phone her family to tell them how unhappy she was with a strange family in London. She would have found it ridiculous to be telling them that she felt the Wakefords regarded her as if she was invisible when they didn't need her for work. She couldn't explain that it wasn't the big things that were making her unhappy, such as the fact that they made her work longer hours than she either expected or was paid for. It was the small things, such as the fact that the family did not think to serve her the dessert they had after their meal.

In Iveta's case there was one more non-disclosure that would lead to the final eradication of her presence among the Wakefords. It is common for au pairs who have had a good experience with families and who are coming to the end of their stay to start to think about passing the family on to someone who would 'deserve' them. In such cases they may also want the family to continue to have a good relationship with their au pairs. They talk about this explicitly as 'inheriting' a family. Iveta had a friend in just this situation, and through her met a family with two daughters. The contrast with the Wakefords was evident from the second time she met them. They had asked her about her birthday and about whether her sister, who was the same age as their daughter, would like to come and stay for holidays. She knew the working hours were rather long there and that the family kept one wardrobe of their own things in the au pair's room and would occasionally intrude – but they were *nice*. She did not mention to the Wakefords she was intending to leave them, planning to tell them on the morning she was going home for her Christmas break. She had heard stories about families who sacked their au pairs immediately after hearing that they wanted to leave early or who did not pay the last month's pocket money for the same reason. While she didn't think the Wakefords would stoop so low, she dreaded a period of bad moods and possible recriminations. So, instead, she intended to leave and not come back in the New Year, leaving the Wakefords to their fate. In the end, as she looked around her IKEA room – the same furniture she had been so pleased to see when she first arrived, the same furniture that had gradually revealed itself as signifying what was cold and anonymous and expendable – she realized that by departing without notice she could at least save herself one last embarrassment.

This chapter has not been concerned with the more formal and systematic issues of exploitation. While there is much evidence of such treatment, the most fundamental problems exposed here have more to do with the underlying contradictions of the au pair relationship itself and with feelings that arise even without necessarily any bad intention or action by the host families. A family that asks an au pair to use Blu Tack on the walls is not trying to humiliate her. The fact that the main meal that in Slovakia is at lunch time in London is in the evening is not a reason for blame. In case after case it was not whether the au pair or the family wanted to be close or distant, but whether the two coincided in their desires. There are quite a variety of responses to their situation by au pairs, as evident in rooms that vary from immaculate to messy, minimalist to crammed. So the critical point of this chapter is to look beyond either intentional exploitation or the differences in custom in order to see a more fundamental problem that seems to emerge in the majority of cases.

The starting point has to be the contradiction implied in the institution itself. This is why the chapter began with the issue of the pseudo-family. It is the concept of being a 'sort of family member' that legitimates the entire arrangement, and it ultimately becomes a major route to asymmetry. Au pairs find they are expected to act as parents to children, and yet are often treated as children by the parents. They always seem to fall on the negative side of a relationship without experiencing the positive. It is a particular shock because they have just come from a situation in Slovakia where it was they who had been in the position of receiving that taken for granted care represented by their own parents. The pseudo-family is commonly the idiom through which the host family cajoles the au pair into doing things for them, while refusing to accept any such reciprocal entreaty. It also means the process starts in mutual denial, since the choice of whether to become, or to have, an au pair is always the least bad option, never a desire actually to take part in this pseudo-family engagement. Once the au pair arrives, this ambiguity creates an overwhelming embarrassment of co-presence – a self-consciousness and fear of how each appears in the eyes of the other. This in turn leads to an increasing tendency to eradicate any impression they might have made on the home in which they now live. So, once again, white melamine from IKEA seems quite prescient as an expression of the situation within which an au pair finds herself.

Snippet

'Last but not least important advice': excerpts from *Important information for your au pair stay*, a leaflet for prospective au pairs issued by the Student Agency (2004).

After coming to England, look after your personal possessions. **London is a dangerous place,** and thus we do not recommend that you walk outside at night on your own. If you have to go out after sunset, always choose the main street and have some company.

If you want to invite your friends home, ask your host family whether they agree. English people are very wary of an unexpected visit by strangers to their house, and this will not lead them to trust you. If you want to borrow anything (e.g. a hairdryer), **always make sure that the family agrees** in order to avoid unpleasant misunderstandings.

The following may make most of you smile, but we are obliged to draw your attention to this problem. Perhaps you would be surprised to find out how little some of us care about our personal hygiene. Hygienic habits mostly come from growing up in our family, so a person does not realize that his or her habits differ from those of others. During you stay with your host family it is unacceptable to neglect your personal hygiene!!! It is essential to take a shower daily, use deodorants, change your underwear daily and never ever let others be aware of your sweat. If that happened, the family would give notice to the agency with a high probability that they will want to change their au pair!

THE HARD WORK AND THE SOFT TOUCH

Hard work

Lucia woke up at half past six. She did not have time to take a shower, so she just washed her face, brushed her teeth and put on her jeans and sports top. She was in a rush, as she was every morning, the busiest time of her day. Everything was geared to one aim, to get the children safely to the school bus. First she had to wake them up. That might seem easy, or at least possible, but while Claire was no problem, John – incredibly clever as he was incredibly sensitive – hated his school. John was cute, John was cuddly. Whether it was academic work or playing classical music, he was probably gifted. But for now all that creativity seemed directed to one end. The task that really stretched John and exercised his mind was the task of not getting ready for school, and ideally not even getting up in the morning.

John would pretend he was sleeping. John would be too sick today to get up. John would have remembered he was supposed to be on a trip or there was some other event that day other than going to school. Worst of all, John might be hiding in his parents' bedroom or in the deep recesses of the wardrobe in their en suite bathroom – the one place Lucia simply could not enter in order to find him. Even though she was desperately busy, she had to wait until his parents noticed him, shouted at him and rushed him downstairs. Lucia did not like quarrels in the morning, especially as she felt that, even when there was nothing she could do about it, it was still somehow her responsibility if the children were not actually ready on time. And John really was cute and nice, and she really didn't want to quarrel with him. She didn't feel quite so reticent about Mrs Christie, who would come into the kitchen without even saying hello, and launch straight into some discussion of schoolbags and similar issues. When her daughter Claire didn't say good morning, Lucia kept repeating it, louder and louder, until Claire finally got the message and greeted her properly. She only wished she had the courage to play the same trick on Mrs Christie. What she hated was knowing that, whenever mornings started like this, an hour later, when everyone had gone, she would sit and brood on this little slight – the fact that Mrs Christie hadn't said good morning. For some reason it felt as though it was not just that she hadn't greeted her, it was as though she had thereby cursed her for the day. It simply confirmed Lucia's feeling that she was invisible in this household, in the same way that her repetitive work was visible only when something was not done, or not done in the proper way.

This time she was lucky: she just had five minutes' conversation with John, telling him he really had to get up, and he finally did, though he deliberately made all his movements *so* slow. She did not understand why his parents wanted her to help him with getting dressed. After all, he was nine years old, from her point of view perfectly old enough to be able to put on his clothes without supervision. She checked the schoolbags and started to prepare breakfast, putting bowls, breakfast cereals and milk on the table. Claire then joined them and asked Lucia to put cereal into her bowl, to which Lucia retorted that Claire could do this very well for herself. So the early morning had been all right – no hiding John, no missing schoolbags or parts of uniforms. Not like the month before, when it was only when getting ready in the morning that they discovered John had actually left his school jacket on the bus the day before. His spare jacket was in the wash, and yet somehow Lucia was expected to magic forth a clean jacket at that instant. The worst of such mornings was not anything that was said directly to her, it was just having to listen to the endless quarrelling and recriminations between mother and son over something they clearly couldn't do anything about. The only good that had come out of that quarrel was that she discovered that the English used exactly the same expression of 'not crying over spilt milk' that Slovaks use at home.

Today they would get to the bus on time. Yet even on such a good morning, Lucia would feel exhausted by the end of the process. There were just so many little things that had to be remembered and checked and dealt with. She had cleaned the children's shoes the evening before. She would have thought children at this age could clean their own shoes, but who was she to decide what tasks should or should not be done by children in this household? So she made a couple of slices of toast and some coffee for herself, and then went to catch the school bus. Previously Mrs Christie had tried to suggest that things were so pressing that Lucia should have her breakfast only after the children had got on the bus. She didn't argue the point; she knew the appropriate British response would have been to tell Mrs Christie to go fuck herself. Instead she just ignored her and continued to have breakfast at the appropriate time while the children were getting themselves ready as slowly as possible.

As usual, Lucia just exchanged a brief hello with the other Slovak au pairs at the bus stop. She did not socialize with them much. She just knew they were Slovak and apparently au pairs, but it appeared that she did not belong to the same 'cliques' as they. So conversation remained limited to these salutations at the bus stop and the occasional exchange of information about work and living conditions. On this occasion she merely put the children onto the bus and hurried back home. It was Monday, a general cleaning day, so she had a vast number of things to do. She changed into her old sports clothes in order not to risk spilling bleach on her jeans. She had damaged one of her favourite T-shirts in this way when she first started as an au pair, and quickly learnt not to even think about dressing well while she was home and working. Old sports clothes seemed to have become something of an au pair uniform. She had noticed this with other au pairs who no longer bothered to get changed even after they had finishing cleaning – except, of course, Mária, who managed to look smart regardless of what she was doing.

One advantage was that all the nice clothes she was buying in England would look fresh and new when she took them back to Slovakia, where her boyfriend and family would appreciate such things. For the same reason she was using her stay in England to go through that horrible transition period from short hair to long hair, which would have really embarrassed her at home, but seemed an ideal thing to get over and done with while she was away. Apart from which, hairdressers are unbelievably expensive in London, and she wanted to avoid having an au pair friend cutting her hair. Once, when she and a friend had gone for confession to Velehrad – the Czechoslovak Catholic hostel and cultural centre – she had seen an ad offering haircuts for £5. This was tempting, but involved the hairdresser coming to one's home, and she couldn't really turn the Christies' bathroom into a temporary salon.

It was in the same spirit that she saw London as the period during which to experiment with funny socks. It sounded stupid, but since she was about eight she had always wanted to try out some of those really silly and colourful socks and stockings that were in the shops but somehow knew she would never wear again once she returned home. And if you ever wanted to indulge this passion, Camden Town provided some of the silliest socks imaginable. It had been great to have a chance to live out this little fantasy and, true to plan, having got this socks thing out of her system she didn't really want to wear them again.

When Lucia first arrived, Mrs Christie gave her a sheet of paper with computer-printed house rules and a *timetable*. At first Lucia found this ridiculous – a useless exercise in unnecessarily formalized organization. What is there to be so organized about, just for cleaning a house? However, after that first weekend acclimatization Lucia thanked God for the timetable. She realized she hardly understood Mrs and Mr Christie's English. They were apparently trying hard, repeating words and phrases until she got their meaning. At least she hoped she got it. But this had proved a strenuous enough task even for basic socializing. When it came to work it was actually much easier to sit down in her room, read the timetable and look up in her dictionary any unfamiliar words. There were quite a few; Slovak high-school English doesn't stretch to words such as 'vacuuming', 'dusting' and 'polishing', not to mention 'skirting boards'.

More comprehensible English was not the only good thing about the timetable. Lucia felt quite unlucky, because the Christies' former au pair, who was Czech, had left before her arrival and could not introduce her to the house rules and all those subtle issues of how to deal with both people and cleaning. The timetable helped, but it was still a poor substitute for a proper transition. Meanwhile she was coming to realize, much to her surprise, that people can have quite different ideas about such simple things as cleaning – that an individual can dust their furniture in quite specific ways, for example, with some special cloth, or first with a wet and then a dry cloth followed by polish, and further that they expected other people to do things in the very same way. She could appreciate this; what was much harder to understand was why Mrs Christie wanted her to do these specific tasks at specific times. Apparently, it mattered that she vacuumed on Thursday and not on Wednesday and between 8 and 10 a.m. and not 1 and 3 p.m. Lucia had once managed to complete her afternoon tasks during the morning and in her lunch break. But when Mrs Christie saw her watching TV instead of tidying bedrooms, she wanted her to polish some silver instead, as Lucia was supposed to work in the afternoons. After this unsuccessful experiment with more flexible working, Lucia decided it was better to follow the timetable dutifully.

Lucia started to appreciate that the timetable was more than just a system and order for cleaning. It didn't just ensure the house was cleaned sufficiently well and often. It was a means to ensure that, while she herself didn't clean, Mrs Christie remained in control of this activity; that she, not her au pair, was the home-maker and child-carer. It had also become a kind of substitute for any legal contract. Lucia's friend Veronika desperately wanted to do a language course in a quite expensive language school (Lucia could not really understand why, as in her opinion English would simply come naturally with living in England), but Veronika's timetable did not allow her to attend it. Veronika's host mother therefore changed her duties and registered this by printing an updated timetable.

By contrast, another friend, Alenka, had a less happy experience. A month after she arrived, her host family had lost their Polish cleaner, whom they had been paying £6 an hour, and asked Alenka to add this cleaning to her work looking after their one-year-old. Alenka was fine with this, seeing it as an alternative to an additional job that would otherwise have supplemented her £55 a week pocket money. But when no extra money was forthcoming she realized that her host mother had assumed this extra work would be accepted simply as part of the original arrangement. Unusually for an au pair, Alenka complained, though refrained from pointing out that the extra six hours a week were in addition to the five hours a day she was supposed to work. Though Alenka's wage did not change, what did change was a printed copy of her *timetable*, as if to mark her agreement to this additional work. Alenka had felt slightly comforted when she met two more au pairs with similar stories. They too had agreed to additional work, assuming additional pay. One, like Alenka, got nothing. The other received a £5 bonus, although the cleaner she had replaced was paid £36 a week.

Lucia's timetable was quite simple. It included a basic routine: things she was supposed to do daily, such as waking up the children and getting them ready for school, collecting them again in the afternoons, making them tea and later supper, and supervising their homework until their parents came back home. Then there were daily cleaning and subsidiary tasks such as emptying the dishwasher, cleaning the kitchen, vacuuming downstairs, watering the herbs in the kitchen and feeding the cat. In addition there were tasks for specific days: washing certain floors, cleaning the oven and fridge on Monday mornings and, on certain afternoons, washing clothes, cleaning bathrooms, toilets and bedrooms, and dusting and polishing. Dominating all was the hated ironing. At home everybody knew she hated ironing, which was shared out among her sisters while she did other tasks. But Lucia did not dare to suggest a similar swap to Mrs Christie. On Wednesdays she was supposed to tidy the window sills and wipe down the skirting boards, vacuum, dust and polish in the lounge and living room, then change and wash the bedsheets. Thursday just repeated Tuesday's tasks. On Friday she needed to clean the kitchen cupboards, tidy the utility room, clean the bedrooms and do more ironing. Saturday was just the usual daily routine, and Sunday was blessedly free. In addition there was babysitting, which was not fixed for any particular day, as she was expected to be at the Christies' behest. This uncertainly was a problem if she ever wanted to plan outings for herself. Fortunately, the Christies usually limited themselves to once a week, mostly Fridays. Lucia even negotiated a free evening for the monthly Czechoslovak party in Camden Town Hall. These dates were now marked in Mrs Christie's diary.

This timetable was supplemented by a sheet of paper with Mr and Mrs Christies' mobile phone numbers, as well as numbers for the fire, police and ambulance. There were also the names of the gardener and of the man who was supposed to come and repair the kitchen drawer. The sheet included a reminder that Lucia should not allow friends into the house if the Christies did not know them and always to close all windows, set the alarm and leave on some lights when leaving the house. Finally there was an assurance that Lucia could use the telephone whenever she needed to call any UK (but not foreign) destinations and that she should feel free to help herself to the food in the fridge, freezer or kitchen.

Lucia would never have believed that cleaning could be such hard work or that it was so physical. After the first week her muscles ached from carrying the heavy vacuum cleaner up- and downstairs. She was left handed, and could only iron left handed. Being afraid she would end up as some kind of lopsided hunchback, she made herself do all the vacuuming with her right hand. It was odd really. It's not as if she hadn't done plenty of cleaning when she lived in Slovakia. Everybody did. It was just part of daily life. But there it seemed to be something you could integrate with various other tasks and it wasn't quite so concentrated. When she applied to work as an au pair, knowing that cleaning was an integral part of the job, she had thought it would be more like the cleaning she was used to at home. The au pair documents had talked of pocket money, not wages. But today there was no doubt that cleaning felt like work, like hard labour, closer to that of her male friends in the construction industry, but they were earning a great deal more money. This was labour she felt in her body, in aches and muscle strain and the need for a shower afterwards to deal with the sweat. The paradox was that it felt like work precisely because it wasn't paid. A real job would be paid by the hour, but this task earned nothing extra just because you spent more time on it. So you tried to get it done as quickly as possible, in order to maximize your spare time, and that too was probably what made it such hard labour.

Lucia wasn't sure if British people had very different ideas about cleaning than Slovaks, or whether this was just the result of having an au pair. Both her parents were working, and housework was shared among them and their three children (well, mainly the women of the house). But one of the main differences seemed to be that Lucia's family cleaned their house when it needed cleaning, when something really was dirty. Here Lucia constantly found herself expected to clean surfaces that could never be regarded as dirty: this timetable of repetitive vacuuming, dusting and polishing seemed to be perfectly useless. Lucia even experimented with her own room; she deliberately refrained from cleaning the surface of a small table in her bedroom, just out of curiosity, to see how long it would take before it actually became dusty.

In addition, as with much of an au pair's work, it seemed that Lucia's cleaning was routinely disregarded by the family. It was almost as though to notice the work of the au pair would be to acknowledge the dirt that they created in the house. The family preferred to see cleaning as simply 'routine' and dirt as an automatic product rather than the result of their own activities. Lucia could easily have cleaned the house within their agreed schedule of six hours a day. It was all this unnecessary repetitive cleaning that meant that, even when working hard, she often took more than seven hours a day.

Lucia found that she now possessed this bizarre knowledge about cleaning materials. This family had four different cleaning implements and detergents just for cleaning the toilet. She knew a toilet duck (why a duck?) from bleach; she knew special cleaning tissues and two kinds of brush. She knew which liquids were corrosive: they bite. Every room seemed to require its own technology, every surface had its own special cleanser. She might not pass an English-language exam, but if there was ever one on English cleaning technology she would get an 'A' for sure. How to open the various tubes, bottles and plastic containers needed one lesson all on its own. She could also see why she needed rubber gloves. Fortunately, Mrs Christie was always providing her with more than enough of both cleaning materials and gloves. Lucia's friend Nina had to ask for every single detergent several times before her host mother bought it. Another friend, Lenka, developed eczema after several weeks of cleaning but was too shy to ask for gloves, so these were being sent by parcel from her mother in Slovakia. Lucia recalled one of her own most humiliating experiences: on her second day, having to stand mute in front of this woman with a bottle and its cap, and with a plaintive 'I just can't open this' look on her face. Everything in the house was so antiseptic she sometimes thought English people would die if they went into a normal environment, since they would have lost their basic immunity to the world at large.

There was another worrying aspect to this. Lucia seemed to have adopted a 'cleaning' mentality. Whenever she saw something that needed tidying away it made her uncomfortable. She was quite fearful that she would return to Slovakia with a kind of obsession that would end up annoying her as much as everyone else. She had a quick taste of this when she had gone back at Christmas and amazed her family with a penchant for cleaning that was pretty much the exact opposite of the reputation she had spent a decade cultivating for proper teenage neglect of such things.

Her adaptation to the Christie household was leading to other more profound changes. As an au pair in London she found that, for the first time in her life, she was not treated as a child. No one else was responsible for her or caring for her. It was she who was responsible for other people's children. This was not a pleasant transformation. She had imagined becoming an au pair as a gentle step towards independence and maturity and had considered the positive freedom from her parents in terms of control and money. Yet with a life revolving around the needs of the Christie family, and without even being allowed guests when and where she wanted, she felt less freedom here than at home. Nor had she really envisaged the sheer drudgery. She was starting to appreciate the old joke about au pairing being the best form of contraception. A few hours with the Christies' children was enough for her to lose those sweet teenage illusions about babies and motherhood. As an au pair you were expected to give the care, but without the reward of a child's love. As it happens there were not too many opportunities to become pregnant, but at this point you would have been very careful to make sure that any pregnancy was carefully planned and desired.

Funnily enough, cleaning things like the toilet did not trouble Lucia, though she might have thought that the sight of other people's shit, vomit and blood would have been a problem. One of her friends had given up a cleaning job where the woman in the house had left used sanitary napkins discarded on the floor. No, for Lucia it wasn't the bathroom that irritated her, it was washing clothes. For one thing, cleaning the bathroom was pretty standard, but families seemed to have very different ideas as to who washed whose clothes. She had friends where the family washed all the clothes, including those of the au pair, and others where the au pair washed her own and the children's clothes – which seemed to her the most natural arrangement. But her family expected her also to wash the parents' clothes. She couldn't put her finger on it, but it somehow seemed that, while cleaning the parents' bathroom was natural, washing their clothes seemed to her to cross a boundary between treating her as an au pair and treating her as a servant. It didn't fit the job description of 'help with everyday household tasks'. There was also a problem of intrusion into intimacy. She could not understand why the Christies did not mind that someone else could see and touch their used underwear.

She knew for others it was still more complicated. Some were expected to wash the parents' and the childrens' clothes, but the parents become quite offended if these were ever mixed up with the au pair's own clothes. One friend was shocked when her host mother ordered her to wash her clothes separately and at specific times. Lucia, like most Slovaks, tended to divide washing colours separately, while English families seemed to wash them together. Lucia could not bear the idea that her beautiful yellow socks with pink teddies would be washed with someone's blue jeans. She realized, however, that in most cases such subtle issues of dirt, disgust and separation did not specify some broad cultural distinction between all Slovaks and all English people. It was probably rather that there was something about liquids and stains that were personal and individual. For example, Lucia thought she couldn't bear the idea of washing the clothes of two persons together. She thought it was unhygienic to wash her clothes with those of people outside her own family. Yet, in practice, she didn't mind having her clothes washed with those of another au pair. In fact she once, when visiting, gave Lenka her knickers to wash with Lenka's own clothes. She didn't read psychology, let alone psychoanalysis, but felt vaguely that there were some deeper *issues* (in both senses of that word) at stake here.

Lucia also had more of a problem with the parents' bedroom than their bathroom. It wasn't any big deal; it was just the problem of feeling intrusive. Should she, for example, be tidying the clothes inside their wardrobes, or only things that were on public display? Sometimes she just felt out of synch with this particular family. They would often tell her not to pick up the clothes left around in the children's room because the children needed to learn to be tidy themselves. This made a change from their usual over-protectiveness, but she needed to tidy the clothes away just to clean the room. In contrast, being expected to pick up the parents' clothes from their bedroom floor made her feel like a servant. After a while she resented the way she had become so concerned with such ridiculously trivial and yet constantly demanding decisions. It was often these which made the whole process of cleaning so tiring and stressful, and she was frustrated that she allowed such things to matter at all. She had heard stories of people who got divorced because the husband wouldn't put the cap back on the toothpaste. She didn't want to become like that.

She started to realize that people could see things in quite different ways, which is why she tried not to rebel against the request to clean the shower tiles with a toothbrush, although she somehow found this confusion of categories somewhat disgusting, not to mention the unnecessary additional labour it involved. It also reminded her of the kinds of bullying meted out to recreant soldiers in the Slovak forces, which could include cleaning the bathroom floor with a toothbrush. Sometimes you just had to let things go. Not everything could be an issue. The worst problem was trying to get away from this underlying sense of fairness, that it was somehow her duty always to get the balance right, even with regard to such trivial issues.

Lucia tended to err on the side of caution. She remembered the horror story she heard from the Christies when she first started, about a Czech au pair who had thrown away some plastic souvenirs, assuming they were junk or rubbish, but which were in fact mementos the Christies had kept from the time they had dated. Lucia had once accidentally broken a small China ornament. She couldn't bring herself to tell Mrs Christie, but had left the pieces out so that it was obvious what had happened. Fortunately Mrs Christie seemed to understand that actually to mention such a thing would be to make an issue of it, which they both wanted to avoid. On another occasion she had damaged a silk blouse she was ironing for the Christies' neighbours, the Grahams, one of her additional jobs. Her first response was to hide the blouse and buy a brand-new replacement. But when she realized that this would cost most of her weekly pocket money, she faltered and decided instead simply to hope that Mrs Graham wouldn't notice. Fortunately if Mrs Graham had ever become wise to the situation she never mentioned it to Lucia.

Increasingly Lucia found herself adopting this technique, which seemed to be common to English homes, of simply not discussing or referring to ambiguous situations. For example, when she had a day off from work, there was still a kind of expectation that certain minor elements of tidying and cleaning, such as unloading the dishwasher, would still be done by her. She somehow knew what they were and did them, without, however, taking on other tasks that would have seemed to her even more a contravention of the idea that this was not a working day. To be frank it was partly the things that she had realized no one would do if she didn't do them – meaning that she would have had more to do the next day. There was a subtle difference between this and the situation with her friend Tomáš. He tended to help on his days off but much more in the spirit of a family member doing their share, and this was reciprocated by the family doing things for him that went beyond the basics. So for them it was almost a case of competitive generosity, while for her it threatened to be more like a competition over who was taking advantage of whom.

At twelve Lucia stopped for lunch and a break. The lunch was just a basic sandwich – today cheese and ham. It took less than five minutes both to make and to eat it and have coffee. She remained a little peckish, and so went upstairs and took a small bar of chocolate from the children's sweet box in their room. They were so small that she could sometimes take several in one day, and it just didn't seem like anything. The children never noticed. They took pride in nagging their parents for sweets and chocolates but didn't seem so bothered about actually eating them. She knew that she should be doing some homework for her language school, but she really couldn't be bothered. She turned on the television, but it was just *Trisha*, and she wasn't in the mood for watching a lesbian couple fighting in public over their private affairs. If it had been one of those programmes about how to choose clothes, she would have watched. She especially liked the programme on home decorating. She did not understand the language as well as she would have liked, but she got the gist of it. The British clearly needed to see programmes by experts telling them how to keep their home, how to decorate them and keep them tidy, since they don't know how to do this themselves. Apparently, this was also why they needed au pairs.

After a few minutes she turned the TV off and went upstairs to use the computer. This was one of the major virtues of the Christies, that when they were out she could have as much use of their wireless internet connection as she liked. This was not that common. Most Slovak au pairs had to resort to the free internet access in the library. Lucia logged on to a Slovak chat room called *Pokec*. She spent a few minutes on another chat room called *Zahraničie* ('Abroad') to write some notes to other au pairs. None of them were on-line at the time, so she couldn't chat, but they would get her notes later on. She did not write anything serious – just hellos and things such as 'I have just finished cleaning and I am totally bored, like always', plus some suggestions for a weekend meeting in a pub. Then she went on to the 'Flirt' room, but there were only silly notices such as the one from a man who wanted to get in touch with a woman who would not mind that he already had a girlfriend and a rather vulgar appeal from someone looking for oral sex. She returned to the 'Abroad' room and found quite an interesting woman who had been in London for several years and was working as a secretary for a politician. They chatted for some time about whether they wanted to stay in London for the longer term. But after a while Lucia became bored again, and in any case she had to get ready for her regular cleaning job with the Graham family.

Lucia was lucky in that the Grahams were just across the road. She had met them one afternoon when they had come to visit the Christie family. She found they had already asked four of the Christies' previous au pairs to clean for them, and seemed to assume that she would agree to do the same. In fact that suited her fine. Of the three families for whom she did extra cleaning they were easily the most conveniently situated. After a couple of months spent in London Lucia decided it was time to find more such jobs on the side. As she put it to her friend: 'I went around Oxford Street and did some monuments for one weekend. And here, I have seen Tesco, and gone once round the sport shops and Homebase. There is not much else to see – it's time to start working.'

It had been more difficult to find the other two families. She had first tried an advertisement at the local newsagent, but hadn't got a single response. She realized that, for cleaners, families preferred to rely on their own and their au pair's personal networking. Similarly most au pairs found work through other au pairs, which was how she then found her two additional jobs. Actually there was an interesting 'market' here. When someone was leaving and there were good jobs waiting to be inherited, those returning home passed on the information to their friends. Better friends could inherit better jobs, or at least were the first to be told about them. Paula felt deeply offended when an au pair who was not in her 'best friends' circle asked her if she could inherit her extra jobs when she decided to return to Slovakia. One of the ambiguities about au pair friendships was that they all recognized the usefulness of friendship as networking.

Some au pairs preferred a regular cleaning slot, so that the house didn't get too untidy or dirty between visits. But Lucia rather liked the arrangement with the Grahams of just a couple of two-hour slots a week, during which she just came over and did what she could. Neither side expected that this alone could make her responsible for the overall appearance of the house. Also, this arrangement prevented her from being given additional unpaid and exploitative work – she stayed in the house only for the hours for which she was paid. Today she did just one hour in the kitchen and a second ironing, and that was it. Lucia cleaned in one other house once a week and babysat for another family once or twice a week. That left her with two afternoons a week with no extra cleaning, which pretty much suited her. The extra cleaning paid £6 an hour, although she had to pay £3 for a bus pass each time to get there. But the Grahams paid her £7, so overall she made an extra £48 a week to add to the £65 a week she earned in 'pocket money' from the Christie family.

Since Lucia's only language learning consisted of free lessons from a local Learndirect, and she therefore didn't need a regular bus pass, she actually found herself a fair bit better off than many other au pairs. She was saving up to pay back her parents the loan they had given her for her travel expenses to London and to pay the fare for her return trip to Slovakia at Christmas. She also still paid her health insurance in Slovakia, given she wasn't employed there for the duration. This all amounted to £450 for six months. Once she had factored in a reasonable amount for drinking and clothes, she wouldn't have been able to save enough money without the additional jobs. True, Lenka somehow managed to save around £30 a week, and Veronika managed to pay for her language school. But Lucia was having a pretty good time, and that just isn't possible in a place like London without spending a significant amount of money.

The other major expense would be Christmas presents. Lucia was looking forward to returning home at Christmas with wonderful presents for her family – not just cheap souvenirs, but real treats: that beautiful watch in Argos she wanted to buy for her mum, some sports clothes for her boyfriend and brother. At a workshop she also painted a plate, with a small elephant and the inscription 'I love you'. That was another present for her boyfriend. And, of course, there had to be clothes for her sisters, one of whom not only had exactly her figure, but also shared her taste in clothing. So when Lucia went to Primark or the more luxurious H&M or the sales at ESPRIT, she was continually buying things for this sister.

Lucia's older sister was herself a former au pair, and they were constantly on the phone or on-line chat, as Lucia wanted advice about her host family and life in London in general – little tips such as a Boots card to save money when buying cosmetics, or the pound shops in

Kilburn. Her sister missed many things from London and would ask Lucia to buy her a particular perfume, some tights, or Tesco orange marmalade and Italian pesto. Lucia couldn't imagine how she would pack and carry all this stuff at Christmas. One thing that had shocked her was how many migrants from other countries were expected to send money back to their families from the little they earned while in London. In Slovakia there was no expectation at all that she should have to give up any of the money she earned to anyone, only that she bring back some presents. Much more went on clothes and having fun with friends than on savings. So, although she hated calling the money she received from the Christies 'pocket money', and insisted on calling it a wage (after all, she was actually working there, not just 'helping' with Mrs Christie's housework), in practice she was treating it rather more like pocket money – to be spent on treats, extras and fun.

After finishing cleaning at the Grahams, Lucia hurried back home, took a quick shower and rushed to pick up the children. She managed to get to the bus stop just in time. Claire and John ran out of the school bus and started walking home, engaged in some banter with other neighbourhood children. They did not pay her any attention. She felt she might as well be invisible. Lucia did not really mind today. She just shouted at them not to cross the road without her. Claire and John tried to pretend they hadn't heard her, but eventually waited and John, finally, held her hand as requested. Lucia was traumatized by such things. She generally hated being with the children out in public and didn't feel she could cope with the responsibility for their safety. She didn't feel self-confident enough to be sure they would either wait for her or obey her. She envied the older au pairs, who did not seem to have this same fear of responsibility, or who didn't share her insecurity about the dangers of the street.

At home, the children went directly to the TV room, where they watched, played, and did their homework. Sometimes they seemed to appreciate her company and they all had a great time together. Otherwise they preferred to be on their own, and sometimes it was Lucia who wanted some time to herself. Looking after the children might involve active participation in their play and homework, but mostly it meant just being in the house to ensure that nothing horrible happened to them (or to the house). Today John was absorbed with his PlayStation and Claire was moody. So Lucia gave them their tea and fruit and left them to themselves. Lucia's room was on the same floor, so she could generally hear if there was something fishy going on.

Her first action in coming into the house was to remove her shoes. She felt quite uncomfortable being the only person in the household to respect what she saw as a hygienic necessity. At home, she would sit on the carpet when watching TV or reading in her room. Here, she felt carpets would never be clean enough, given that everyone was tramping all over them with their outdoor shoes on. This was the source of one of her first misunderstandings with Mrs Christie. When she arrived she had asked Mrs Christie where to put her shoes, looking for some niche or shelf next to the front door. She was shocked to be told that she was expected to put them in the same cupboard in her bedroom as her clean clothes. In the end she placed them under her bed, although even this felt unclean and she imagined her visitors could smell them there. Until she saw for herself that they all kept their shoes in their own rooms she had assumed they were somehow excluding her, but, as with many such misunderstandings, she came to realize that often there was nothing personal intended. Mind you, she envied Tomáš, who had actually persuaded his host family to adopt the Slovak custom and to take their shoes off before going upstairs. It had been partly his self-confidence and partly his assumption that this was part of his new responsibility for keeping the house clean. But Lucia was not a man, and there was no way she would ask Mrs Christie to take her shoes off when entering her bedroom.

Like most Slovak au pairs, Lucia didn't feel she could challenge her host family about anything. She wouldn't contest unpaid extra hours or unwanted babysitting, let alone little issues such as shoes in the house. Similarly, she found it easier to lie about some of her extra paid jobs, letting Mrs Christie think she was actually going to language school at that time. She couldn't quite work out why she thought this was necessary. After all, Mrs Christie wasn't too interested in Lucia's free-time activities, but it just seemed like a sensible precaution to make sure that she did not know too much about her.

Suddenly Lucia realized it was time to make dinner. Dinners didn't vary much. It was mostly chips and chicken nuggets, fish fingers or pasta. Lucia was relieved she was not expected to cook – she couldn't. Her mother did all the cooking in her home. It was fine that dinner was just a routine reheating of ready-made food in the microwave. She was just a bit surprised that children and parents did not eat the same food, and that parents seemed to buy healthier food such as vegetables and fish for themselves and not for their children. In fact she liked much the same food as John and Claire – chicken and chips. The problem was not the meal but the way it was prepared. For her

74

meals should be freshly made, as her mother always made them. Lucia thought microwaved food couldn't be as healthy as home-made cooking. She feared it would soon make her sick. Nevertheless Lucia liked chicken and the children ate early enough for her. Being used to big lunches and smaller dinners at home, she was starving by the early evening. Also, she found the company of the children easier and less embarrassing than eating with their parents. She also sensed the latter might need some time together and she would be distinctly *de trop*.

Tonight Lucia reheated pasta and chicken and took the food to the TV room, where she ate it with the children. Then she put the dishes into the dishwasher. She planned to go to Alenka's place sometime during the evening. Alenka's host family had a great selection of DVDs and allowed her to watch them whenever she wanted. Alenka could even invite her friends to watch with her. So they could snack and eat sweets and watch *Friends* or perhaps the second part of *Bridget Jones's Diary*, which Lucia hadn't seen yet. She changed her clothes to be ready to leave the moment Mrs Christie returned. She was already due, but predictably she was a bit late. Less predictably, not only did Mrs Christie actually say hello, but she seemed to want to speak to her. It turned out that the issue was Lucia's phone calls. Mrs Christie asked her whether she used the land line a lot. No, Lucia did not; she just used it when she phoned home with a phone card she had bought at a corner shop. What Lucia couldn't have guessed was that, apart from the card fee, these cards also charged the land lines from which they were used. Lucia felt horrible. Mrs Christie was evidently annoyed, noting that she allowed Lucia to use the phone for UK destinations but not for calls abroad, while Lucia was confused as she hadn't known that pre-paid cards would also charge the Christies. Mrs Christie counted through the individual items on the bill until she arrived at a total of £64.35. Lucia was shocked that it could be so much, and also surprised to see Mrs Christie counting every penny. Mrs Christie concluded that she would pay Lucia £8 less every week until the sum had been paid back. Lucia didn't like the sound of this. She thought she could save the money and pay it back in one instalment. She also felt Mrs Christie was making way too much fuss, given even she must have realized that this was the result of a misunderstanding.

Mrs Christie was rich enough to have been a good deal more gener-ous in her accounting – at least to have rounded down the amount to £64. After all, Lucia was working more hours than she was supposed to in this house. Wasn't this precisely the time for a bit of reciproc-ity? If she had been paid the minimum wage for the extra hours spent working, she would have earned at least £35 more each week. Lucia could see she had cost them the £64, but she was far more resentful that Mrs Christie couldn't put this in the context of those extra unpaid hours of work. She just couldn't say any of this out loud – at least not to Mrs Christie. But she ended the day going off to Alenka with a real sense of the injustice and the hypocrisy of these English people. But, to understand why Mrs Christie insisted on being paid back the full amount, we need to turn to the way she saw the encounter, and in particular the idea of the soft touch.

The soft touch

What Lucia would never really know, and frankly wouldn't appreciate even if she had known, was how much of Mrs Christie's attitude and behaviour was a consequence not of her attitude towards Lucia, but of her experience of several previous au pairs. The result was a perspective that bore little relation to that of Lucia and had formed itself around one overwhelming anxiety in the mind of Mrs Christie, who firmly believed that, as far as au pairs were concerned, she was a 'soft touch'. She shared with most host families the expectation that an au pair could work up to twenty-five hours. With Lucia, as with all her previous au pairs, she was convinced that her demands fell far short of this requirement. But the phrase 'soft touch' is important, because it means much more than her simple assumption that she had treated her au pairs well and fairly. It means that in some way or other she felt that her au pairs treated her unfairly and did not respond to her general expectations of reciprocity. To be a soft touch is to imply that the relationship is failing because the family gives way too easily to the various demands of the au pair and after a while grow resentful at the way they are being treated by her. Mrs Christie would say: 'They see how flexible I am and now they take me for a ride.'

Typically Mrs Christie felt that she started off her relationship with all new au pairs with a series of generous gestures, such as informing them they would be paid even when the family was on holiday. She would offer to stay in when an au pair had a special party to go to, and spend hours helping arrange their tickets to go home, even paying with her own credit card, hoping that such gestures will be met by generosity and concern by the au pair. Instead she considered that she was systematically taken advantage of by au pairs who kept pressing for more and more benefits at the expense of a woman they had now learnt would give way.

For example, there was one au pair who then just assumed she would also receive some money towards her language school, while another constantly prioritized having fun over work. She would start with occasional requests to leave early in order to go out with friends. But these would become more frequent, and agreement was taken for granted, until she would just leave and expect Mrs Christie to take over regardless. Another variation was the au pair who had wanted to take jobs with several other families. By the time she left, Mrs Christie felt her home had become just a convenient resting place and food supply for the entrepreneurial au pair, who was making money through the sheer number of jobs she was holding down at any given period. She felt especially affronted when it seemed the au pair prioritized these other jobs and left her without childcare in order not to let down some other family.

As for Lucia . . . well . . . Mrs Christie thought that giving an au pair unlimited internet access as well as free phone calls within the UK was really pretty generous. Although the pocket money was not vast, when you added in all the free food, accommodation and extras such as this, it wasn't a bad deal at all. So, given all that, why should Lucia do the one thing she had told her not to do, which was to use the phone for foreign calls? She needed to show that she could draw the line somewhere, which is why she insisted on being paid back every penny. It was the same when she came home and found Lucia watching television. After all, she was paying £10 a week more than the basic £55, and for just one extra hour a day. So why should she pay just for Lucia to watch television?

Mrs Christie complained that several of her previous au pairs had started cleaning conscientiously, but over time had got away with work that was less and less effective. After a while she agreed with her friend, who declared that everything the au pair did had to be done again by her. Of course, Mrs Christie did not do cleaning after her au pairs had done it – that would mark a final giving way, but she was always on the lookout for what she took as the classic Slovak pose in the face of unwelcome authority, which consists of simply standing dumb. For example, the au pair repeats verbatim, 'No I didn't vacuum', but with such an empty look of incomprehension as to whether this statement has any further implication that there is no real way of the situation developing into a quarrel or further admonishment. The au pair stares astonished in mutual surprise at the fact that the act appears not to have been carried out, as though this has absolutely nothing to do with her. As it happens, this wasn't something she had ever experienced with Lucia, but she bore the legacy of the previous au pair who had treated her in just such a manner.

Another form of exploitation by the au pairs – one that has not actually happen to Mrs Christie but that she had heard about from others – was seen as abuse of the home while the family were away on holiday. A family might come back from holiday to a complaint from the neighbours about some rowdy party held during their absence, and a rather more extreme case had led to the dismissal of an au pair. Although she had been told clearly not to hold parties during the family's absence, she gleefully showed her employer the photographs she had taken on the occasion, which revealed, among other things, the use of the best crystal glasses by various au pairs and boyfriends posing in advanced states of drunkenness. When followed by confirmation of who had been sleeping in the parents' bed, and photographic evidence that the guests had included a man who had on a previous occasion been banned after being drunk and sick in their house, the host mother felt obliged to terminate the au pair's employment, even though the latter was completely shocked at this consequence. Many au pairs confirmed that there could be some peer pressure to hold a party in the house of a family that was away on holiday. But mostly these were quite restrained occasions, mainly involving collective cooking and watching DVDs. In fact most au pairs are remarkably discreet about activities such as drinking.

Things can get a good deal more serious. Most of Danny's experiences with au pairs were entirely positive, but with one exception. One particular au pair managed in a short time, among other things, to leave his children on the bus and routinely cross roads leaving them behind on the other side (he discovered this after she had left). She also ran up a phone bill of over £1,000 in a month and left the house phone number with a random number of male check-out operators at the local Tesco, leading to a certain amount of confusion in subsequent weeks. As it became clear that the au pair was simply unable to cope, an arrangement was made by which her parents came over from Norway to collect her.

None of the families that Danny worked with believed that they exploited their au pairs. They were genuinely convinced that none of them even worked as much as the legal limit of twenty-five hours, and anyway were paid for additional time. In general most feel, as does Mrs Christie, that they are a 'soft touch'. This is the precise opposite of Lucia's view, and her real disappointment that her attempts at trying to be generous were met only with greater exploitation. Lucia would have pointed out that £10 for six extra hours was nothing, even by the standard of the minimum wage, and actually in practice she was working more like seven hours a day. When it comes to evidence there is no doubt as to which of these two perspectives is supported. Zuzana spent her time actually with the au pairs and was able both to observe their work and to confirm the accuracy of their accounts. In fact, Zuzana found out that, in eighty-two out of eighty-six cases, many of which included those employers portraying themselves as a 'soft touch', the families were in fact expecting their au pairs to work beyond the hours specified by law or failed to respect other parts of the legal arrangement.

Consequently most au pairs felt that much of the work they were doing was not properly paid, was unnecessary and seemed more an expression of the families' power than the needs of the house. So it was not surprising that they did indeed find ways of trying to extricate themselves from certain tasks where they could. With exceptions, there will be some aspects of the au pair's labour that they do not particularly welcome, and some au pairs will learn over time how to get away with, for example, minimal cleaning. They may work out that the mother is fixated on having a clean bath but never really worries about the floors. At a party one au pair gave an almost formal lecture to a newcomer on the tricks of the trade and how to appear to have worked a great deal more than one actually had. She treated the new au pair as a kind of naïve 'newbie' who would not understand such things, which comes only from experience. She explained something the au pairs generally mentioned in interviews: that the new arrival might be tempted to show herself as willing and offer some extra service such as cooking. But inevitably the family would then just take her for granted.

As a result, both sides feel that they have been made a fool of by the other. Rather, as the classic housewife, they note how they give not just time but emotional energy and concern for the other party. But this is simply either not recognized or rejected, leading to a strong sense of hurt followed by resentment and bitterness. Both host mothers and au pairs will argue that they should really have found some way to take a stand, to show they wouldn't be a doormat, and that their failure reflects on them as a person – specifically as a weak woman or, as au pairs commonly saw this, as typical Slovaks, who are hard working and non-confrontational and, as such, easily exploited.

At dinner parties Mrs Christie's friends could talk for hours about the behaviour of their au pairs, such as the time when the family had even allowed the au pair to have friends over when they were away for a weekend, but on the strict condition that they didn't smoke, and yet there were fag ends in the garden when they returned. Some of these dinner-party conversations seemed to hark back to an earlier time of talking about servants. But more often such conversations are more analogous to the way au pairs share information in order to try and find out, by comparison, what they should regard as typical or acceptable. They dwell on the details of childcare and house maintenance. Where they become personal in reference to the au pair, they can extol as well as denigrate.

Some of this discourse about au pairs did seem specific to Slovaks. Typically host families first judge their au pair generically as an au pair, then quite often as a Slovak and only then as an individual. For example, they might be slightly surprised or offended when they find their first Slovak au pair does not seem to want to join them in a family meal, which they see as part of the proper integration into home life with the children. But after having had several Slovak au pairs they realize that Slovaks have a lighter and earlier evening meal. So Mrs Christie was not at all surprised that Lucia, after a while, did not usually take her meals with the family. Sometimes it also becomes clear that not everything being encountered is familiar. Mrs Christie remembered the Slovak au pair who had once cooked the stalks and thrown away the tops of the asparagus. Particular ethnicities are often compared. For example, Mrs Christie had a standard conversation in which she used to compare Lucia with her previous Czech au pair, whom she described as a 'princess'. A 'princess' is either an au pair who clearly has no expectation whatsoever that they might actually have to work for their keep while in London, or one who felt that labour such as cleaning up young children or bathrooms was far too demeaning. Such an au pair 'gives herself airs' and is particularly offended that anyone would expect her to deal with the less pleasant detritus of childcare. By contrast, according to Mrs Christie, the problem with Slovak au pairs was not that they were afraid to work; it was always that they took on too much other work. Actually Lucia knew of one Slovak 'princess', who came to au pairing from her degree in philosophy. The family waited and waited for her to start cleaning, which apart from washing dishes just didn't happen. So eventually they employed a cleaner as well.

Mostly, however, discussions of au pairs involved nothing that pertained particularly to Slovaks and concentrated much more on how to deal with a generic twenty-year-old from a place considered *foreign*. Many families would also temper their generalizations about au pairs with individual quirks. One noted that the period of a particular au pair coincided with the only time in the history of the household that they never seemed to accumulate odd socks. But such mysterious skills would not usually be attributed either to au pairs in general or to Slovaks in general.

Many host families genuinely see au pairs as an opportunity to demonstrate, as much to themselves as to others, their capacity for kindness and sensitivity. This provides a deeper insight into the use of the specific term 'soft touch', since it manages to convey just as much about the softness of the family and their potential generosity as the exploitative character of the au pair. Families will talk about the expensive holidays in France or elsewhere on which they took the au pair, usually with many compliments about her good company – though often with a footnote as to how much better the holiday was with someone else there to look after the children. On the other hand, au pairs very often point out that they are not paid their pocket money when they are taken on such a holiday and commonly have to share a room with the children they look after. In direct contrast to the au pairs' own accounts, mothers also often claimed to give the au pairs extra money for various additional services such as overtime. They would often claim their general remuneration was above average for that paid locally to au pairs. Again, obviously not all families made such claims. Some almost celebrated their studied indifference to the au pair as simply an employee who happened to live in the house. Others would tell long stories about the generosity of the au pairs themselves in terms of constantly wanting to work more hours than asked for, or never minding if the children went to play with them at times designated as leisure. Such stories rarely, however, showed any awareness that this could be a form of exploitation, or that the au pairs were, in effect, thereby being portrayed symmetrically as a 'soft touch' in their willingness to acquiesce to the increasing demands of their host families. Not surprisingly, children are rarely understood by their own parents as the perpetrators of such exploitation.

Nevertheless, relationships tend to remain relatively impersonal. Mrs Christie's lack of interest in Lucia was pretty typical. Very few mothers seem to have built relationships with their au pairs around the discussion of outside interests such as films, clothes, sports or politics. One mother did go out with her au pair on occasion, although the latter was slightly ambivalent, since she had never revealed that she smoked and therefore couldn't light up on these excursions. Occasionally a very warm relationship develops, especially around the combined love and affection felt for the children themselves. Not surprisingly, most mothers respond very positively to the clear evidence that someone other than themselves can have such strong affection for their children and valorize their sense of how special they are. It is probably this more than anything else that results in long-term relationships with an ex-au pair, who may pay visits for many years and continue sending gifts to the children and exchanging e-mails to keep up to date with their progress.

Host families vary considerably in how prescriptive they are towards the au pair. One will establish a rule that says only that no males are allowed to visit, or even that an au pair cannot return to the house after 11 p.m.; in such cases she should stay somewhere else for the night. For the family this may simply suggest an obvious concern for protecting the moral environment of their children or the security of their homes. They described such rules in terms of common sense or common decency, not as modes of constraint or discipline, though one has to wonder when, as in some extreme cases, the rules speci- fied that the au pair should not use the living room, as well as what brand of deodorant she should use and what time she should be in bed with the lights off. Hosts such as Mrs Christie knew of a number of stories circulating about the poor treatment of au pairs by employ- ers, ranging from very extensive extra work to turfing them out into the street with no notice, but these were always 'other' families. What Lucia found most difficult about Mrs Christie was not intentional exploitation as much as simple indifference to the point of coldness. But Mrs Christie could have told her that, in her experience, this could certainly be matched by the behaviour of particular au pairs.

The perception of the relationship is not necessarily determined by the actual remuneration or treatment. It can often depend upon a more subtle concept of fairness. For example, Mrs Murray, a divorced mother, showed great concern for her relationship with her au pairs. Both her Slovak au pairs stayed for two years and continue to have a close association with her. This suggests that Mrs Murray's repre- sentation of her caring and friendly relations may have been accurate. Nevertheless, she brought over au pairs on the basis that they would be paid only for the time when she needed them to work for her, and that did not include pocket money during periods when her children were staying with her divorced husband, which was half of the school holi- days. Since she had very little money and no social life and spent all the time she could with her own children, she even saw school half-terms as times when she didn't need to pay the au pair. She remarked that the au pair was welcome to stay in the house, but could not expect to be paid.

As it happens, this was a woman who as a single parent really didn't have the wherewithal to pay the au pair, and was having to work much longer hours than she would have wished. Nevertheless, from the point of view of an au pair, the idea that somehow you are employed only when the family happens to need you, and that even staying in the house is a kind of privilege at other times, would strike most people as absolutely outrageous. It is extremely expensive for an au pair simply to keep moving out at regular intervals, and she may well have a commitment to her language school. So, on the one hand, this represents highly exploitative conditions of employment. Yet this was a mother who could quite accurately see herself as generous and caring, and whose au pairs stayed with her much longer than is the norm when they were obviously entirely aware of their situation relative to other au pairs.

One can only assume that, while they were well aware of the conditions of their own exploitation, the au pairs put this into a context in which it was easier for them to relate to Mrs Murray's difficult circumstances, and to some degree sympathize with her position. Many others simply walked out when faced with similar conditions or constraints. These two au pairs, however, were prepared to live in a house with rooms that were probably a good deal smaller than those of their own childhood. Mrs Murray's two daughters, though both teenagers, were still sharing bunk beds, and there was only a single small television in the home. Mrs Murray generally lived on reheated fish fingers and other leftovers from whatever the au pair cooked for the children. So compatibilities of character and attitude can on occasion cut across issues of exploitation and power.

In fact Mrs Christie, like many of the middle-class women in full employment, was well aware of academic, journalistic and left-wing writings about the exploitation of domestic labour, and was happy to discuss with Danny her treatment of au pairs in relatively academic terms. Such families were tentative in making claims about the positive way they felt they had treated their au pairs. But they argued that, when an au pair decides to stay an extra year beyond that originally planned, comes back frequently to visit, or invites the host family to meet their family back in Slovakia, this seems pretty good evidence that they do not feel they have been the victims of exploitation. To take an extreme case, one Slovak stayed for four years with the same family, left for two years and has now returned. Her host family have visited the family in Slovakia, and both sides would claim to be fast friends. They remarked that, as a Jewish family in London, once they had visited the au pair's Slovak family and seen that her parents argued just as much in front of her as they did, they could now fully understand why they got on so well.

Curiously, the single most important factor one might have thought would determine the behaviour of the host family was very rarely mentioned to Danny by host mothers. As one South Asian mother put it, after describing various gifts she had bought for her au pair, 'I am leaving the single most precious thing with her, and if she is not happy . . .?' Yet this sentiment was otherwise almost never expressed. Although it was said by some that they didn't want untrained au pairs looking after their very young children, the idea that the way they treated their au pair would or could rebound upon their own children seems to be both unspoken and apparently unthought. This is one of the most striking conclusions of our research. After all, one might have expected that parents, devoted to the welfare of their children, are already, in choosing to have an au pair, opting for essentially untrained childcare. But at least they could help ensure a positive attitude towards their children by their own positive treatment of the au pair. After all, if they treat their au pair badly, how should they expect the au pair in turn to treat their children when they are alone with them – especially if the children are very young and unable to report back to their parents any ill-treatment?

If this whole aspect of employment is almost completely absent from parents' discussions of their relationship with their au pair, it seems most likely to mean one of three things. Firstly there is what is now commonly called *denial*: the logic is so unpleasant that people simply don't want or are quite unable to think about it – a side effect of their pragmatic choice of an au pair as their least bad option. Secondly, despite their avowed care and love for their own children, parents are actually a good deal more bothered about their own personal convenience. In most cases denial seems more likely, given the sacrifices parents can be seen to be making for those same children in other areas. But there is a third possibility: we think the fact that families are convinced that they do not exploit au pairs and see themselves as a soft touch helps them to overcome the potential worry over the welfare of their own children. Clearly all this is speculative. What we do know is that, for whatever reason, the likes of Lucia and Mrs Christie manage to inhabit the same house, sometimes for a year or more, and end up with totally incompatible representations of the relationship of which they were part.

Snippet

The timetable below comes from 'A guide to living with an au pair' by the Universal Au Pair agency, www.universalaupairs.com/family/living_with_an_au_pair.html.

Induction to duties
It is well worth taking the time to be very specific about the duties you are expecting the au pair to complete. Do not underestimate the cultural differences that may be highlighted when you have someone new living in your house. If you like things done in a particular way, then these will need explaining and demonstrating to the au pair. Remember, the smallest of habits can lead to misunderstanding so, if you like the dishwasher loaded in a certain way because that works best, you will need to explain this. This area is particularly critical where an element of childcare is involved. We all bring our children up slightly differently, and you will want to ensure that the au pair reflects your desires and standards in all activities relating to the children.

An example of an au pair's timetable as suggested by the agency

Monday
8.30 Take children to school
1.00 Ironing and dusting
3.30 Collect children from school
5.00 Prepare tea
Evening free

Tuesday
8.30 Take children to school
10.00 College
1.00 Clean children's bedrooms
3.30 Collect children from school
5.00 Prepare tea
Evening babysit

Wednesday
8.30 Take children to school
1.00 Empty dishwasher
Wipe around kitchen
2.30 Free
Evening free

Thursday
8.30 Take children to school
10.00 College
3.30 Collect children from school and take to swimming club
5.00 Prepare tea
Evening free

Friday
8.30 Take children to school
3.30 Collect children from school
5.00 Prepare tea
7.00 Bath children
Evening free

Saturday
Daytime free
Evening babysit

Sunday
Free

— 4 —

SORT OF ENGLISH

There are still many families in London who, when they first contemplate employing an au pair, have in their minds a cross between Heidi and Mary Poppins. But, equally, when young Slovaks first consider becoming an au pair, their imagination of an English family is not so removed from the Banks family of Mary Poppins. They are certainly not thinking in terms of the diversity or cosmopolitanism of contemporary London. They presume that their host family will, or at least should, be a white, middle-class, Christian or secular, affluent, nuclear household, living in a red-brick house with a nice garden where they will drink tea. The assumption that most people who employ au pairs are wealthy households living in places such as Hampstead is also evident in the academic literature, and was pretty much what we anticipated when we started on this project.

The reality turned out to be very different, not in the exception but as a rule. The fifty au pairs who were our respondents were contacted through their Slovak networks irrespective of the composition of the eighty-six host families for whom they worked. Yet, in terms of the categories they use for such families, only thirty-two were 'English' (*Angličania*) – meaning British, white and non-Jewish. Twenty-nine were Jewish (*Židia*) and were to a certain extent also regarded as 'sort of English'; six were 'Indian' (*Indovia*), denoting South Asian and taking in Pakistanis and Bangladeshis; nine were black (*černosi*), and included seven Nigerian and two Jamaican families; one was Slovak (*Slováci*); and in two more families one partner was Slovak and the other English. There were seven others, among which was one Iranian family and other European and American nationalities. Moreover, of the 'English' families, around a quarter were single parents (consistent with national statistics) who, along with the Nigerians, were some of the least affluent. Danny's sample is harder to characterize, since much of it was based on discussions with friends and relatives who have hosted Slovak au pairs, as well as seven families that were selected largely to coincide with the au pair sample. These families were all either English or Jewish, apart from one South Asian and one Slovak family. In addition, Zuzana interviewed one more Slovak family and informally met a couple of other Slovak families who have had Slovak au pairs. This degree of diversity in London contrasts with the relative homogeneity of Slovak society, where the major minorities are Hungarians and the Roma and other immigration is very recent.

As a result, less than a quarter of the families who hosted the au pairs we interviewed would have approximated the model and expectations of Slovak au pairs. Although there is increasing awareness of the presence of Asian and black families in London, the Slovak au pairs inevitably regard them as in some way anomalous and not really English. Furthermore, au pairs are rather unforgiving of the degree to which London is no longer the homogeneous population they had imagined. It's as though London has betrayed itself, or let itself go. And this sense of disappointment is directed just as much at families who are not affluent or are single parents as it is at non-white or non-Christian families. Clearly an exception is the absence of any strong feeling that the very large numbers of Eastern European immigrants is currently contributing to these changes. It is suggested that, since London has already given up on being properly English, their own presence is hardly an issue – that Londoners desperately need Eastern Europeans to look after their homes and children, since the English are too lazy to do the manual work involved in keeping a house or lack the emotional sensibility and care to spend the proper amount of time with their own children. Assuming that Asian and black families would be both dirty and lazy, and Jews would be mean and calculating, the general feeling is that moral, hard-working and properly emotional Eastern Europeans are somehow saving this city, its families and their children.

Any initial speculations and anxieties of the au pairs prior to their arrival tend to be focused on racial issues. When the agencies allowed for preferences to be expressed, prospective au pairs showed little reluctance to being settled with English or Jewish families. But they were clearly averse to being placed with an Indian or black family. The entirely unfamiliar rituals found among very religious Hindu, Jewish or Muslim families are actually less of a barrier, since the au pairs have no real reference point from which to assess their potential influence. For example, Katka claimed to have no racial prejudices, although initially she didn't want to be placed with a highly religious family as it might clash with her secular and 'new age' lifestyle. On the other hand, she had read widely about Hinduism, was curious about it and in the event was enchanted by the family she ended up with. More problematic was the situation for an au pair who was placed with a family of Jehovah's Witnesses, who were desperate to convert her and expected her to help them with distributing missionary journals and leaflets.

Other au pairs actually prefer the idea of a placement with a religious family because of their own beliefs; there is a Roman Catholic au pair agency dedicated to making good matches between Catholic au pairs and families. It is also one of the very few agencies that demonstrate real concern for their au pairs, looking after them when they have problems and taking pride in their conscientious treatment of them. Not that all such matches worked. Magda, who insisted on a placement with a Catholic family, found the Connors, though baptized, were non-practising Catholics. Magda was very unhappy there, insisting she wanted to pray before all meals and go to church with them several times a week. The Connors thought she was completely mad. Practising Christian au pairs sometimes preferred to stay with Christians of other denominations or with religious Jews. For example, Barbora saw Jews as people of the Old Testament – and thereby sharing part of her own tradition, since, as with other Slovak Protestants, she referred to her community as people of the Bible. Monika wanted to learn about Judaism, and was disappointed that the host family did not discuss their beliefs with her.

In contrast we did not encounter any evidence that particular British ethnicities wanted particular types of au pair, the exception being the most religious families, who are concerned lest they end up with girls that are too 'loose', especially if they had children of an age that might fall under their influence. The Rowlands, a very religious Catholic family with six children, wanted and obtained a Catholic Slovak au pair. Mat'a was indeed religious but, as with many Slovak Catholic au pairs, did not relate her faith and religious practice to clothing, and walked around the house in shorts or mini-skirts. Mrs Rowland was horrified and asked Mat'a to change her clothing. In this case, although the explicit grounds were immorality, Mrs Rowland clearly had a problem with the constant reminder of the difference between the au pair's young svelte body and all the weight she herself had put on after having six children, not to mention the presence of her husband.

The Hosseins, an Orthodox Muslim family, were quite explicit about not wanting the kind of au pair that spends all her leisure time dancing and drinking. They felt that in general there was no particular tension or issue around religion apart from some mild curiosity from the au pairs' side. The au pairs did not seem too put out by the ban on alcohol in the house. The one clear point of contention was again clothing, where au pairs would often wear short skirts or low tops that were viewed as unseemly. In Slovakia, conservatism and revealing dress are completely compatible in a way that they are not in Britain. Youth and a slim body are regarded as beautiful and worth showing off – Slovaks have a strong sense that they are generally an attractive nation. Revealing clothes are connected with youth, and not seen as opposed to any religious views or lifestyle. Mrs Hossein requested more modesty in dressing within the house. She noted that her daughter was starting to point out that she was being stopped from wearing clothes that the au pairs were free to wear. Mrs Hossein could also see this becoming a potential issue with regard to going out clubbing all night, with her daughter again already wishing to emulate the au pair. She began to dread Friday afternoons when the au pairs seemed to her to change suddenly from respectable and sensible young women and begin wearing things she would associate more with ladies of the night.

In all other respects, the Hosseins swore by Slovak au pairs, whom they saw as conservative and therefore more compatible with their own lifestyle than au pairs from other countries. The nearest thing to a complete clash of cultural expectations came with this same family and this same issue of clothing, or the lack of it. One afternoon Mrs Hossein returned home to find Vierka sunbathing topless in the garden. This is not unusual in Slovakia – people commonly sunbathe in their gardens, often in underwear and sometimes topless. The mother was mortified. She couldn't decide what was worse: the idea that her neighbours might have seen this or that her husband might have come home. She fully appreciated, however, that Vierka, of whom she was very fond, simply had no idea about how offensive her actions had been in the midst of this deeply religious Muslim family.

Many writings on paid domestic work reveal that employers of domestic workers, including au pairs, regard particular nationalities as possessing certain qualities which make them more or less appropriate for cleaning or childcare. What has not been addressed to the same extent are the stereotypes and prejudices held by these same domestic workers. On both sides such expectations have consequences for the subsequent relationship. Our evidence shows that the actual behaviour of families and au pairs has much less of an impact upon these stereotypes than one would have imagined or hoped. Even though the two parties are living together under one roof, experiences are constantly interpreted through the lens of ethnic prejudice. It is these stereotypes that result in subsequent generalizations. While we would not shy away from such generalizations if the evidence warranted it, this chapter will show that the overall experience of au pairs is neither better nor worse with English, Jewish, non-Jewish, Afro-Caribbean or Asian families. This would be the case with respect to formal conditions of labour such as working hours and informal treatment such as sharing meals, or indeed standards of hygiene and cleanliness. Since these stereotypes operate in both directions, this chapter will start by directly juxtaposing the key relationship – what Slovak au pairs think about the English and what the English think about Slovaks. Given that most of the host families are not what Slovaks regard as 'standard English', the focus will then move to all the other categories of host family that emerged in the fieldwork, ending with that of Slovak host families.

The English

The critical difference when working for 'proper' English families, as against Jews, Nigerians or, indeed, Slovaks, is that the English are the least 'marked' population. They are merely the ordinary, expected category against which all others are held as different or special. Au pairs generally feel that any family that chooses to have an au pair – that is, to employ a young, unqualified, foreign stranger to look after their children – must, by definition, be either lazy or lack proper care and consideration for children and for people in general. This confirms an assumption that indigenous English people are unusually cold and uncaring. When it is added to the mix of conflicts and exploitation that arise during their stay with the families, this initial concept of cold becomes a more general accusation of hypocrisy or falseness that is a flaw in the 'English' character. Coldness and lack of emotion are seen as generically English. So, when 'sort of English' families – minorities – are accused of being cold, false, hypocritical and incapable of true emotions, these traits are often seen as aspects of their Englishness rather than of their ethnicity.

Au pairs provide various examples to demonstrate this lack of care. Jarmila noted that the host mother was employed part-time and worked from her home selling antiques on eBay. Though the mother was therefore present in the home a good deal of the time, even when she was not working the child spent all his time with Jarmila. Jarmila was particularly shocked when the mother just seemed to be playing games on the computer and failing to take an opportunity to be with her child. Marika was equally horrified when she was regularly employed as a babysitter, essentially so that the couple could stay at home and watch TV together without interference from their children. This failure to act as a proper mother was seen as further evidence for the general lack of femininity, already evident in English women's refusal to make themselves beautiful through make-up and clothing. The au pairs use this as evidence to assert their own general superiority, as people who possess a proper degree of emotionality and are proficient at care. Furthermore, Slovaks generally believe not only that their women are beautiful but that they are the world's most beautiful nation.

The other possibility, and a slightly more positive one, is that English women do love their children, but they just are not able to combine childcare, housework and their own career. This is seen as being in marked contrast to Slovak women, who 'can cope'. The au pairs we have worked with are the children of late socialist or early post-socialist families, which is the generation of women who had to cope. Their mothers did most of the housework with very little help from men, yet it is claimed they managed to combine their work with greater involvement in childcare. In making such comparisons the au pairs constantly construct an idealized version of their own background which suppresses the many problematic features of the Slovak family during this period, including the details of their own families and upbringing. What is often forgotten is that most au pairs spent their early childhood in nurseries and kindergartens, where children were frequently placed when only eight months old, as well as the degree to which in Slovakia it is grandparents who generally undertake a good deal of the childcare and sometimes also the cooking, laundering and other domestic tasks in families where both parents work.

In line with this interpretative framework, au pairs constantly refer to the apparent slowness of English women: Marika said it seemed to take as much time for her host mother to prepare the carrots for cooking as it takes her to clean the whole house. In another case the mother was said to spend all morning making plans of what she would have done if she hadn't been busy making plans. Fortunately, English women rarely had to exert much labour in cooking, since the vast majority of food preparation seemed to consist of putting supermarket foods in the microwave, and, as such, was amazingly quick. This too was taken as a combination of lack of care and chronic inability actually to cook. Opinions of this kind tend to dwell on extreme examples or cultural 'misunderstandings'.

Slovak au pairs have all sorts of issues with the pattern of politeness and greeting. As might be expected, they have difficulty realizing at first that 'How do you do?' is not a question. Au pairs insist that, whatever is being communicated in this general English greeting behaviour, it isn't warmth. Overall English politeness is seen as false, since the initial interpretation of smiling and apparent interest as genuine signs of friendship is soon replaced by the discovery that politeness is simply politeness. Accusations of hypocrisy or falseness are reinforced by the central structural contradiction in the au pair institution – the largely misleading ideal of a pseudo-family relationship. Given the overall structures of power of which they are part, it is perhaps not surprising that au pairs tend not to see the positive side of fairness and moderation in the pattern of polite behaviour that is usually generalized by others as English.

If there is a 'sort of English' that Slovak au pairs seem on the whole very happy with, it is probably the Irish. Several au pairs commented favourably on their relationship with a people they consider to be a bit like Slovaks. Irish are commonly Catholic, they drink (this was stressed as highly positive by au pairs) and they know how to have fun. They are generally regarded as more open than the English and are said to be more caring and friendly both to the au pairs and to their own children. Radka, who was staying with an English family but babysitting and doing ironing for an Irish family in the neighbourhood, was constantly contrasting the two. The English family was described as cold and non-emotional. A common term is 'dry', which doesn't refer to humour but implies simply 'not having any juice' – that is, lacking in any form of emotion or expression. Radka was extremely happy when the Irish family phoned her when she was babysitting to say they would be late relieving her, since they were drunk. She saw it as proof of their humanity and openness.

As with other representations discussed in this chapter, we would like to stress that there is no necessary link between the development of a negative discourse and the actual behaviour of that section of the population that is being categorized. Au pairs pick examples that they see as proving the point. In the case of stereotypes about the English there is an additional powerful mechanism at work. During the time when they are living in London, the vast majority of Slovak au pairs have almost no social contact with any other English people who might balance the awkward hierarchy of their relationship with their host family. They see the English as the single most difficult group in London actually to get to know socially or informally. As a result, they naturally extrapolate from the behaviour of their host families, so that an encounter with people as employers becomes generalized to assumptions about the English character in general.

Slovaks – 'sort of Eastern Europeans'

When it comes to facing in the other direction and considering how host families conceptualize the Slovak au pairs, the findings have to be viewed within a general field of prejudice about what people from different parts of the world are naturally 'good for'. By now there has grown up a series of assumptions that, for example, associate Filipinos with caring work or Scandinavian au pairs with sexuality. As far as host families are concerned, Slovaks are part of a generic Eastern European lake which stretches without significant differentiation from Estonia to Macedonia, from which they fish for au pairs.

Even families that had had more than one Slovak au pair showed little interest in the origins and homelands of those who had stayed in their house over the course of a year. They found it difficult to answer a question about which other countries shared borders with Slovakia. Not only did they have no knowledge of the country of origin, they did not seem to know much about the particular person staying with them. About three-quarters of the families seemed to show this lack of interest, in contrast to the remaining quarter who became actively involved in learning from their au pairs. They saw the au pair as giving them an interesting link to a new place, and in some cases used them as a reason to visit Slovakia and perhaps meet with their parents.

Given the lack of information on and interest in particular individuals, host families start by seeing Slovaks in turn as 'sort of Eastern Europeans', which was taken to mean typically rural. As such they are expected to be natural with children. If they had had the relevant experience, then families commonly defined Slovak au pairs through a comparison with Czech au pairs and especially those from Prague. Families assimilate the Czechs as a kind of national middle class and the Slovaks as a kind of national working or even peasant class. This could have both positive and negative qualities. On the one hand, Slovaks were seen as hard-working, honest, authentic, conscientious and agreeable. As previously noted, at least some Czech au pairs were described as 'princesses' who saw their work as demeaning. They were said to be full of conceits and to have a sense of themselves that made them difficult and unwilling to enact their side of the 'contract'. Slovaks, by contrast, were never seen to be what the English call 'stroppy'. Typically, Mrs Gibson, describing Slovak au pairs, said:

> They were clean, quite respectful of the family situation, trustworthy, worked very hard, and keen not just to do au pairing. They all went out and got other jobs. Did more ironing, cleaning, waitressing. Merely being an au pair just seemed to imply a place to live and a core income, a safe haven. But during the day they were off working as much as they possibly could.

On the other hand, Czech au pairs were seen as comparatively sophisticated, educated and knowledgeable. Generally, Slovak au pairs were not considered as likely to engage in the vast range of 'activities' that middle-class parents in London now expect of their own children. So, the occasions when it emerged that a Slovak au pair had spent some time at a university appeared as entirely incongruous. Slovaks were seen, if anything, as anti-culture. One mother stated: 'Like when English girls go to Germany and France they learn about the life and culture. And I didn't feel they wanted to at all. They were just in it for the money and had great social lives. They weren't coming to further themselves or educate themselves. Just to get the money.'

The other generalization that seemed common to host families was that Slovak au pairs had remarkably little idea of what they were going to do subsequently. A kind of inertia set in, such that even when families would question them or offer to help them make plans, the Slovaks seemed resistant to any form of planning. Several families suggested they found a striking lack of ambition. They felt that their au pairs neither really knew what they wanted for themselves in the future nor took any steps to obtain it. One common observation was that their au pair could have become a student, but didn't bother with the basic tasks required in order to obtain a place in college. This was often mentioned in comparison with au pairs of other nationalities. It rather ignored the degree to which the same families seemed to define Slovaks as anything but intellectual. There was no sense of the number of au pairs who were already university graduates. Rather this idea of passivity complements their characterization of Slovaks as calm and quiet and stable, a general condition that could mean solid or could mean stolid.

Au pairs themselves may comment on the way that au pairing leads to this kind of inertia and passivity. For example, Elena was keen to stop herself gaining weight, which she associated with having to have her meals with the family, but she simply could not bring herself to explain this. Similarly, Ľudmila, who detests cats and found that the children not only brought the cat into her room but commonly onto her bed, simply felt unable to explain the problem to her hosts. Au pairs realized for themselves that they had become less inclined to plan for the future. But while families see this as an intrinsic aspect of Slovak behaviour signifying their peasant origins, the concluding chapters of this will book will show how it emerges from the institutional structure of au pairing itself. Even within this chapter it will become clear that the behaviour of Slovak au pairs can be entirely different when they are working for Slovak families.

This stereotyping of Slovak au pairs as passive and 'anti-culture' has particular consequences for the relationship between families and au pairs. The fact that a particular group of au pairs are portrayed as passive economic migrants who are in a way less civilized or cultured than others is likely to legitimate exploitation. We found cases where Slovak au pairs were discouraged from going to language school or encouraged to do more work because it was assumed that they were in the UK to earn money and not to learn English. All such stereotyping can degenerate into a more negative racism. Most families would be less inclined to see Eastern European au pairs in terms of pseudo-family relationships than say Scandinavian au pairs.

'Indian' and black families

The main result of the degree to which, in the last fifteen years, some awareness of the presence of 'Indian' and black communities in the UK has filtered back to Slovakia has been a determination that prospective au pairs should avoid such families. These people are generally regarded as in some manner or other 'dirty', and the assumption is that children from such families come home from school with lice, and that the homes will be messy and unclean. These were the two groups that were most commonly refused by au pairs on their application forms. However, as noted in the case of Barbora in chapter 1, agencies put considerable pressure on au pairs to accept host families, telling them that finding alternatives will take ages or may not be possible. As a result a fair proportion of au pairs do in fact agree to work for 'Indian' and black families in London, especially if they have already quit their jobs and the agency tells them that they might otherwise have to wait for months. Also most of these families are based in London, and London itself is such a powerful draw that it may outweigh the prospect of a more conventional English family based somewhere the au pair has never heard of. Furthermore, for many of these au pairs, such fears and prejudices are relatively superficial. Once they see pictures of children that humanize the prospective family, they quite quickly come to feel there is no good reason to reject such a placement.

In general English, Jewish and 'Indian' families routinely mentioned ethnicity in their correspondence, but some of the black families, probably sensing this prejudice, did not. Blanka had exchanged letters and extensive conversations with her prospective family, the Jameses. Since they had never made reference to being black, she was somewhat surprised when they finally met at Victoria station. The host father had told her by phone that he would be wearing a blue scarf, but when the only man there with the blue scarf was black, she assumed this could not be him. Blanka had written on her application form that she had not wanted to be placed with an Indian family (as she had thought Indians were messy). In the end she accepted that she was about to stay with a black family as an irony of fate. Though her subsequent relationship with her hosts was a good one, she never wrote to her parents that she was staying with black people because she thought they would be upset. After returning to Slovakia she confided this to her mother but never told her father, hiding from him the photographs of herself with the children. She therefore had a shock when after a couple of years the Jameses contemplated a holiday in Slovakia, and was extremely relieved when ultimately they chose another destination. Blanka couldn't imagine her father's reaction, not only to this black family, but to the discovery that she had been lying to him for two years.

In this instance, and in two further cases where the au pairs were unaware of the Nigerian background of their host families, the au pairs assumed it was an intentional withholding of information rather than the families seeing it as an irrelevance. Slovak au pairs do not necessarily see their refusal to countenance 'Indian' or black families as racial prejudice. Race is often hidden behind concerns about language and whether it will be possible to 'read' the faces of coloured people. The kinds of argument au pairs put forward, and very likely believe, is that, given all the other elements of this process that will be new and difficult to understand or get to know, such families represent a whole series of additional burdens that would make the transition that much more difficult. For example, it will be assumed

97

that for such families English is not their first language, and after all the au pair is coming to London to learn English. Or they say that they will not like hot and spicy food – a point of some significance, given that Slovak food is spectacularly bland. There is also the general objection that they are coming to London in order to experience English culture, and they do not recognize such families as an integral part of that culture. Whatever the grounds for such fears, they are clearly influenced by a history of more specific prejudice based on the analogy with the familiar Roma – still generally regarded as gypsy – population in Slovakia, who help give form and content to these fears. Slovaks routinely assume that the Roma are both 'dark' and 'dirty', so they are not inclined to acknowledge that actually Asian and black families have much the same standards of cleanliness and are messy in the same ways as other families.

Yet from such prejudicial beginning things can develop in widely differing directions. Svetlana found herself with a family from Pakistan in an old house, full of dust and with a wall half torn down. It felt like she was living in the middle of a construction site and immediately confirmed her prejudices. Her response was to stay there, but simply to use this as her base in London. When she was telling other au pairs she was picking up the children she referred to them as gypsies. As she put it: 'They fuck me and I fuck them.' When she left, she gave no notice. On the other hand, many au pairs grew immensely fond of the Asian families they lived with. In one case both sides simply gave in to their mutual curiosity. Nela has an undergraduate degree in museum work and was overjoyed to have this immediate experience of education in cultural diversity. Nela taught the mother Slovak recipes (something very rare for au pairs) and in turn learnt to cook rice and chapati, and there was constant chatting about food. She was included when the family went to a wedding and learnt about putting on bridal henna decorations, and soon she was being taught rituals for *puja* (prayers) and other ceremonies. In turn, at a function in their house she ended up with ten Indian matrons being shown around her room avidly discussing her underwear, which she had left lying around on the floor. About the only problem that arose was that the grandmother began to worry about just how close the au pair was becoming to the grandchild. The problem was solved when she decided that this au pair must have been a reincarnation of the child's mother in a previous life. Nela was even more charmed by this strategy of inclusion.

These two au pairs represent the extremes, but there were other cases where au pairs discovered elements of Asian culture increasingly attractive. In such instances the host families function as their au pairs' windows to 'exotica'. Despite her initial caution about spicy food, one au pair became a virtual addict to South Asian cooking. Beata working for a Bangladeshi family and, responsible for taking the children to see films, soon became an expert on the Bollywood actors and actresses, with a special penchant for Shahrukh Khan. Her friend staying in the neighbourhood found the music initially intolerable, describing it as half screaming half weeping, but also ended up as a complete convert to Bollywood films and music. These same au pairs, however, would still have particular persons or behaviours that they didn't take to. One was complaining about the grandmother of the house, who was untidy and seemed to expect the au pair constantly to tidy up after her. Others might not like the food or indeed the films.

More specific issues arose in relation to black families. It was only with respect to black families that there were cases of au pairs actually walking out as soon as they arrived and discovered for the first time that the family was coloured. In one case an au pair stayed all of three hours before leaving. Although, as we will note in a later chapter, there is a complex and ambivalent relationship to black men in terms of sexuality, this didn't feature as an issue in relationship to host families, who were seen as outside of the frame of reference that designated potential sexual interest.

Most au pairs saw Nigerian and other black families as effectively anomalous not simply because of their ethnic origin. Being placed with them usually involved staying in the rather less desirable London districts of Acton, Lewisham, Peckham and around Heathrow, rather than in the more trendy or upmarket areas they were hoping for. These are areas where very few people employ au pairs, so they were much more likely to feel isolated. Most Nigerian families that employ au pairs are themselves first-generation migrants and among the least wealthy of the host families. The most extreme example was that of Mrs Adenaike, a single mother employed as a nurse, who lived in a council flat with her three-year-old boy. Zdenka was shocked to find there was no room for another bed and that she would be sleeping in the same bed as the boy, who was still using a potty, and that she was expected to spend virtually all her time within the confines of the flat. On the first day she was given a broom made from twigs of the kind that she associated with the old peasant women of Slovak villages. There was no vacuum cleaner or cleaning materials. Zdenka was expected to work all day, with only one day off in a fortnight. In addition, although she was completely secular, she had to accompany the mother and son weekly to the kind of church that for her was entirely bizarre, replete with customs such as laying on hands, ecstatic dancing and fainting that she found quite frightening. The mother was also convinced that her son would fall ill if ever taken outside the home. Zdenka became desperate to go out and buy some Tampax, having been unable, owing to her limited English, to explain this to the mother. The mother became extremely angry when she discovered that Zdenka had left the house with the child for the time required to obtain the Tampax. In effect her whole time there felt like a nightmare in which neither side could really hope to have any comprehension of the other.

Darinka also recalled staying with a Nigerian family as one of her worst experiences. The problems started when she found the food for dinner so spicy that she simply couldn't eat it, even if she had wanted to. She subsequently felt that the Abedayo family were deeply offended, taking this failure to share food as a basic rejection of any possibility of friendship. From then on they stopped inviting her to eat with them and expected her to cook her own food – which might have been fine, but the only foods supplied were Tesco value-brand corned beef, tuna, canned tomatoes and rice. Firstly Darinka didn't know how to cook these, and secondly they were evidently much lower in quality than the foods the family were eating. In this instance she remembered one Afro-Caribbean father who claimed to have sacked an au pair on precisely the grounds that to fail to share food was to refuse the basic 'African' mode of sociality.

Again there were cases that went in quite the opposite direction. Another Nigerian family who worked in advertising were quite unusual in that, although they had already had seven au pairs, they showed none of the typical fatigue of other host families but were extremely friendly. Iveta really liked the food, and after a short while they were regularly cooking and eating as well as spending leisure time together. There was constantly a fun atmosphere, with lots of joking around. When the family discovered that Iveta had a sister the same age as their daughter they invited her to come over and spend her vacations with them.

Overall, au pairs tended to leave these black families quite quickly, but it is impossible to separate this from the critical factor of being in a district where there were no other au pairs. The choice then was either loneliness or perhaps travelling for an hour and a half to find another Slovak au pair. Six of the seven au pairs who left Nigerian families went to Jewish families, who tend to live in areas with the highest concentration of Slovak au pairs.

100

One of the factors that could result in a closer bonding and camaraderie between Slovak au pairs and Asian and black families was precisely the degree to which neither side considered themselves as English. This might be a practical bonding, for the diction of some migrant families was relatively slow and clear and therefore much more helpful to an au pair with limited English. In comparison an English-born family would often speak too fast. Yet such positive experiences did little to limit the persistence of generalized prejudice about these groups. The reason is that Slovak prejudices do not emanate from their own experiences but from wider stereotypes about black families which are emerging as a growing negative discourse in Eastern Europe generally. The relative unimportance of actual experience is found even more clearly with respect to Jewish families.

Jewish families

The fact that twenty-nine of the host families were Jewish was quite unconnected with Danny being Jewish, since the recruitment of the au pairs was conducted entirely by Zuzana through a variety of networks. Rather it reflected what seemed to be a very high degree of employment by Jewish families, something confirmed by the au pair agencies. Another reason may be that Jewish families tended to live in concentrations based on walking distance from synagogues (since religious Jews are not supposed to drive on the Sabbath), which meant that au pairs in Jewish families usually found themselves in areas with many others within easy reach. Such concentrations of Slovak au pairs then gain their own momentum through those already employed in turn finding families for friends and relatives. So through networks of personal invitations a district of Jewish host families may end up with a concentration of au pairs from one small region of Slovakia. Also Jewish households tended to be in exactly the kinds of areas that the au pairs had hoped for – that is to say, leafy suburbs with good transport connections to the centre of London. In places such as Finchley there were also specific restaurants, bars or shops that specialized in Czech, Slovak or often Polish food and drink (many Slovaks seek out familiar 'childhood' sweets or vegeta – a spice mixture used for soups. They may also swear that Slovak mustard is special or that English flour is harder to bake with than Slovak flour).

None of the au pairs had any previous experience of Jews in Slovakia, where the Jewish minority of around 3,000 is restricted largely to Bratislava. None revealed any self-awarenss of an actual or even latent prejudice against Jews prior to this experience. Indeed, the prospect of working with Jewish families was not seen as particularly problematic. However, by the time we met them, many Slovak au pairs explicitly laid claim to anti-Semitic sentiments which they attributed directly to the experience of working for Jews. At the extreme, Olívia claimed that previously she was horrified by what the Germans had done to the Jews during the Holocaust, but stated that she now fully understood the attitude of the Germans. Similarly, a group of Slovak au pairs and builders were passing by bus through Stamford Hill, an area settled by very Orthodox Jews. One of them looked out the window and simply stated: 'Those people should be killed.'

These are extreme examples of a more general trajectory that starts with the claim of being free of anti-Semitism but ends up being quite explicit about a specific set of prejudices centred on the idea that that Jews are particularly mean and exploitative. Not all au pairs follow this trajectory towards anti-Semitism: we also recorded many cases of sustained and very positive relationships between au pairs and Jewish families. But a growth in anti-Semitism was the norm. The au pairs insist that what they now feel is simply an objective description of what they have learnt about the nature of Jews from their experience of living with them and reject any idea that this is prejudice.

Au pairs clearly showed prejudice against English families as being cold and false, and their prejudice against black families was so strong and explicit that they sometimes just refused to stay with them under the same roof. Yet there is a contrast in the case of Jewish families. Only in this instance did we witness a growth of such fierce generalized prejudice. We are thereby faced with a difficult question as to why we should find this huge increase in anti-Semitism, given that it did not correspond to any objective assessment of their conditions.

The irrelevance of being Jewish

Within the ethnography, incidents commonly cited as grounds for resentment by au pairs against their Jewish hosts seemed to fall into two basic categories: those where being Jewish seemed to us irrelevant to the accusation and those specific to a Jewish context. Our evidence also shows no difference in the final form of anti-Jewish sentiment between those who lived with Orthodox families and those who lived with those who were entirely secular. Most incidents that caused resentment had nothing to do with the Jewish identity of the family concerned and were equally common as part of the general

102

experience of au pairs living with all families. However, it is essential to our argument that the au pairs themselves make absolutely no such distinction.

Since they are common to non-Jewish encounters, many of the problems are the same as those found throughout this book. For example, with respect to food, they range from au pairs finding they are not welcome to eat with host families to where the provision of food is inadequate. For example, the Mandels appeared to be generously permitting the au pair to take all her meals directly from supplies left in the fridge. However, when Zuzana photographed the contents of the fridge in question it was found to contain only margarine, jam, some fruit, a cucumber, half a pot of pickled cucumbers and some drinks – hardly the ingredients for a sustaining meal. In this case the paucity of food was a result of Mrs Mandel's obsession with dieting rather than anything to do with her being Jewish. However, if we examine the interpretation of such incidents carefully, we find that au pairs have a propensity to turn such general complaints into an exemplification of what they regard as specifically Jewish traits – meanness, exclusivity, distance and calculation. For example, one week, when the family had no change, Mária was given £70 instead of the agreed £67 for doing an extra cleaning job, But she found this £3 deducted the following week. This was seen as specific evidence for Jewish meanness, notwithstanding that this family were in many respects particularly generous to her – for example, volunteering to pay half her school fees for quite an expensive language school in addition to her wages. The concept of being mean was in turn associated with the inhuman face of the market. Later, in discussing the current transformation of the Slovak health system to one of more market-like provision, Mária suggested first that this would make it more American and then, on further reflection, felt the most appropriate expression would be more Jewish.

This orientation towards money could also become associated with Jewish exclusivity. For example, Barbora interpreted the Cowans' efforts to keep their relationship professional and fair as evidence of their desire to remain distant and to have their relationship based on strictly monetary terms. She felt highly offended when Mrs Cowan wanted to pay her for spending her free afternoon looking after the children following the death of their grandmother. Similarly, she was offended by attempts to pay her back for food she had bought for herself. What was seen by the families and by other au pairs as fair treatment was viewed in this case as Jewish calculation and exclusivity. In effect, Jews were being blamed equally when they did give extra money and when they didn't.

When following severe health problems Hana gave notice to her family, she was shocked that their response was apparently to see their investment in kindness as no longer worthwhile. They stopped paying her for the time she was unable to work as result of sickness, gave her no additional time for packing, no longer left her food despite her illness, and refused to help her with her luggage when she came to leave. This was notwithstanding that she had previously extended her stay at their request, although it had already been apparent that she was ill. Our evidence is that such deterioration in treatment, once the au pair had made it clear that she would be leaving, was quite common, even if this particular example was extreme. But here it was interpreted as 'typical of Jews – what else would you expect?', a comment supported by several of Hana's au pair friends. Our documentation suggests that there is no aggregate difference in the treatment of au pairs by Jewish as against non-Jewish families. What is clear, then, is that au pairs respond differentially to perceived ill-treatment by Jewish families, especially when this can be linked to conventional stereotypes such as meanness and exclusivity.

The relevance of being Jewish

Jewish families were divided equally between those whose religious practice was largely tokenistic and those who were deeply religious, for whom even the most minor element of domestic life is seen as an expression of their belief. Just as we could find no distinction between Jews and non-Jews in terms of overall fairness, the treatment of au pairs by religious and secular Jews proved identical, with good and bad practice equally evident in both cases. But even in what might be seen in terms of religious practice as middle of the road families, there were many activities au pairs found difficult to comprehend. For example, Danny belongs to the centrist Masorti tradition of Judaism. Au pairs in his household still had to come to terms with basic Jewish dietary and other restrictions. These include the use of entirely separate kitchen equipment for foods associated with milk and meat and the inspection of all foods coming into the house for vegetarian labels in order to avoid the presence of non-kosher items. They also experienced restriction on activities associated with work on the Shabbat (Saturday), such as not turning on the computer. In one instance Danny's Norwegian au pair complained to her agency when forbidden from eating bread within the house during the eight days of Passover. In more religious households these restrictions become

104

still more complex and confusing. For example, the restriction on work during Shabbat may include things such as not turning on lights or tearing toilet paper (which is therefore pre-torn). The au pair may find in some cases she is allowed and indeed asked to do some things that the family are not allowed to do, while in other instances is asked to share their prohibitions, especially when this is seen as important in demonstrating consistent religious practice to the children.

Au pairs found particularly confusing the extreme differences in religious practice between Jewish households. Sitting in coffee shops, they would often compare their experiences. When one noted that in her family she was forbidden to turn on the cooker, her friend was astonished because her own family, which she regarded as equally religious, seemed to have no problem with her use of the cooker. These common differences in degrees of religiosity were often interpreted by the au pairs as signs of hypocrisy or fanaticism. The Christianity with which the au pairs are familiar places far more emphasis on belief compared with Jewish families' emphasis on practice and interpretation, which also confused them. The emphasis on rules and strict prohibition is in stark contrast to the understanding of sin and repentance that is prevalent within the dominant Slovak Catholicism. A major cause of misunderstanding is that, in the Christian traditions familiar to au pairs, rules apply to individuals rather than to homes, while many of the rules they have to deal with in Judaism are conceived of as the creation of a kosher home and thereby applying to any individuals who happen to be present within it. In more general terms, they found it difficult to understand why dietary prohibitions on food and drink in the household should apply to them, as non-Jews.

Renata, living with the family of a rabbi, found the sheer quantity of these rules unbearable. After a while she became almost obsessive in her constant complaints to other au pairs about what she saw as particularly unnatural restrictions – for example, the prohibition on eating foods containing milk together with or after eating meat. Au pairs may also be shocked by the reaction of panic when families examine a gift of food that has been bought for them and immediately demand that this present must be removed from the house. Or an au pair may feel she is making a real effort by, for example, putting bread and butter on a 'milk' plate and the salami they would have placed on top of the bread on another plate and eating from the two plates simultaneously, only to find this still didn't conform to requisite religious rules.

Au pairs who feel that such rules, while fine for the family, should not apply to them are quite likely to observe them only when the family is present. At other times they will happily bring in non-kosher food and use whatever plates come to hand, especially if they have not been treated with consideration – for example, if there has been no attempt to explain these rules. The critical problem for the au pairs is the burden of being made responsible for overseeing the children's conformity to religious practice, which they feel distorts the relationship they are trying to establish. In some cases the infringement is accidental – for instance, when Miša gave children the yoghurt they had asked her for, even though they had just eaten meat, and was duly reprimanded by the mother. But au pairs may also happily give their non-kosher food to children, with the comment that 'Maybe they are no longer so Jewish, so it is better not to tell the parents.' Many au pairs felt that kosher restrictions also led to people focusing on rules instead of people. They see a concern for religious dietary conformity as sometimes taking precedence over areas such as nutrition or the health of the children. They considered such things as questions of choice, and that the family was therefore being capricious.

While a few au pairs were interested in understanding the theological background and a few families were interested in explaining such things, it was very rare that the two coincided. In any case, few au pairs possessed the fluency in English for such discussions. Some of the more centrist religious families, who often tended to be involved in welfare professions such as social work or development organizations, tried to be sensitive by presenting the au pairs with a choice. They encouraged them to participate in Friday-night rituals of bringing in the Sabbath before the special meal, and in some cases the au pairs visited a synagogue either for a more 'fun' festival such as Purim or on the occasion of the bar- or batmitzvah (coming of age) of the children. Au pairs could participate but also remain separate from religious activity if they preferred. Some of these Jewish families included some of the best relationships between family and au pairs that we encountered in the whole study, with families coming from Slovakia to stay with the host family in London or the London families going on holiday and meeting the au pairs' family in Slovakia.

Jewish families could envisage the possibility of prejudice but in general assumed it would be based on entirely different issues. They have many stereotypes about themselves, but one of the most common is that they engage in much more heated and high-volume argument than the English more generally. While for them this is part of their normal lifestyle, they could see that this might disturb the au pairs. As Mrs Stern put it, 'The most difficult job for them, since they

106

don't understand it, is all the screaming and shouting. I am sure that's why the last one left. They had had enough.' In fact anti-Semitism bore no relation to such behaviour, which au pairs generally preferred as evidence of a normal emotional repertoire.

In no case did any of the Jewish families show any awareness of the anti-Semitism of their au pairs. All those asked specifically denied this possibility. Even a Slovak host mother, who had converted to Judaism, was becoming quite Orthodox and could understand every word of the au pair, saw no evidence for anti-Semitism among the three Slovaks she had employed. They had joined her in the Friday-night prayers and generally seemed quite positive that they had learnt something from the experience. The Nymans were rather disconcerted when the au pair joined a missionary group called Jews for Jesus, which was specifically targeting Jews to convert them to Christianity. Being quite liberal and not very religious themselves, they were more amused than threatened by this situation, seeing the various mission-ary tracts left around the house by the au pair as more a source for dinner-party stories than anything more serious. On the other hand, some highly Orthodox families could be quite worried by even the slightest sign that the au pair might represent the importation of Christian influences upon their children.

The separation of prejudice and experience

It is not possible to explain our findings only by reference to the ethnographic evidence. We need to turn to the much deeper roots of Slovak anti-Semitism. Briefly, there are many sources of quite virulent anti-Semitism within Slovak history, even before the Second World War, when the Slovak government was unique in actually paying the Nazi Party to remove their Jewish population. During this earlier period it was also common for anti-Semitism to be couched in terms of employer and employee relationships, and many of the accusa-tions against employers could be matched by our evidence from these contemporary relationships. These included prejudice about Jewish meanness and orientation to money, as well as power.

It was common in pre-war accounts to find accusations that Jews controlled professions such as the law, so that Slovak servants could not obtain redress for any mistreatment. Olívia, the au pair who now claims sympathy with the Nazi perpetrators of the Holocaust, took this stance despite evidence that her relationship with her own Jewish (and religious) host had on its own terms been fine. The problem arose when she was cleaning for another Orthodox Jewish family. The woman of that family accused her of stealing clothes and CDs. Fortunately, a friend was able to prove to the police that she was innocent. But Olívia bitterly resented that her host family seemed to assume that she was guilty. This was one of several cases where au pairs felt that the trust assumed in having a stranger care for one's children was not extended to the more general relationship, which in the case of a Jewish family was much more likely to be read as a sign of inherent Jewish exclusivity. In addition, in this case Olívia expected there would be an assumption by the police that the word of 'a rich Jew' would take precedence over that of a poor Slovak.

Although au pairs do not see themselves as arriving with such prejudices, Zuzana's previous study of a contemporary Catholic village in rural Slovakia found that anti-Semitism was ubiquitous today, even though no Jews have been present since the Holocaust. She discovered that even the way she greeted people could be construed as 'too Jewish', where the concept of 'Jewishness' has increasingly become synonymous with that of ugliness, and has become opposed to the beauty associated with the Church. Anti-Semitism has become an integral part of villagers' vocabulary and cosmology. Renata, the au pair who worked for the family of a rabbi, wrote a diary of her encounters with Jews, which she hoped to publish in Slovakia, to reveal the horror of her experience. Similar diaries were occasionally composed in Slovakia just before the war, and au pairs' comments on Jewish families commonly rephrase motifs from these diaries, although the au pairs would not have been aware of the precedent.

So, unbeknown to themselves, these au pairs arrive with deep-seated structures of prejudice, centred upon quite ancient suppositions as to the negative character of Jews. There is no such structured prejudice about the English, black or Asian families. Contrary to the au pairs' claims, the precise form of anti-Jewish sentiment does not derive from their experience of living with Jewish families in London but repeats traditional and historical accounts of Jews as particularly calculating, mean, orientated to money and cold. So, despite all the issues that arise from the specifics of Jewish religious practice, these are not central to the expressed anti-Semitism, which is applied to secular as much as to religious Jews, while the specific accusations that do emerge, such as an emphasis on money and meanness, seem entirely removed from the kind of middle-class social workers that are often their actual host families.

These established genres of accusation therefore make sense only as part of the anti-Semitism that developed over several centuries in Eastern Europe in the context of political restrictions, such as the Jews being forbidden to own land, which led to the association of Jews with certain trades, including money-lending. Specific complaints of mistreatment, exploitation and meanness are equally common in accounts of Christian English, Asian or black families, who are exposed to different forms of prejudice described above. This chapter does not contain similar discussions about the historical relationship with Asians or English because there is no direct analogy. The particular problem with Jews derives not from their being 'sort of English', but rather from the fact that they form the one group that is also seen as 'sort of Slovak', having been a significant minority within the Slovak population for centuries. However, this has become a kind of bitter shadow, since the actual population against which the prejudice is directed has been almost entirely destroyed.

Slovak families

We have tried to be careful to keep apart generalizations made about behaviour from claims that certain people, such as the English, the South Asians, the Nigerians or the Jews, posses a certain character as a group. The same applies equally to generalizations about Slovaks. The idea that the descriptions host families make about Slovak au pairs is itself a sign of some inherent character or disposition is flatly contradicted by the evidence that they may behave very differently when the host family is also Slovak. In fact, among the worst treatment of a host family occurred with Agáta, a Slovak single mother. She attributed this partly to the au pairs' envy of the fact that she was relatively wealthy and established in an up-market location of London. Because she was Slovak, the au pairs saw this as a condition that could naturally become theirs. This led to the expectation that they would be treated equally, in the sense of sharing all the household resources, rather than merely being paid as an au pair. In one case this created an expectation that one individual should not have to bother paying rent after she ceased working as an au pair, but rather simply stay on in the house for free if she chose to do so. One of the things that most shocked Agáta was the degree to which the au pairs seemed to empathize with her non-Slovak husband, rather than with her, when she went through her difficult divorce.

Slovak families, or families where one of the partners is Slovak, tended automatically to look for Slovak au pairs, often through personal networking rather than through agencies. One couple, both of whom had themselves previously worked as au pairs, asked Erika – a second cousin from the wife's village – to become their au pair. The relationship started well: Erika seemed to love children and was friendly with the wife. But later on tensions arose around their divorce, which created a greater sensitivity to the 'allowances' they had found themselves making for their au pair. In particular, they wanted her to spend creative quality time with the children, such as painting dinosaurs, but began to realize from the children's reports that she spent much of her time on the phone, or at least not particularly involved in such play. It was also evident that she was scrupulously avoiding even the small amount of cleaning they had expected of her. After a while they felt they had to ask Erika to leave. Even though they then helped her to look for a job and offered to let her stay until she found something else, Erika felt offended. She stopped doing any work she had previously carried out and in the end left the family without paying for a very large phone bill. The situation was closely paralleled by another case where the initial period was benign, but the au pair simply would not countenance actually doing any serious work. When asked to do so she theatrically rolled her eyes and made it apparent that the family was becoming bothersome and irritating. However, the relationship of this family with their next Slovak au pair was one of the most successful we encountered: both the family and the au pair described themselves as being 'in heaven'.

These stories of employment of Slovaks by Slovaks, some of which came from outside our main research group, seem to form a pattern. With one exception, the relationship failed after a relatively short time. Apart from one case where the au pair was treated badly by the family – and physically mistreated by the children – it was the au pair who exploited her hosts, refusing to take seriously either their childcare responsibilities or the expectation that they would undertake at least some cleaning. The au pairs could become rude and offensive to the host mothers, or simply ignore them. Although we have examples of exploitation and ill-treatment of non-Slovak host families by au pairs, these are rarely as extreme or systematic.

What is striking, from the point of view of this chapter as a whole, is how all the generalizations about Slovak au pairs as docile and hard working are here entirely reversed. While non-Slovak host families could never even imagine that Slovak au pairs could be stroppy, that's exactly what some of them were with Slovak host families. The presence of a Slovak host family complicates the au pairs' portrayal of English families who employ au pairs as lazy and cold because they don't look after their own children or do their own housework.

110

Issues of inequality are more evident and more unacceptable. Slovak au pairs, in general, resist any sense of class distinction and do not think there is any intrinsic inferiority or superiority in the relationship. They prefer to see being an au pair as a kind of apprenticeship in learning to live with the more affluent conditions to which they themselves aspire and in some ways expect.

Clearly the au pairs felt that the fact that these Slovak employers were not 'foreign' made their work appear much closer to that of a servant, something that they found very uncomfortable. Unlike their relationships with 'foreign' hosts, those with Slovak families had signs of both open class antagonism and class competition. Another possible misunderstanding came when au pairs endeavoured to cast the employer into an idiom of family relations in which there was an expectation of equal sharing of resources and work – a possibility refused by the host families.

There are several clear conclusions that emerge from this evidence. The first is that academic discussion needs to confront not just the racism and prejudices of those who employ domestic labour, but also those of the people employed in that work. Although there are considerable differences in power, there are consequences for these relationships that emerge from the assumptions and expectations on both sides. It has also become evident that the specific relationship that exists through the institutional structure of this employment commonly becomes misconstrued, on both sides, as the character of the group. So au pairs who fail to meet English people other than their host family see all English people through the lens of their treatment within the home. They infer a generic English coldness, laziness and lack of love for children on the basis of the au pair institution itself, while in turn host families see Slovak character according to the specific behaviour au pairs adopt in order to cope with their role – for example, an increasing passivity in the face of lack of control over their lives.

There is a striking contrast in the consequence of any feelings of resentment against slights and exploitation, and it seems that these will tend to be cast in ethnic terms only where such structures of prejudice are previously available. So if an Asian family can be viewed as dirty, this will be assimilated into an ancient prejudice against Roma as gypsies, whom Slovaks believe migrated from India in ancient times. Or Slovaks holding a university degree find this ignored as they are subsumed within a wider set of assumptions about the natural care or docility among the children of Eastern European peasants. The final and perhaps most depressing conclusion is that these structures of prejudice are largely unaffected by the actual experience of au pair and family living together for a year within the same house. The specific form of anti-Semitism bears no relation at all to the behaviour of the Jews against which it is directed, so, far from being diminished by this discrepancy, it flourished. Of course there are always exceptions: there were a great many positive encounters, and people change their views over time. But we cannot pretend that they do so consistently in the directions we might have hoped for.

Snippet

This is taken from a well-known Slovak blog, www.blog.sme.sk. The author preferred to remain anonymous.

It seems that a Slovak mother is superman . . . or what English mothers do not know.

An English mother . . .
. . . has three wonderful children, a dog and a beautiful, especially tidy, house. She works only from home, by phone and from her study. Her children are only at home during five weeks of holidays. They spend the rest of the year in some prestigious boarding school. But when they all are at home, the English mother has an extraordinarily hard time. Fortunately, she has an au pair, because to spread butter on toast for all three children at breakfast, or to make their beds, prepare their snacks for their tennis lessons, or to defrost their ready-made food for dinner, to vacuum, iron, sweep the floor, walk the dog . . . this all would be really, really too much for one English mother. When windows need cleaning, the boys from a company come. When carpets need washing, the boys from a company come, when roses need cutting, the gardener comes. So when the children finally sleep sweetly in their beds, and English mother is dead tired: housekeeping is very hard work . . .

A Slovak mother . . .
. . . has three ordinary children and an average, tidy family house. She wakes up at 5 a.m. to catch her bus to work. Her children are at home every afternoon and every morning they take public transport to get to their ordinary Slovak high school. Once their mother made their school meals, but then she taught them how to spread butter on bread without her help. A Slovak mother works all day, shops on her way home and walks back with food for her permanently

hungry family. A Slovak mother is dead tired in the evening, but does not need to talk about it. The reason? Who does the cleaning for a Slovak mother? Who cooks (not only defrosts), who does the ironing, vacuums, washes windows, the laundry, digs the garden? Something is wrong here. A Slovak mother has to have some special quality. So I reach a simple conclusion. England may have high salaries and an important position in the map of world politics. Slovakia has high beautiful mountains and extraordinary mums.

— 5 —

BORED IN BEDDLINGHAM

You could not even claim that Beddlingham is dramatically ugly, it's just plain. In many respects the high street looks like that in hundreds of other British small towns, although in most such towns the main aesthetic complaint is that they are dominated by the likes of McDonald's and Tesco. While in Beddlingham the single most attractive building is the local McDonald's, and far and away the best Beddlingham coffee is to be found in Tesco's café, it has one of the those main roads that has been reworked to ensure the easy flow of traffic, as though the planners were trying to guarantee that drivers pass through the place as quickly as possible. From this main road, side streets lead out to charmless, though reasonably affluent, rows of semi-detached and detached houses. To be fair, as everywhere in England, you will find oases of pretty front gardens or districts of more interesting homes. But other roads lead to council estates of unremitting ugliness.

There is nothing, then, that gives a sense of history or character to the place. To be honest, charming and authentic architecture is probably not the au pairs' main concern, but for them too Beddlingham is a place of isolation and boredom, alleviated only by gossip. Above all it's a place of disappointment. The problem is that so many au pairs imagine they are coming to London, and yet they mostly end up in places such as Beddlingham. For Slovak au pairs, Beddlingham is *paža*, literally 'an arm'. The English equivalent would be 'the middle of nowhere', but the Slovak term is both more active and appropriate; it means landing, or being dumped, in a nowhere that is an appendage to a somewhere. While Beddlingham is a pseudonym, an astonishing number of the Slovak au pairs we encountered seem to have ended up at equally *paža* places – Watford, Borehamwood, Ickenham, Hadley

Wood or Orpington – sufficiently middle class to require a reasonable number of au pairs, but sufficiently outer suburban for au pairs to realize that, whatever place it is, it isn't really the kind of London they expected. Some of them, unlike Beddlingham, are actually quite pretty, but they are all pretty boring from the perspective of an au pair. One of the things that surprises au pairs is that the condition of Beddlingham is not a sign of lack of affluence. They visit other centres where the average house might be smaller but somehow there is some character. Possibly there is an ethnic element such as a Bollywood cinema, some night life such as a couple of clubs, or some more interesting shops. At first they don't understand why a place such as Beddlingham has none of these. After a while they realize it is because these are true commuter sites, where both work and shopping is done elsewhere. It is only for the people left behind during the day – the housewives, the unemployed and the au pairs – that the lack of amenities becomes defining of the place. Worst of all, such places tend to be 'sixth zone', which means that it is seriously expensive in terms of transport to and from the centre of London.

It's like – where do you go in Beddlingham? OK, so there are three pubs, but at lunch time these are filled with working men, and if au pairs go inside they are liable to be about the only women there. This is not so true of Weatherspoons, but then Weatherspoons is the au pair pub, from Ickenham to Ilford, from Sevenoaks to Stratford, the pub that has special deals at lunch time, a two for one, even if the choice is pretty much limited to fish and chips, chilli con carne, lasagne and a Caesar salad. Beddlingham does have a Weatherspoons and its equivalent café, Jenny's, with its plastic tables and plastic pretty much everything else and a particular smell of disinfectant that signals its presence even before you enter. There is also a Jenny look-alike café, but that's where the Polish au pairs go.

Of course this is all relative. Au pairs in places such as Radlett flock to Beddlingham for an outing, since it has a swimming pool, charity shops and a twice-a-week open market with gypsy skirts at knock-down prices that look just the same as ones from the shops. Actually there is even a sort of highlight: a proper pizzeria, which – even if they don't like the way the manager treats his Czech workers and gets grouchy when they order only coffee, or share one pizza between three – is still a sort of restaurant. And, oh, one of the pubs has a karaoke on Wednesday night, worth getting drunk for.

Another significant asset is the Learndirect centre where, if you are from the EU, you can take courses that range from English language to the use of computers, and, as long as you finish the term, they are free. As they are computer based, they allow for flexible hours, which fits au pairs perfectly, although it means there is little practice in spoken English and the contact with teachers and class-mates is limited. This is a distinct advantage compared with some places, which simply don't have affordable English classes and from where it is too expensive to commute to ones in London. Many individuals mention language as their motivation for becoming an au pair. Foreign languages, and especially English, command high cultural capital in Slovakia, where people joke that these days even to get a job as a cleaner one will be asked about one's proficiency in English. Zuzana met an au pair who declared, with some surprise, that English is almost as important for finding good work in England as in Slovakia, though some au pairs thought having fluent English could lead potential host families to suspect they would soon quit and migrate to a proper job (one au pair was rejected on these grounds). For all this, Slovak au pairs were unusual in comparison to au pairs from other regions in the proportion that don't end up in formal English-language training. Only around half them were registered at a language school – though if Beddlingham had had a language school, many au pairs would have gone there just to escape boredom and meet people.

Beddlingham's one really successful facility is its public library – not its books, though it seems impressive on that score, but the free inter-net access. Within a couple of days, families who don't particularly want their home computer colonized by some foreign language have pointed their au pair in that direction. The librarians support them as best they can. Users are supposed to have evidence of a fixed address but, rather than bother the family, if an au pair returns a letter sent to her address they allow her to register. Once there, the connections to be made off-line are just as productive as the ones on-line. If you peer over the screen and spot someone using www.post.sk, www.azet.sk, www.london.sk or www.pobox.sk, you know you are going to stop for a chat. So, while Radlett may be pretty and surrounded by open countryside, having a place to look at is just not the same as having a place in which to do things. Beddlingham at least has excuses for killing time and, above all, it is cheap, as cheap as anywhere au pairs are going to find. In turn, from Beddlingham one can migrate north to the likes of St Albans or south to Finchley, other worlds where things cost more, but where you will also be paid more for cleaning and other additional jobs.

The one skill that au pairs in Beddlingham cultivate is the art of killing time. There are various methods. One could go around Tesco's shelves and look at the goods on display. And the next day go back and do the same thing. One could communicate with home as much as possible, write long e-mails and letters, and postpone 'real' life until the moment of one's return to Slovakia. One could go daily to a local café, have a cup of awful coffee, a daily dose of gossip and a bit of a flirt with the Turkish waiter, who would look just as bored by the activity as the au pairs. One could start learning English fervently, or try jogging in a local park, perhaps find a boyfriend. The other possibility is not to fight boredom at all. One could let it seep into the body, cultivate lethargy, stop doing even the tasks one used to do at home, and then inevitably find that one was eating sweets and other rubbish, and realize that the main thing one was really going to gain in Beddlingham was weight.

But the most exciting thing to do in Beddlingham was to gossip: to gossip with fellow au pairs about families, men and other au pairs, talk of who went with whom to Tesco, who refused to acknowledge whom, who was invited to eat the sausages brought from Slovakia and who was not, who phoned whom, who did or did not answer. As each came to know the others better, the claims could reach down into deeper recesses and shadows: who was sleeping with whom, and maybe how, who was flirting with whom and what was likely to come of it. Then there were always comments about clothes, ways of dancing, make-up. One group of au pairs had stopped talking to another group of au pairs entirely. They wouldn't even greet them if they saw them in the street – a studied indifference that was bound to elicit comment. It helped that alliances could shift. Moving from one camp to join another meant bringing all sorts of intimate information to add as ammunition. This steamy incestuousness among au pairs as a language group is really the by-product of their situation. Slovak au pairs don't come to London to gossip about Slovak au pairs. It's simply that they soon feel an intense isolation, worse than they had ever imagined. When they first arrive, they may not know anyone other than their host families. They assume at first that this family will be the centre of their social life. However, most families have neither the time nor the inclination to socialize much with their au pairs.

There were, of course, exceptions: single parents who occasionally expected au pairs to become a captive audience and genuine friendships between au pairs and families with common interests. Lýdia felt she had had a year's holiday with a young couple, who were as sporty as she was and took her with them whenever they went sailing. Or there was Slávka, who was going clubbing with her host mother, whose husband did not like dancing, or Dora, who came to London for a 'gap year', having failed in her dream to qualify for a university course in international relations. She was placed with a divorcee who was studying part time at university, and they became excellent friends who could discuss anything from books to men. But more often families and au pairs were like pieces from different jigsaws.

It was understandable that many families were interested in the au pairs only as part of their household arrangements. Much more mysterious was the apparent impossibility of au pairs developing friendships with English people of their own age. Apart from being chatted up, which often deteriorated into incredibly crude and drunken invitations for sex, there seemed to be no way of developing a dialogue with an English man. It seemed even harder with English women, who seemed cold and aloof, although the Beddlingham au pairs heard that English people in rural areas were a good deal more friendly. At least Slovaks could then join in that conversation that bonded all foreign residents in Beddlingham. Why are the English so cold?

The main exceptions were the elderly, who make up the other quotient of frankly 'bored in Beddlingham', and are happy to find anyone who will talk or listen. Often they would effectively 'adopt' lonely au pairs and keep a little corner table at the pub where they could have regular chats, at least some human company. They could also turn out to be the people who would rescue an au pair in an emergency. For instance, Marcela found a job on the side cleaning for an elderly man. Her conscientiousness in cleaning reminded Mr Hutchinson of his deceased wife. Indeed he frequently told Marcela that she should put on some weight in order to become as beautiful as his wife had been. After a while they developed a friendship. Marcela was coming to his house twice a week for cleaning, but she usually stayed longer than the period of her paid employment to have tea and a chat. The Stephens family she was staying with hardly communicated with her at all and didn't even comment on her work. Talking with Mr Hutchinson showed her that there must be English people who could be friendlier, and she decided to leave the Stephens. She gave them a month's notice, but they were so incensed by this that Mrs Stephens told her to leave within a week. Marcela did not know what to do, and in some distress called Mr Hutchinson, who said she could stay in his home where she would receive free board for cleaning. This was much more than she expected, and she happily accepted his offer. She stayed there for a couple of months until she found five small jobs (a mixture of cleaning, ironing, babysitting and distributing newspapers) which enabled her to pay rent for a room she shared with a friend. Of course she still continued cleaning for Mr Hutchinson.

Although most Slovaks come to London with the idea of meeting people from anywhere and everywhere other than Slovakia, they incvitably end up with other Slovaks and Czechs. Their initial halting English limits their communication not only with the English but equally with a Moroccan or a Filipino. After some time feeling increasingly frustrated at the sheer superficiality of their everyday conversations with their host family, they are desperate to be able to converse again as proper adults without being inhibited by a foreign language. One of the principal effects of the small places such as Beddlingham is that pretty soon one knows precisely how many other Slovak au pairs are working there and what the relationships are between them.

Time as well as language can be a constraint upon socializing, as free time is often at the behest of the host family. Even if there is a general rhythm of daily work, it is hard to visit au pairs in other areas. Marika was at first delighted to find that there were now more of her schoolfriends in England than back in her home town of Banská Bystrica. But, while on the map it seemed some of them were located with families in nearby suburbs, in practice she found that during either of the two leisure slots available to her, early afternoon or evening, it simply wasn't worth the journey there and back again for the amount of time they could have spent together, since buses across London seemed to take forever. The problem was exacerbated since her nearest friends worked for religious Jews, which meant having Friday off and babysitting on Saturday night, while Marika worked for a secular family who went out Friday nights, leaving her babysitting when her friends were out clubbing on Saturday nights. She realized that if she wanted company she needed to find someone who was already in Beddlingham, or to persuade her friends to come as au pairs to Beddlingham itself.

There is some help. The agencies will usually supply a sheet of local contacts for all other au pairs in the area that were placed by them. There are au pairs who attend (especially free) language courses, not in order to learn English, but so as to have at least someone to speak with on that particular day. Fortunately many of the families who employ au pairs come from a particular social milieu in which they know other families who also employ au pairs. Such networks of families may then gravitate to au pairs from a particular area of origin, partly through reporting to each other favourably about a previous experience, and consequently become a good source of contacts.

Hana's host mother had a wide circle of friends among Orthodox Jewish women and was very effective in making these kinds of contacts for her. In her case this extremely successful 'matchmaking' had unintended results. As it happens, Hana had a very good friend nearby and was far from lonely. But she started to discover that the new au pairs, who arrived with limited English, were expecting her to help them with finding a language school and with many other such tasks. Hana would have to spend time and money visiting, explaining things such as library access and how local transport worked. Increasingly she felt exploited, as when she took considerable time integrating Nina into the neighbourhood, only to find that Nina then refused even to go for a walk with her in the park at the weekend.

Some families try to organize a week's overlap with a departing au pair, who can then explain routines and tasks in Slovak, saving them endless trouble. This also means the departing au pair can introduce the newcomer to a ready-made network of friends. Alenka shared her first week at the Green family with their previous au pair, but found her irritating and patronizing and would have preferred to have learnt directly the Greens about her duties and responsibilities. On the other hand, she admitted that the contacts with other au pairs were invaluable – how else would she have found out about them? She would not have dared go to the pub on her own. How can you meet someone in a totally unknown place when your job does not provide you with any obvious opportunities? But although you might 'inherit' an au pair group from a previous au pair who had spent some time in that area, there was no guarantee that they would welcome you. Indeed, an established group of settled au pairs may even have fun being difficult or downright nasty to a newcomer.

Under these conditions, it is not surprising that there is a palpable sense of relief when sometimes in a shop, in a pub or at a bus stop one happens to overhear someone talking to a friend, or on the phone, in Slovak – even more so if the accent suggests the speaker may come from the same district of Slovakia as oneself. An individual in Slovakia would no more go up and start a conversation with a stranger in the street than would someone in England or France. However, a situation in which it is difficult to meet other people and there isn't the money to travel to other areas gives licence to such impromptu communications and expectations of friendship. It is equally unproblematic simply to pass on telephone numbers, names, addresses and contacts that might just result in a person to go out with for a drink, or go shopping with.

By the end of our fieldwork, the use of the internet to locate local au pairs was becoming more established. Websites devoted to Czechs and Slovaks living in London, such as www.pohyby.co.uk or www. londyn.sk, have introduced local advertising. Those interested can look for, or offer, accommodation or a job, and there is an extended section for matchmaking. Within this, most advertisements are found in the section headed 'Friendship'. This comprises questions such as 'Are there any au pairs around Orpington?' or 'Are there any au pairs who want to go shopping in Oxford Street with me this Saturday?' A much frequented Slovak chat site, *Pokec*, at www.azet. sk, hosts permanent rooms called *Zahraničie* (abroad) and *Anglicko* (England), and many au pairs are logged in at *Pokec* for the entire day, taking a peek whenever they can get to a computer, just in case they find someone they know logged on, writing short messages to their friends, or simply trying to find someone new who is staying in or close to their area.

Such networking was even easier at certain regular meeting spots for Slovaks and Czechs such as the weekly Czechoslovak Roman Catholic masses at a church next to London Bridge, or the Czechoslovak restaurants and pubs – *U vrány* in Willesden Green, *Jasmine* in Finchley Central, or the oldest London Czechoslovak restaurant in West Hampstead. These are places where, all for very reasonable prices, one can get Czech beer and local soft drinks, such as *Kofola* (an inexpensive socialist imitation Coca-Cola) or the grape-based *vinea*, as well as local foods such as dumplings with sauerkraut, potato pancakes, or deep fried cheese. At such places, clientele, waiters and waitresses are all either Czech or Slovak. On most evenings, but especially on Friday nights, there could be discos with Czechoslovak music, so it was easy to talk to strangers, and this might lead to invitations to parties or barbecues on Saturday. The fact that most Slovaks staying in London are twenty-somethings makes such communication even easier. Compared with her previous field-work in Slovakia, Zuzana was amazed how easy it was to approach strangers and how prepared they were to talk to her or to give her phone numbers of their au pair friends. People were generally friendly and cooperative, whether participating in research or socializing. During the entire year's ethnography only one au pair refused her an interview. All the others willingly participated in research they hoped might help future au pairs in their conditions of employment, and were happy to find someone with whom to share their leisure time, to have a coffee, or go clubbing.

Au pairs often gained most from their initial encounters. Most commonly, when they first meet, the conversation takes on a rather particular form – pragmatic and neutral. It starts with a basic description of their conditions of employment: the family, where they live, their facilities, pay, expectations and behaviour. Given the diversity and informality of arrangements, it is only through such comparisons that one can judge one's own situation. Au pairs were desperate simply to know how they should feel about their circumstances. Should they feel exploited and undermined, or accept what was really the expected and appropriate conditions of employment? Do 'household tasks', for example, imply just washing the dishes and taking the children to school or a daily thorough cleaning of the whole house? Thanks to this shared information they could feel they now had some sense of what was fair and how to cope. They could find out how easy or hard it was to change families but also general information such as where (should they ever need them) contraceptives could be found for free – well, they could always stockpile them for their return to Slovakia!

Such conversations, while useful, also brought home the more negative aspects of their situation. Since the conversations were about the relationships between the general categories of families and au pairs, there was something dehumanizing about being reduced to an example of a category. But also it made them realize how the consequences of coming to London can diametrically opposed to what they had expected. Before they arrive there is a general feeling that being at home in Slovakia is claustrophobic and the opportunities there are too limited. Going to London will lead to a huge expansion of their lives and entry into an exciting and cosmopolitan universe. But in practice a typical au pair settled into Beddlingham soon ends up with a tiny group of about three other au pairs, all from Slovakia (or perhaps the Czech Republic), with whom she spends the vast majority of her leisure time. It doesn't follow that they will necessarily get on with each other. The problem with this enforced networking is that it consists simply of those au pairs who happen to find themselves in the same area. This is far more parochial and restricted than anything they had ever experienced at home. What's more, the few au pairs in that group are likely to come from quite disparate regions and backgrounds. Each may well represent the kind of individual another would never otherwise have dreamt of spending time with. They often share little by way of common friends or experiences; they know their stay in Beddlingham is temporary, and that they will probably share nothing more in the future.

Barbora made numerous attempts at socializing. At first things looked promising. She quickly met Slovak au pairs at the bus stop while waiting for children coming from school, and found out about the café they were frequenting. She also met a Slovak au pair in the library whom she had noticed using a Slovak mail provider. So one evening, after finishing the washing up, she went to Jenny's. She ordered a coffee and spotted the library au pair sitting with two others. They seemed to be surprised when she asked whether she could join them, but agreed. After exchanging basic information about their host families, the number and age of the children, their duties and pay, the three au pairs returned to their previous discussions and seemed to ignore her totally. She couldn't join in their gossip – she couldn't even follow it, so she just sat there silent for half an hour.

As usual the initial conversation had been helpful on practical issues, such as the latest cheap phone cards which could cut the cost of communication back home, the location of cheap or free language schools, and information about Czechoslovak parties and live music. But she simply couldn't comprehend why the others had then excluded her from any further discussion. She persevered for a while, but they refused to spend a single evening with her. Perhaps they were satisfied with the contacts they already had? Perhaps they just did not like her personally? She could not grasp such crass impoliteness. Later on she came to find that this was not untypical – that somehow being in London generated rudeness between au pairs that was unthinkable back in Slovakia.

As it happens, Barbora soon came to see reasons why she might, in any case, not have wanted to go much beyond the polite exchange of useful information. She understood that she was dressed very differently, in the same unpretentious, unfashionable sportswear she used to wear back home, without make-up or jewellery, while these other au pairs spent most of their time shopping, or window shopping, deeply interested in things she thought superficial. She found their conversation boring and vulgar and was shocked by the language they used. Mostly, though, she was shocked by her own reaction to them. Later, reflecting back on this period, she said:

> I have always believed that everyone is equal. I have always behaved like that. I used to have some friendships, lasting from primary school, with people who have never had A-levels. I always thought that education is not important and what matters is what kind of person you are. But I just cannot stand being around these people. You know, I have never believed in class. I thought English people were pretentious freaks with their obsession with class. But now I am afraid that class does really exist.

This is quite a common finding. Given their socialist background, most Slovaks start with the strong assertion that they do not come from a class society. It is these unexpected encounters in London that force them to recognize that actually Slovakia has powerful and buoyant class divisions. But at least in acknowledging their existence they are at the same time coming partly to transcend them. One effect of these London experiences is probably to help open out Slovak society as people develop relationships that have to cross class, regional and other boundaries. Sometimes they retain this increased openness when they return to Slovakia. If not, at least they have gained some knowledge about how other Slovaks live, think and drink.

In the end, though, Barbora's only au pair friend was Tinka, and this wasn't based on class. The former au pair had worked for the Cowans, and had initially introduced Barbora to them. But Barbora had wanted to find her own friends in her own way. Later, when she became lonely, she remembered Tinka had seemed nice, and decided to phone her. Tinka was from the north of Slovakia, had some vocational training and before coming to the UK had been a factory worker. There were, however, two things which brought them together: firstly a shared love for walking and the countryside, which separated them from the majority of Beddlingham's au pairs, who preferred shopping, drinking and clubbing; and, secondly, they had similar expectations about socializing. What Barbora saw in Tinka was empathy, tolerance and a willingness to listen to other people's conversation and needs. So they became friends.

Most often, in a place such as Beddlingham, relationships between au pairs become extremely intimate, based on constant companionship, leading to an abstract commitment that these people must be your close or best friends. And yet in retrospect, as Beata observed:

> You know, friendships here are crazy . . . you know, people, who are your friends here . . . you would never ever have met them back in Slovakia. If by chance you met, you would never have spoken to them. If you had spoken to them, you would have thought they were total idiots and never have spoken to them again . . . And here . . . here they are your best friends. And it is real. I really phone them every evening to find out whether they are fine and how was their day. And I really mean it. And I really want to meet up with them.

This discrepancy between the need to be friends and the artificiality of it could lead to underlying tensions. On the surface they seemed to give rise to a kind of regression to childhood concerns with trivia and slights taken much too seriously. Beddlingham had become like a school playground. This was the backdrop to those endless conversations about whether another au pair had slighted you because the greeting wasn't warm enough in Tesco, or two au pairs who spontaneously decide to finish some homework together thereby inadvertently greatly offend a third au pair whom they didn't invite to join them.

Alenka and Ľudmila spent an evening discussing whether Monika, who used to go out with them but seemed to be less enthusiastic about their shared programme, was or was not being rude to them and whether her behaviour really amounted to some kind of betrayal. Was the problem Monika or really themselves? They dissected the exact level of reciprocity in past phone calls, invitations to various kinds of gatherings, shopping trips to Tesco, writing English homework together, or clubbing and parties. It wasn't just levels of friendship and betrayals that were monitored but also certain scarce resources, such as food or cigarettes brought from Slovakia. During one evening in Beddlingham, Alenka had just arrived from her visit back to Slovakia and brought sheep's cheese (*bryndza*) with her. This kind of cheese was unavailable in England and is a popular Slovak national dish. So the two of them spent the evening working out the appropriate distribution. Alenka wanted to give one to her host family, keep one or two for herself and distribute another two packs among friends, but then decided she didn't really want to give any away, and instead discussed organizing a party where the cheese and *bryndzové halušky* (the Slovak national dish – a kind of potato dumpling served with this particular cheese and fried bacon) would be on the menu. Then the discussion turned to those au pairs they wouldn't invite to this party, individuals who after they had had some food from home had not invited Alenka and Ľudmila. They decided they would only tell them afterwards that there had been such a party. Of course, they would not forget to tell them, to make sure they knew what they had missed.

Au pairs learn some curious lessons thereby about friendship: that one can have a real commitment, that one can struggle to try and find common interests and topics of conversation, but that sometimes commitment is just not enough. While you are constantly with someone, at the same time both of you are constantly (though largely unconsciously) wishing you could 'trade up' to someone more interesting or more compatible. One of things one could be most bored with in Beddlingham was one's fellow Slovak au pairs.

There are alternatives. Some au pairs decide that they actually prefer their own company and choose relative isolation. Others cultivate an intense internet life, keeping in constant communication with their parents, friends, a partner at home, or strangers in chat rooms. For example, when Radka settled in Richmond, she spent most of her free time on-line, or on the phone to her boyfriend, her mother and her high-school friend Adriana. She felt lonely and did not know how and where to meet other Slovak au pairs. The first group she did meet were welcoming, but seemed rather too interested in picking up men for transient relationships, which she could not comprehend. She tried a couple of other contacts but then found that the internet provided her with both sufficient social life and something deeper and more meaningful than anything that was likely to arise from chance encounters at the pub or in the language school. The one thing that might turn this around was to bring one of her proper friends out to join her in Richmond. So, when Adriana lost her job, she was easily persuaded by Radka to take up an au pair place which Radka found for her conveniently situated also in Richmond.

Another possible solution to this problem comes when a whole circle of high-school or university friends manage to migrate to a relatively specific region of London. We uncovered, for example, many au pairs originating from a single girls' school in Banská Bystrica settled around Radlett, a group from Hlohovec in the Finchley area, and a group from Michalovce in Richmond. These transplanted networks are generally highly successful and end up being something more like shared holidays – where these women can meet, go clubbing together, gossip and talk with or about men. Even if they had not known each other before, it appeared that au pairs who discover they come from the same region seem to have that much more in common, such that they form close groups within the London context. Zuzana found that women from her own home region were much more accepting of her. If, however, one is subject to the kind of claustrophobia that we characterize as 'bored in Beddlingham', then there is yet one more alternative – to escape from the whole issue of peer relationships with other women from Slovakia and instead look to developing relationships with men, ideally to fall in love, or at least to have a lover. But this is the subject of the next chapter.

In the meantime, within the confines of Beddlingham, where a daily visit to Tesco is the only potential source of warmth and companionship, it really does matter whether a friend agrees to come with you or decides to prefer some other company or activity. Actually a walk around Tesco was surprisingly effective as a bonding ritual for au pairs. Tesco itself is now an established store in Slovakia, so au pairs encounter it as one of the Slovak features of London – what, England also has Tesco! Going around the shelves examining the cakes and desserts, you could discuss their advantages and disadvantages with regard to taste or putting on weight. You might end up with some curried chicken, a huge tiramisu, banana with chocolate and cream and, of course, beer, even if the drink didn't go too well with the sweets. Somehow the companionship that built up through these trivial discussions and decisions as to what to buy felt 'real'. They had a depth and some warmth, especially if you could then slowly walk back to someone's house, where you could eat, drink and have a giggle over the trifle. Then the day hadn't been too bad.

It was precisely because these events were significant and successful that they could also be fraught and sensitive. In a sea of loneliness and exploitation, where for most of the day you seemed to have lost your name and personality under the suffocating position of being a family's seventh au pair, Tesco was an oasis of true feelings and respect for your own individual preferences and whims that reminded you that you were a particular person again, where you as an individual, and thus making your own choices, could buy yourself a little treat, just to remember that someone cared about you, even if that someone was yourself. At best a group of au pairs could develop banter and silly comments and make the whole shopping expedition quite glorious fun. Yet at the same time there was an awareness that the mere fact that thirty minutes' looking around shelves, punctuated by coffee, was the only real humanity in the day was also a sign of just how lonely, narrow and pointless life had become for some. This great adventure to discover another world that was supposed to make you grow in stature had somehow shrunk you down to Beddlingham banality.

So if au pairs seemed to have regressed to schoolgirl bitching and pettiness it was because of how much their relationships mattered, not how little, because there was another side to these Tesco friendships, whether with au pairs or others. If often people were much more petty than in Slovakia, then on occasion they could also find themselves going further out on a limb to help each other: to rescue someone who had been thrown out by their host family and ensure they had somewhere to stay; to spend ages talking to people in language schools they never knew or could never have met before; or just to keep faith in a friendship with someone whom at the back of their minds they knew perfectly well they would never really like.

To London, to London, to buy a fine . . . Primark sweater

But, of course, if you were bored in Beddlingham, then providing you swallowed hard when it came to paying for your train fare, you could always go to London. For most au pairs, London was already present as a kind of map of sites that they more or less expected to visit at some time or other. These sites are not just those listed in the Lonely Planet guide; they also included the monthly Czechoslovak parties at Camden Town or clothing chain stores such as Primark. Most au pairs have little interest in conventional tourist sites such as monuments, museums or parks. Only two among our fifty participants regularly visited galleries or museums, one of whom had been a member of a creative art society at university and was herself a painter. She was completely delighted to have an opportunity to see some of her beloved old masters in the National Gallery.

More commonly, au pairs take what they regard as their one obligatory tour, to places such as Buckingham Palace, Big Ben and Tower Bridge, where they can take the pictures with other au pairs that will become London 'memories'. They will often postpone such tours until they can afford the requisite digital camera. Although the photos were partly to share their experience with their family when they returned home, it was usually good fun posing in front of Big Ben, with a street artist at the South Bank, or with the wax celebrities at Madame Tussauds. Quite often they end up taking such tours when their parents or partners come to visit them for holidays, since somehow when one is working around London one never gets around to being a tourist.

Gabriela was saving like mad. Her mother had never been abroad before, except for shopping trips across the Polish border to Nowy Targ. So when Gabriela's host family said she could invite her parents while they went away for their summer holidays, she did not hesitate for a moment. Using the money from her extra jobs, and borrowing even more from her friend, Gabriela was desperate to give her mother the best time possible. She paid for her air ticket, took her to all the expected sites, such as the London Dungeon, Westminster Abbey and the National Gallery, and even went on the London Eye. Of course, they also shopped around Oxford Street, buying a present for Gabriela's father, who, as most Slovak fathers, did not come with his wife on this visit, saying that he was happier to stay at home than to travel and spend all this money. Eventually all her savings were gone, but it had been worth it.

It was similar with Jarmila from chapter 1. While she was addicted to Oxford Street, she stopped herself visiting any tourist spots until she could go with her fiancé. It was one of first things she asked her host family – Would they mind if he came to visit? Could he stay with her in their house? No, they wouldn't mind, and, yes, he could stay. To go on her own to such places sounded quite a cold and expensive experience, but to go with her fiancé was like a dream come true, especially on seeing those pictures of the two of them with Big Ben or Buckingham Palace in the background.

But cultural tourism also had an important function with respect to less established relationships. Danka met Dušan, who worked in a factory packing CDs, at a weekly Czechoslovak party in Covent Garden. They spent part of the night dancing together and at the end exchanged phone numbers. Often such exchanges were entirely forgotten, or entirely regretted, when people sobered up the next day. But when Dušan phoned and asked Danka to go out for a drink she felt she liked him and agreed. However, dating needed some kind of content. Somehow, for both of them, a 'real' relationship had to include more than drinking, dancing and sex, even if they clearly enjoyed all three. A 'real' relationship needed some other kind of shared experience. Movies are expensive and their English was limited, but many of the museums and galleries in London are free. When an au pair friend teased Danka about her sudden interest in paintings, she responded that they were not going to do 'this museum thing' for good; they would take in some culture for now, as otherwise it would look as if they were only meeting to fuck. Once it was clear that this was a genuine relationship, they could dispense with such activities. Then they could just relax together by watching DVDs, go for an occasional drink or to a party, and cook and sleep together. Anyway, as it happens, there were a lot worse ways of spending time than passing a rainy Sunday laughing at dinosaurs in the Natural History Museum, gazing at the mummies in the British Museum, or wondering why pieces exhibited in the Tate Modern were considered art and how people managed to keep such a straight face when they looked at them.

The rather more 'authentic' tourism that made London such an important destination was shopping. Sometimes shopping itself could become part of such cultural tours, when the aim was not to buy but to have seen those monuments to designer labels and luxury such as Selfridges or Harrods. It was a chance to mix with the rich and perhaps even the famous – a very different side of English culture to karaoke at the local pub. Furthermore, with a shop such as Selfridges, one could touch, try on and, at least occasionally, own and use a treasured item. One au pair bought her Dior sunglasses there, while Jarmila bought a special brand of sports shoes for her fiancé.

More generally, though, for au pairs, shopping means above all shopping for fashion, because the contrast with clothes shopping in Slovakia is even greater than they expected. It is not just the vast range of clothes; it is that the same clothes are often cheaper in London. There are cheap clothes in Slovakia, if one goes to so-called Chinese or Vietnamese shops, or shops specializing in Turkish or local production. But there is nothing in between these clothes, which look as cheap as they are, and, at the opposite end, very expensive urban outlets with international brands. What au pairs are delighted to find in London is that they can buy decent quality and very fashionable clothes at places such as Primark or H&M at prices they could afford. Some au pairs even started a business, buying these clothes in London and selling them to their grateful friends in Slovakia at a small profit.

It was also noticeable, at least at the time of this fieldwork in 2004–5, that there was still enough of a general fashion lag between London and Slovakia for au pairs to be in fashion twice – once when they wore their new purchases in London and again when they returned home. In the winter of 2004, Lucia could buy pink summer clothes as sales bargains in London because they were going out of fashion but be pretty sure that pink would be just coming 'in' when she returned home for summer in Slovakia. Of course, there was also something about 'foreign English fashion' associated with most recent trends in the world of fashion – as seen from Slovakia, especially in countryside. Another huge plus when shopping in London is the much greater variety of sizes than can be found at home. Slovakia is generally more normative in judging the size of young female bodies, which are assumed to range only from size 8 to size 10. Many au pairs are not just pleased to find larger sizes in fashionable styles, but also to discover that such sizes can be considered as 'normal'.

Shopping was perhaps the au pairs' most important free-time activity. It was not uncommon for them to spend nine hours of their day off shopping or window shopping. Nine hours? Well, when Darinka went shopping with her friend Adrika, they met in Finchley at 9 a.m. Darinka had come from Golders Green and Adrika from East Finchley. The initial goal was Finchley's QS, where, if you were lucky, you might find jeans for a fiver and a top for £2. On a previous trip Darinka had bought a pullover and three tops there, but was by no means finished. Adrika was looking for jeans, but then decided on a pair, spotted a week ago, in a sale at Le Pop in Golders Green. They spent about an hour in QS, discussing every single item they were interested in. One of them might disappear into the changing room for a while; sometimes they could both be heard giggling together in the changing room, and sometimes, when there was a queue for the changing room, they would just try things on in the middle of the shop.

Darinka simply couldn't make up her mind between a dark blue or white jersey until Adrika convinced her that the blue better fitted her complexion. Anyway, she already had a white one, intended for cold nights. Adrika bought two violet pullovers, one for her sister, and one for herself, to match with something pink. From Finchley they took a bus to Camden town via Golders Green. The underground fares were too expensive, but by now they had an encyclopaedic knowledge of London buses. Their gossiping slipped to an undertone when passing through Golders Green, as this was a haven for Slovak au pairs and you could never tell who might overhear what. The thing about Camden market was that clothes here were 'crazy'. This was alternative culture, which could mean huge colourful hats, clothes for clubbing, getting a piercing or buying magic mushrooms (although more often they got these from male friends). Darinka headed straight for ethnic styles – she was totally into Afghan embroidered skirts. She tried on a couple, one blue with pink flowers and one dark green with red embroidery. She bargained hard, but not hard enough. So she decided she could get them still cheaper later at sales.

Darinka loved to chat to the stall keepers, about clothes, their countries of origin and possible bargains. She generally loved talking to strangers. Adrika was shy and knew Darinka was showing off her better knowledge of English. Darinka thought the man selling Tibetan coats was being flirtatious to the point of rudeness. But then Adrika noted that Darinka had been asking him whether her figure looked slim enough in the coat, smoothing her hips and smiling. But who cared? They were already starving, but then cheap Chinese or Thai food was always a highlight of trips to Camden market. It could be made exactly to order and was among the cheapest food in town. They tended to experiment with Chinese, but not Indian, which was too hot. With their chicken and seafood they sat at a wooden table outside. Darinka immediately embarrassed Adrika, and startled the English family sitting next to them, by chatting to them about the weather and how they liked Camden. But there was always something charming about Darinka's openness.

Fortified by lunch, they tackled nine other Camden shops. Adrika found everything too expensive, but Darinka bought a blue top for

£22. From Camden they moved to Kilburn, as Adrika wanted to go to Primark, a regular haunt. This time Darinka did not buy anything, but Adrika found a black skirt with a red pattern and a sports top. Though they were quite tired, they still had their bus passes, so they decided to finish with a hypermarket in Cricklewood. Once there, they browsed the shelves. Adrika decided to return a week later and possibly brave a mini- (almost a micro-)skirt. She had never worn such a thing before, but felt London was far enough from her gossiping village to try this shockingly short skirt with boots. Completely exhausted and completely satisfied, they parted at half past five and took buses to their respective homes. They had in effect paid for nine hours of entertainment and had a number of new clothing items into the bargain.

Church, sports and partying

Other than shopping, many of the activities for which au pairs will spend the money and time to travel into London are either Slovak or Czech. This concerns primarily parties and pubs but also religion and sports. Though a Protestant herself, Barbora often went to activities organised by Velehrad, the Roman Catholic institution that originates from the period before the break-up of Czechoslovakia in 1993. Velehrad is essentially a cheap hostel in Notting Hill for labourers and budget tourists and a useful place for exchanging news and putting up advertisements. It was founded by an elderly Czech priest, who is a living legend of post-war Czechoslovak migration to the UK, with compensation money from his time in concentration camps. Owned by the Church, it is where Catholic services and confessions take place three times a week, though on Sunday there is a larger congregation at a church next to London Bridge station. In general the church service alternates between the Slovak and Czech languages. Slovaks, not all of whom are Catholic, fall somewhere between the Poles, and their intense identification with Catholicism, and the Czechs, among whom secularism is dominant. For religious Czech and Slovak au pairs, Velehrad and the fellowship around the church provide a strong sense of community and hominess and even Protestants such as Barbora sometimes drop in, either for religious or for social reasons.

Barbora in particular was touched by the sense of a youth service based on mutual kindness and informality: there is apparent affection for both the old Czech and the young Slovak priest and for the institution itself. The church itself does everything it can to encourage a sense of community development. Sunday masses are followed by coffee in the refectory, and every other Sunday coffee is in turn followed by a Christian class, and then practice with Karpaty, a folk dance group. At the beginning Barbora was surprised that on a typical Sunday the church was pretty full, with around 120 seated and another thirty standing at the back, mainly young people, several of whom were taking a role in the service. After an hour's service she was one of about fifty people who would mingle for coffee and a chat. She felt relief that everybody there shared similar values to her, even though she was sceptical towards Catholicism as such. In the refectory she bumped into people whom she knew from elsewhere – a man from her university and a woman from the language school. On the other hand, sometimes Barbora would actually rather avoid yet another newcomer, who would immediately latch on to her in order to gain an instant London survival guide and instant best-friendship. Coffee, though, was a bargain here, and sometimes nice little things happened. Once, on a cold November Sunday, a woman in her twenties, a church regular, went around the tables, offering people bread and apologizing that this was Polish, not actually Slovak. Though people usually offered chocolate or biscuits, there was definitely some Central European sentimentality around bread (Slovaks generally complained about the poor quality of British bread), and in this context, Barbora felt, it had also a deeper religious meaning.

Spectator sport is even more important for creating a sense of community, since both Czechs and Slovaks are keen on watching ice hockey. Both have successful teams, taking part in the world championships. Au pairs would know of the few pubs which screened key matches (not just the Czechoslovak restaurants; there is also one English pub in Finchley and another in South London). Queues form outside the pub well before the game, with many fans sporting national flags or dress, usually brought from home. After one Czech–Slovak game (Slovaks inevitably lose) the two groups sang songs and anthems at each other competitively from either side of a street.

But the largest gathering of young Czechs and Slovaks in London is undoubtedly the monthly Czechoslovak party held in the Camden Town centre. Many au pairs never miss these events, and Ivana was definitely one of them. The ticket (£5 when there was a DJ and £7 when there was a live band) was a bargain in that it also included a serving of food (almost inevitably either goulash, *kaustnica* – a saurkraut soup – or sausages), along with the 'socialist' chocolate wafer, *horalka*. All of this Ivana loved and could not usually get in London.

Food was served in a café area away from the main dance hall, and two additional bars were selling Slovak and Czech beer and local spirits such as *borovička* – a juniper-based equivalent of gin.

Typically, the DJ plays new Czech and Slovak hits as well as music from the socialist period, but given a 'house' or other dance-music beat. For Ivana, as for the most of this audience aged mainly from eighteen to twenty-five, it has the feel of 'retro-pop' that repackages songs they can recall from their own childhood or from Slovak media. This makes it highly effective as a memory of home and also the kind of old-fashioned village disco which everybody throughout Czechoslovakia once shared. In comparison, most parties in Slovakia would have far more international pop music. There was always a DJ, but sometimes also live music. Ivana saw more well-known Slovak bands in London than she would have seen back home, even if she also had to suffer the occasional pretentious Freddie Mercury clone. But once, in the bar area after the concert, she bumped into Jarek Nohavica, one of her favourite Czech folk singers. And, guess what? He asked her how she liked the concert! She said it was really, really great, but also that she was disappointed he had not played her favourite song. And then he took his guitar and played it there, just for her! One just had to come to London to experience this.

The situation at parties is the exact opposite of that in the host family home. Here au pairs are visible, want to be visible and want to be visible to men. So, while clothing is casual, mainly jeans and tops, the emphasis is clearly not on fashion or expense, but on either conspicuous or more subtle erotic strategies to draw attention to whatever looks good about one's body – perhaps the tan from sunbathing, a new tattoo or the flatter tummy that has taken so much discipline to achieve. So before their arrival Ivana spent hours with Miša and Lenka at Lenka's place: they were changing clothes, discussing various possibilities, exchanging accessories and helping each other with make-up. Their main concern was to look pretty, but also not to look like 'English women', whom they saw as either overdoing make-up or not using it at all and as being too dressed up (though without consideration of the shape of their bodies) for their evenings out. Ivana also refused pieces she considered 'too elegant', so finally she chose her new pair of skinny jeans and a sleeveless sports top she had bought at Primark. Happy with the result, they shared a gulp or two of vodka on the bus while travelling to the party in order to be in an appropriate mood for such an event.

For the first couple of hours, while there may be plenty of people on the dance floor, it is mostly an opportunity to check out who else is around and what they are wearing, and also to get a sense of whether the man someone came with is just accompanying them or is spoken for, since such a party is the key time to meet potential partners. This is also the time, after a drink or two, when you might come across people that you never knew had also come to London, resulting in squeals of recognition and enthusiastic embracing, even though you barely knew them back home. There is a general acknowledgement that women are more interested in dancing and men like to sit around a table and drink. So a female might alternate between sitting with her boyfriend and finding someone else to dance with. There is also a general asymmetry in drinking. The men earn higher wages but are also keen to follow a Central European style of buying drinks and somehow distributing them so casually to women that one hardly notices that they have done it. There is no specific intent here; it is more analogous to the English custom of buying rounds, and it reinforces the idea of the male as the generous provider.

As the evening wears on, the dancing itself becomes more important. This is where a man can most easily make a 'move' on a woman who seems to be unengaged at that time, and each can see how attractive they might be to the other. There are further erotic potentials in the occasional group of slow dances, where people can form clear couples, though the interest may not be in the potential for anything further, but just who is good to dance with. As at most parties, there is etiquette in whether a man is prepared to read any subtle hints of lack of interest, which a woman feels should be all that is required to get him to move on. These monthly parties are complemented by smaller weekly affairs, for example, at Czech and Slovak restaurants, which are generally quite low key, and in practice not as exclusive to this particular group; some au pairs even avoided the Friday parties at Jasmine in Finchley because they were both ethnically mixed and more overtly sexual. Even in Beddlingham there might be an occasional party, either organized in a local pub or in someone's household, given the strong pressures on au pairs to host a party when the family is away.

These experiences – the church, the ice hockey, the Camden Town party, and even the shopping expeditions – reinforce a point made back in the depths of Beddlingham itself. Au pairs come to London and may have unforgettable memories: they might finally see their favourite band, might have a significant relationship, might buy what end up being their favourite jeans. Yet all of this is contained within a social environment that is in many ways more parochial than anything they would normally experience at home. Slovakia has become reduced to a few key signifiers – the socialist wafer biscuit, the drink *Kofola*, shared cheering of the national hockey team (without having any deeper interest in ice hockey) and a few other token au pairs whom one would probably have avoided in Slovakia itself. There was a refuge in other people with whom one could have a full conversation in one's own language, who could laugh at old jokes and at the recitation of full passages from Czechoslovak film classics, who could be equally offended or delighted by new London experiences, or with whom at the end of the day one could watch a DVD, cook a meal and just relax, and for a while at least alleviate the boredom that is Beddlingham.

Snippet

Greater London described at www.studentagency.cz/mainpage.php?switch=538.

Perhaps most of our au pairs spend their English adventure in Greater London. So, for example, popular Kent, situated south from London – in cities such as Sevenoaks, Tonbridge, Maidstone or Tunbridge Wells, you will soon find friends among local au pairs. What about the areas north of London? St Albans, Watford, Radlett or Bushey – these places also occupy high positions in the hit parade of favourite localities. You can visit many interesting places, you have a lot of culture to choose from . . . and, if you need a change, London is not far.

— 6 —

MEN

The au pair world is to a large extent a female world. Many experience being an au pair as a period when they need to create a close bond with fellow females. It is a girlie time. They spend all their free time together, sharing their boredom, worries, joys, gossip and petty quarrels. This creates an almost sacred female space with its own aura. As illustrated in the previous chapter, this forms largely because au pairs come to depend upon each other much more than they had anticipated. They never know when a capricious host family might unexpectedly ask them to leave, at which point the only thing they have to rely on is their friends. Nevertheless, men have a central place within this female sociality. Not only are men, along with host families, the main topic of discussion, but au pairs in general go out and meet men in groups. In conversation men may appear as boyfriends, whether left behind in Slovakia or recently acquired in London, or discussed as idealized partners for the future, tempting transgressions. Especially important are those men whom au pairs know a little, and it is therefore worth dissecting every detail of that little, to decide how best to proceed. Similarly, in long-distance relationships, every text message and e-mail could be brought to the group for collective interpretation. Even the religious Catholic Magda, perhaps feeling a little left out of such discussions, raised the question of quite how Jesus Christ, as the main man in her life, compared to any men she was actually likely to encounter. Of course, the less benign side of all this was competition over men.

In this female coterie, real men could often seem like visitors, slightly alien others, with whom one could have sex but could never achieve the same kind of intimacy that was created among women. Faced with this, men may feel uncomfortable, sensing that they are

137

being excluded, and respond by suggesting that this group of giggling yet intimidating females is best left to its own devices. It was evident that men who were developing relationships with au pairs sometimes found it difficult to extricate their particular partner from the wider female society, but felt it essential to do so – if only because, given the limited amount of freedom available to many au pairs, they could find themselves in direct competition for their time. Au pairs who had become dependent on a 'best friend' could feel almost betrayed if this meant there was no one to go out with, especially as a newly formed couple tended not to go out very much. Juliana, who was nineteen, started a relationship with an Albanian man who was quite possessive, and in effect prevented her from continuing to associate with those in her previous circle. She moved to his place and left it only to work for her host family. After around three months she wanted to break away from these constraints and contacted her au pair friends, hoping to go out with them again. However, those friends, having felt rejected by her neglect of them during this period, simply refused to accept her back into their company.

This female sociality is also enforced by the host families' household rules. Most host families do not allow their au pairs to invite any male visitors into their homes. They seem to regard men as a security risk, and may even be fearful just realizing that men know where their au pair lives. Beyond this there may well be unspoken issues concerning the acknowledgement of her sexuality. This deeply affects the au pair. It not just about access to sex; rather, it precludes the whole arena of romance that should be part of a proper relationship and having an exciting life in London. There is nowhere to have long discussions over coffee or candle-lit dinners. This is one reason why au pairs may give up their work when a relationship starts to develop.

This avoidance of men is even stronger when it concerns men within the host family. It is as though merely to raise the issue of the relationship between a husband and the au pair would be to countenance the possibility of there being such a relationship. Perhaps this is precisely because there is a legacy in popular culture of the 'friendly' Swedish au pair. In practice, husbands were much more subject to the opposite complaint: that they conspicuously failed to help deal with the au pairs' practical, emotional and other concerns. There are exceptions, where men dominate domestic work, including the relationship with au pairs, but these were rare. In our research gender relations generally emerged as highly conservative. Men might strive to mediate in tense relationships between their wives and the au pairs, or redress the balance when they felt their wives were being unduly harsh. So, for example, when her host mother reprimanded Ol'ga for taking an additional piece of meat at Sunday lunch, the father countered that Ol'ga could eat as much as she liked. In another family it was also the host father who ensured that a dinner was left for the au pair during her days off or when she was coming home late. It seemed, however, that men could more 'afford' to come across as the benign partner, since they had mostly absolved themselves from the day-to-day responsibility of working with the au pair.

Nor did au pairs see men in the families as possible sexual partners. Fathers are regarded as an occasional, almost shadowy presence, and there is a certain degree of mutual avoidance. The situation was more complex on the rare occasion when there were grown-up sons present, for example from a previous marriage. Mrs Christie knew of one mother whose grown-up son had started a relationship with a neighbour's au pair. While the son was very open about this, the neighbours, by contrast, managed never to bring up the topic.

Overall in this sample of eighty-six households there were three cases of family members making sexual advances to au pairs. One was a single mother and her male au pair and one a single father. The only case within a nuclear family concerned Petra, who found her new host mother to be exceptionally hostile but could not understand why. After some time the mother informed Petra that she needed to put some things straight from the beginning: she said she knew what Slovak women were like and what her husband was like. The au pair was there to do her job and should keep her hands off her husband. Petra felt offended, but decided to stay. After a month, when her host mother went out for an evening, the father told Petra that he would be waiting for her in the jacuzzi. She told herself he could indeed wait, and went out. The final straw came later when the host mother asked Petra to translate the letter she had written to the mother of the previous au pair, who had apparently actually slept with her husband, at which point Petra left the family for good. No other cases were admitted to within this research, although the only person who refused to take part in the project was an ex-au pair who had fallen in love with a host father. He had then divorced his wife in order to be with her, and she was now struggling to be the step-mother to the children she had previously au paired. More common were problems with respect to single fathers with au pairs – a situation about which au pairs themselves were very wary. Eva complained that the single father for whom she was working apparently saw the au pair company more as a kind of dating agency in his quest to find a new mother for his son.

On balance, then, both the amount of direct sexual harassment and the number of consensual sexual relationships was probably lower than we anticipated at the start of our research. Nevertheless, both parties are clearly influenced by the prominent discourse (see Snippet at the end of this chapter) of promiscuous au pairs being sexually available and lecherous fathers who were either sleeping with or trying to sleep with vulnerable, innocent au pairs. For instance, when Danny joined Zuzana in field research, the au pairs always asked her whether he was married, and implied that an older man must inevitably have some sexual interest. Furthermore, it has been almost impossible for Danny to inform people of his research topic without eliciting a smirk, at least from men. What this makes clear is that the very concept of an au pair seems to imply an intrinsic sexual ambiguity. One additional facet is the Slovak au pairs' belief in their own particular beauty and attractiveness.

Relationships with men

Most of the literature concerning au pairs focuses on their relationship with work and host families. In this book we have also emphasized the relationship with other female au pairs. But, for the au pairs themselves, their present or potential relationships with men might be equally if not more important. The reasons they become au pairs in the first place are often connected to their partners or the absence of partners. Becoming an au pair could be a powerful gesture within a relationship. For example, Vlasta was in love with Juro, who was married and could not decide whether to divorce his wife. By choosing to become an au pair, Vlasta was able to force the issue and show she was still capable of making important decisions for herself. When he was still undecided, despite visiting her in London, she formed a plan to continue as an au pair in the USA. At this point Juro divorced his wife and married her.

Au pairing is often important in demonstrating that there are other trajectories in life than marriage, or at least a bad marriage. Natália was engaged, but the relationship had deteriorated into constant quarrelling. As often happens in such cases, the couple exchanged many threats. During one quarrel Natália announced she was going away for a year as an au pair, mainly because it was the first thing that came into her head. She then found herself unwilling to admit that she hadn't meant what she said, especially when her family got wind of the idea. She therefore turned up at the British Embassy ten minutes before it was closing, assuming her request for a visa would be rejected (this was before May 2004), but, much to her surprise, the embassy granted her an instant visa. In her case there were no economic grounds for leaving, it was merely a side effect of a complicated personal relationship. Janka found herself facing an apparently inexorable trajectory towards marriage with the boyfriend she had had since high school, who lived in the same village. When she realized she no longer loved him, she hit on the plan of becoming an au pair as a means to break up the relationship, but indirectly and diplomatically. By contrast, Lívia became an au pair when she found out that her boyfriend was having an affair with another woman. She did not want to stay in their small city, where too many places and people were related to their history together.

Although some women become au pairs to escape relationships, others remain in love with a partner in Slovakia, and come to London because they hope this man will follow them, because they need to work abroad for economic grounds or they want to learn English. This doesn't always work. Júlia, aged twenty, was unemployed and could see the advantages of learning English. She decided she could manage a year abroad, but after four months of daily phone calls she realized she could simply no longer remain apart from her boyfriend and returned to Slovakia. Romana came to London convinced that her partner Gregor would join her when finances permitted and when she would know the place well enough to help him to find a job. But for month after month Gregor avoided the topic in their conversations and even suggested he would much rather they ended up in Germany. Though annoyed, Romana returned to Slovakia after a year, as her relationship with Gregor was more important to her than her life in London. Since there were several similar cases, it is possible that underlying them is a general reluctance by men to allow women to dictate the trajectory of their future lives. It could also be that they fear that coming to London when their partner already knows English and the city would place them in a subordinate or dependent position.

Clearly an important factor in these relationships is rapidly changing technology and the cost of international communications. Lucia's boyfriend Matej was such a sweetheart – not only were they exchanging daily 'good night' text messages and longer e-mails, he was also writing her 'real' letters by post. They had their own special ritual based on the phone cards at the Turkish corner shop that she used once or twice a week. They always had to speak for the exact fifty minutes allowed by the card – it was funny, they both knew when there were five minutes left. After they had exchanged all their news,

141

Matej might turn up his CD player, so that she could hear some recent Slovak song. Each medium had its own meaning. With the texts, you could feel your phone beeping or vibrating in your pocket, and you knew that your boyfriend was thinking about you at that very moment. As for letters, there was something serious about them – they were real and material, and there was a commitment in the way they both had to sit and write down properly what they wanted to say to each other. Neither could have any doubt that they were still in love.

Au pairs with boyfriends at home would constantly gossip about how much and in what way they were in contact. Did he phone you? Was he sending texts? How often? Rather as in their relationship with their hosts, they found they could best evaluate their relationships with their boyfriends comparatively. Lucia was shocked when a friend of hers confessed that her boyfriend had just sent her one text in the last month, and yet she seemed to think that there was nothing untoward about this. Actually Lucia was worried by Matej's last letter, which mentioned his anxiety about whether she was meeting other men. He was repeating to her what he had just heard from a close friend recently returned from England. This friend described how Slovak women in London were getting drunk all the time and going out with foreigners, either English men or even Albanians, Pakistanis, Arabs and other blacks, and that these men had much more money than Slovak men could offer and could buy them things. Matej could not imagine that Slovak women could confuse this with love, or have any doubt that they would end up abandoned or abused. Surely they weren't whores?

Lucia felt terrible. No, she never went out with any foreigner. She did not find darker men attractive. Everybody knew that English men were only interested in you for sex, and they talked so fast you couldn't even have a proper conversation with them. But there was something she couldn't tell Matej: how at a recent birthday party she had got drunk with one of the Slovak builders from her native region and ended up snogging him in some corner. The next day she had felt horrible. Nothing more was going to happen. The builder was looking for a 'serious' girlfriend, and understood when Lucia had to explain she loved someone else, someone back home. But reading Matej's letter Lucia felt such remorse. She never thought this could happen to her. She despised people who cheated on their lovers. Now she could see how weak she was. She had needed a hug so desperately that she slipped this once, but it would never happen again.

If men in Slovakia were worried about these tales of promiscuity

– Slovak 'sex in the city' – au pairs generally felt that men who remained in Slovakia had an even greater tendency to stray. So tensions and anxieties about infidelity inevitably developed in these long-distance relationships. A common story was of the relationship that breaks up when the au pair returns for Christmas. This happened to Natália. One effect of the new technologies was that people could gain a better sense of the current state of their own relationship. Sometimes, when Natália phoned Jožo, he did not pick up the phone, and it was unlike him to have turned it off or left it at home. Also his e-mails were growing shorter and colder. It was not that he did not write, but she could sense that something had changed. So she was not that surprised when on her return for Christmas she discovered from her friends that he had indeed been sleeping around. Generally partners seemed to prefer breaking up in person during such visits rather than dumping one another over the phone or via e-mail. The downside to this preference is a whole lot of presents intended for the boyfriend, and now unwanted, which may be given to friends or kept, but quite often have become too poignant for any fate other than the dustbin.

Partners in London

Whether au pairs do or do not have a partner at home, London offers them numerous possibilities to meet men and experience various forms of relationship, from one-night stands to something involving a more long-term commitment, either with migrant Slovak men or with foreigners. In Slovakia, the man in a normative long-term relationship has many facets – lover, potential father, friend, income provider and householder. But in London, while there is a continued search for the ideal long-term partner, there is the possibility of stripping out those elements and instead experimenting with shorter-term experiences. In the final chapter we will consider the specific issue of transgressive behaviour as an aspect of au pairs' time abroad. Short-term relationships may not, however, be seen as particularly transgressive, since there is a pre-existing model in the example of the summer holiday fling. Short-term need not mean fleeting, as it could be a commitment for several months; it is just different from an expectation that the partner might be the one to spend one's life with and with whom one has children.

While there were au pairs who certainly used this period to experiment with both different forms of sex and different kinds of relationship, this should not be over-emphasized. It continues to be exaggerated in contemporary Slovakia, where a discourse has arisen implying an almost inevitable promiscuity among Slovak women abroad – and particularly au pairs. This is evident in Slovak magazine articles with titles such as 'If you want to lose your virginity become an au pair' (see snippet to chapter 7). In fact many au pairs spent their time looking for much the same kind of relatively straightforward and sustained relationships for which they would have been searching in Slovakia. This was evident at the various Czech and Slovak parties and in much of the au pairs' conversations. It would, however, be an exaggeration in the other direction should it be suggested that there were no marked differences between the two contexts. Probably the most important of these differences concerns the kinds of men to whom au pairs were drawn and why they were interested in them.

The behaviour that probably creates most discomfort within Slovakia is that of some au pairs who quite specifically and deliberately avoid Slovak men. Such au pairs reason that these are relationships they can experience 'any time' at home and are therefore beside the point with respect to potential relationships in London. For example, Želka would never go to Czech and Slovak parties, and had a boyfriend, not just a sexual partner, who was Turkish. One of the obvious alternative relationships to look for is with English men. However, English men were generally seen as usually interested only in sex. Au pairs resented finding that even mild flirtation seemed to be deliberately misinterpreted as an invitation to full sex. This was reinforced by the inability of Slovak women, with their limited English, to participate in the standard pub banter and irony, which meant that they felt uninteresting for anything beyond sex. A saying often heard in Slovakia is that an ideal girl is made for 'the coach and for the cart', meaning that, while she is cultured, polite, educated, etc., she is also practical and skilled at keeping house. The idea of love and care in Slovakia is very much connected to the second ('the cart'), in that love is shown through doing things for people: a woman should spend time with the children, cook proper meals, etc., while the man should look after the house. Slovak women felt that, even when the relationship deepened, English men seemed either to need less or be less appreciative of the kind of care and concern that Slovak women associate with love.

Mostly, therefore, English men were avoided unless the au pair was herself equally interested in showing that she could 'pull' one. For example, one au pair came to England in order to create a break from her serious relationship in Slovakia, so that both sides could consider their longer-term commitment. When she returned for Christmas she found not only had her boyfriend left her, but her parents had moved to a house with the clear expectation that she would not be returning, since there was no room for her. She systematically went in search of a temporary English boyfriend as a kind of rebellion against this fate. Obviously there were exceptions, including more rounded and successful long-term relationships. While our research was concentrated in the London region, we heard that the situation could be quite different elsewhere in the UK, where there were fewer other minority groups present. Here English men were often seen as showing a more serious interest and commitment, and were much more important as the source of potential friends and partners.

Relationships in London were therefore most common with men of Albanian/Kosovan, Pakistani, Ukrainian and Moroccan origin. In many cases au pairs simply fell in love, even if they knew that either or both might not stay for long. Others, such as Jitka, developed a relationship with a Kurdish man, knowing that this was largely just to have someone for sex and to go out with. Even to her friends she referred to him only as 'a sort of a boyfriend', without really introducing him. In such cases au pairs would often say they just needed someone to hug and hold. This might be said even when there was a boyfriend back in Slovakia to whom they intended to return. One justification given was that they felt in particular need of this kind of comfort at a time when they might be staying with an unfriendly family where the children were calling them names such as 'stupid bitch'. Also there could be a feeling of common companionship with men who were themselves in London as temporary or recent migrants. Au pairs might acquiesce in such relationships when the men in question proved particularly generous with their gifts.

So it is often the case that au pairs engage with men from different regions initially as part of their transient setting as short-term migrants. But, once this occurs, the consequences can be deeper and longer lasting, especially as they find themselves increasingly occupied not only with a particular man, but also with the wider cultural background he represents. Sometimes the attraction is precisely the history and depth of that culture as an antidote to feelings of transience and alienation. We encountered two au pairs converting to Islam, one from within our sample. She came from a broken home, converted first, and was then found an arranged marriage by the London Pakistani Muslim community. This was very successful, as she embraced the warmth of her new husband's close extended family. Another au pair lived for several years with her Jewish boyfriend, but finally broke up with him as his family was unwilling to accept her unless she converted, and this she was unwilling to do. In her case the relationship also ended because this very extended Jewish Iranian family came to feel too intrusive.

Although relations of love or sex are personal and intimate, the possibilities for au pairs to meet potential partners in London are embedded in larger political and economic conditions, in particular pertaining to EU enlargement and British immigration policies. Before Slovakia entered the EU, au pairing was one of few ways a young Slovak could obtain a British visa for a longer stay in the UK. Marriage with a British citizen was then a means to prolong one's stay. Before starting fieldwork Zuzana met a former au pair who had married her English gay friend in order to stay in London for longer than the two years of her au pair visa (later on she went on a quest to try and find some equally effective means for her boyfriend to stay in London). British immigration politicies also affected already existing relationships deeply. Bibka, outside of our sample, fell in love with a Pakistani male and became pregnant by him. When she returned to Slovakia for a couple of weeks to prolong her visa, the British Embassy unfortunately refused her request. As her partner was staying in the UK illegally, he could not leave Britain. Despite the pressure of her family, Bibka refused to have an abortion – a courageous act, given both the racism of the Slovak countryside and the uncertainty of her partnership. Fortunately the couple met again after EU enlargement, when the baby was several months old.

When Slovakia joined the EU, along with nine other countries on 1 May 2004, only Sweden, Ireland and the UK granted Slovaks immediate free access to their labour market. One result was a rapid increase in Slovak migration to the UK, particularly of men, as a result of which there was a proliferation of new Czech and Slovak pubs, clubs, restaurants and parties. This provided far more opportunities for au pairs to meet and form relationships with Slovak or Czech men, so that by the time of our fieldwork the issue was no longer one of unavailability but rather whether au pairs were looking for, or avoiding, men from their own homeland. Overall, what was striking was how far the personal and intimate lives of people are influenced by larger political transformations.

Slovak men

Our fieldwork coincided with this rapid increase in migration. The main focus was on the au pairs, and our knowledge of male migration is much more limited. Most Slovak migrants in London are young – individuals in their twenties and early thirties, usually unmarried and often single. (The simultaneous migration from Poland seemed to involve older people and families.) Slovak males tend to come to work in the UK essentially as a form of circular migration through which they can fulfil their obligations to obtain sufficient funds to buy a flat or build a house and establish a family and in some cases a business. By working as manual labourers in London they might hope to reach this goal in two or three years, while if they remained in Slovakia it might take much longer. While in London they see little advantage in using the time to become integrated into the wider society, and find it easier to hang around and drink with other Slovak men, hopefully develop relationships with Slovak women and then return home. As such they are less likely than au pairs to experience their time in London as a distinct moral and social condition.

We found little evidence that men experience any of the radical changes that we will describe and discuss in the next chapter. For men there is less sense of transience and transgression and it is more likely that their time in London is experienced as just one more example of a period of work abroad. Compared with Slovak au pairs, Slovak men are much more reliant upon their relationships with other Slovak men, because they tend to work on building sites in groups and also stay together. Quite often they gather around the individual who speaks English the best and in effect communicates on behalf of the group. While relationships between them could be tense, they could not afford to let these undermine the group because of their mutual dependence.

There are a series of highly significant differences in the abilities of Slovak men and women in London to form relationships, and these are particularly marked when compared with the situation in Slovakia. Women (and men) generally form serious relationships and get married earlier in Slovakia than in Britain and, while cohabiting is not unusual, it doesn't seem to be as common for couples to live together for several years without getting married. Although during socialism most women were married by the time they were in their early twenties, now the mean age is rising for both sexes. Combined with the premium put on female youth and beauty, women in their mid-twenties in Slovakia are likely to start worrying about their future, while men, who are usually slightly older than the women they marry, will tend to feel, if they remain single, that there is a greater pool of younger females from which they can choose. By comparison, when in London, these women feel much less constrained and sensitive about their age. They find a whole culture of 'singles' so that, even without a partner, they are able to go out and enjoy themselves. In fact the situation is reversed, because in London it is the Slovak women who find a much larger pool of available men. One of the main reasons for this is that the Slovaks tend to mix with a series of other low-income minority communities such as Moroccans, Albanians or Pakistanis. Among all such Islamic groups, women are generally highly protected and not normally available as potential partners for Slovak men. In contrast, the men in those communities are much less constrained and quite often are precisely those with whom Slovak women form relationships. Muslim men are generally brought up to believe that they can marry women from other mono-theistic religions such as Christianity, while a man wishing to marry a Muslim woman is usually expected to convert.

The basic power asymmetry is again reversed in relation to the confidence with which people can approach relationships. In London it is the Slovak women who generally have a better command of English, and this matters as much for conversation with non-English minority communities as with the English themselves. Their work depends upon this facility with language to a much greater degree than for Slovak men. Au pairs have much more time to go to language schools than manual labourers working throughout the day, but also, working in isolation within English households, they may well feel a much greater need for such wider companionship. One way in which continuities in gender inequality now come to favour women is that, even in London, it is men who are expected to have the money and resources, while for women this is much less of a consideration. There is also a shift in surrounding gender relations. While au pairs may not espouse any particular feminist ideology, they are certainly exposed to greater equality. The mere presence of single women in pubs, clubs and various forms of work, combined with sexual equality, may be something of a revelation. However, once they become embedded in relationships – for example with men from Islamic societies – women may experience quite another dimension to gender relationships within the domestic sphere.

Igor, aged twenty-five, was working as an electrician. He came to London because he wanted to experience a new country and travel for a bit: his dream was to go to the USA to see the national parks. Though he was happy with his salary back to Slovakia, he also hoped he would earn enough to start a small hotel somewhere in the Slovak mountains. Igor has never had any problem with women. He knew he was fairly good-looking, and he was outgoing and pleasant. He didn't have any girlfriend at the time, but he thought it would not take long to meet some nice Slovak girl in London. He was shocked when it transpired that after more six months he was still on his own. It was not that he did not meet women. He was going out a lot, but he did not like English women – he did not find them pretty and feminine enough – and in particular he did not like the way in which they dressed up for evenings out and how much they drank. He also thought they were too proud. He generally did not consider other foreigners, finding them either not suitable or unavailable. So basically he was looking for a Slovak or Czech partner. He went for the Czechoslovak parties and also met some friends and friends' friends who happened to be in London. The problem seemed to be that the friends' friends were mostly someone else's girlfriends, and he found that the only woman he really liked was his friend's partner. Igor hoped to have what he saw as a normal, steady relationship with a woman, much as he would have had back at home, and was frustrated that, while Slovak women he met at the parties would sleep with him, they seem to have adopted a more promiscuous and to his mind shallow character that seemed odd and new to him. At one point he quoted from a well-known film, *Poets in Czech Countries*, involving a scene where a mother is trying to introduce her son to one of the girls she has seen in church. She is enthusiastic about how there are so many decent and nice girls in church. He replies to her, 'You know, mum, all girls are decent and nice in church.' By the same token he recognizes that now he only meets au pairs in pubs, and 'You know all girls are drunk and indecent in pubs.' Igor also felt bad about his own behaviour, as when once, after having a one-night stand with a Slovak au pair he met at a party, he could not remember her name. This was not the kind of love life he wanted to have. But, again, once he invited an au pair he met at a party for a date and was told by her, when they went for a walk, that she wouldn't meet him again, since she wanted to practise her English. He noted sarcastically that he could perfectly well speak English with her, but fully appreciated the wider evasion that lay behind her remark. In the end he met a nice woman during a Christmas holiday at a party in Slovakia. They liked each other and, as she had lost her job recently, she suggested she could join him in London. He felt considerable relief that he was finished with dating in London and happily settled.

Slovak men faced with such dramatic shifts in gender relations can find solace in their continued sense of themselves as good-looking, well-built men who have many basic skills that they can use to construct and maintain a house and family, knowing that, whatever their behaviour while in London, this positive view is shared by Slovak women. Tóno, a male au pair who felt it was difficult to find a girl-friend, thought it was because he could not earn as much as English men or other foreigners staying in London. With his male friends he would swap stories about the bad treatment meted out to Slovak au pairs who have succumbed to the temptation to form relationships with, for example, English, Albanian or Pakistani men, whom they have subsequently discovered to be cold or violent. They presume such women will eventually return to Slovakia, having learnt their lesson and, if anything, come to appreciate better the positive qualities of warm, considerate and reliable Slovak men.

In the meantime Slovak men certainly welcomed any possibility of developing relationships with Slovak women. Au pairs found it was considerably easier to meet interesting men, who were also inter-ested in them, than would have been the case at home. At Czech and Slovak parties or restaurants the au pairs found a generally relaxed atmosphere where they could very easily meet and chat to men. They felt they had more control over the type of commitment, which could mean just an invitation to a barbecue, but could also be a one night-stand or a long-term relationship. These men tended to be manual labourers and were less likely than the au pairs to include gradu-ates. While there is an additional migration of both male and female middle-class Slovaks, these tend not to frequent the same places as au pairs.

Male au pairs

This book has up to now been written in an entirely gendered lan-guage which identifies au pairs as female. In fact five of the au pairs (10 per cent of our sample) were male. We have no way of knowing how representative this is. Another study suggests that up to 25 per cent of applicants are male, but it is clear that British families were still very reluctant to take them, and so the proportion who actually work as au pairs will be significantly less. Also the discourse around the au pair remains resolutely female. However, even in our small sample, the distinctive attitude to male au pairs was striking. In each case there was initially a good deal of caution about whether a male was a safe or sensible option. It was still generally regarded as quite a radical departure from the norm, and one that would generally cause eyebrows to be raised by friends, neighbours and relatives.

The problem was felt to be particularly serious if there were girls as well as boys to be looked after, but even when only boys were involved there was an initial fear and hesitancy about taking the step. Two male au pairs whom we interviewed were wrongly accused of paedophilia at some time during their employment. Jozef knew British society was very conscious about possible child abuse, but hadn't realized how obsessive this could become. He had been aware that the thirteen-year-old boy he was taking to school was shy. So while they were out in the school yard he had asked the boy about the girls from his class – whether he liked them, which of them he found pretty. Jozef remarked on one particular blonde girl who was nicely shaped. The boy had apparently been scared to death and immediately after coming home had run to his mother telling her that Jozef was interested in young girls. Jozef was told to leave. He hadn't the slightest interest in sleeping with a thirteen-year-old girl. He had simply been trying to have what the English called a 'laddish' discussion with the son. In the other case there was clearly more ambiguity, such that the family may have had good reason to err on the side of caution. So evidently, although the relationship can be very positive, these initial fears remain. In several cases there were clear reasons why a male had been preferentially selected. One was a single mother who wanted an au pair that could also help in the garden and with physical labour. Another was a couple where the husband was in a wheelchair and needed transporting. A third was a single father with only sons. In a fourth case, the Borgersons, who had a twelve-year-old girl, were quite deliberately challenging what they felt were prejudices in asserting the reasonableness in having a male as readily as a female au pair. In fact this was one of the most successful pairings.

Once the plunge had been taken, and a male au pair employed, it seemed in several cases that, after a while, the host mothers felt as though they had discovered a hidden treasure in the world that had brought them untold blessings. They didn't so much talk about these au pairs as gush. There was simply so much a male au pair could do. Quite apart from looking after the children and cleaning, it meant there was someone living in the house who could repair things, undertake DIY jobs and help in the gardening or with moving furniture. All of these things are significant because of the sense of 'crisis' in urban domestic life in affluent areas of London, where access to manual labour and associated skills is limited. This is a ubiquitous topic of middle-class dinner-time conversation. Does anyone know or can anyone recommend a man who can 'do things' around the house? Slovak men are generally highly experienced at household repair work. So the families found that they had hired an au pair but somehow managed to get the 'Polish plumber' into the bargain.

Under these conditions the eulogies for male au pairs poured forth: 'With Radik, I could not stop him working. Phenomenal, incredibly strong. I would ask him to do something small and he would do vastly more. If I asked him to mow the lawn, he would do all the gardening and erect a fence, and carry on till nine o'clock and get offended when you asked him to stop.' Radik is reported to have done painting and decorating jobs for houses for miles around, but on returning to the family home would still clean the coffee cups and sort out the kitchen. These external jobs were never at the expense of his care for the home and the children. Equally important to this enthusiasm is the reflected admiration of boys. Within a very short time, young boys at school realized that having a male au pair was a kind of trophy that gave them a huge boost in their endless rivalry with their peers. Only they have an au pair who also plays football, wrestles and can lift them on their shoulders, who plays computer games – violent computer games – and who basically understands, shares and enhances their worlds. One mother noted how her son's friends constantly wanted to share or borrow the au pair and were clearly envious of her own sons. It appeared we had finally met Mr Poppins!

Another advantage of the male au pair was the feeling that they had much fewer problems with cleaning. While they might be expected to work just as hard, and even be as submissive, they simply didn't tend to take such things personally or relate it to some ideal of how a good mother or carer ought to be. For them it was just a job, and if their work wasn't always appreciated it was no big deal. They didn't seem so upset when the kids managed to reproduce in five minutes the mess that they had taken hours to clean. Tomáš didn't mind being the only male waiting for the children at school. Indeed he knew the other kids were all jealous of having this young sporty man. At the same time the mothers would not see a male au pair as a threat, in the sense of a substitute mother who challenged their position as primary carer of their children. At least from our small sample it also seemed that families were less concerned about male au pairs bringing girlfriends to the house than they were about female au pairs bringing men.

The topic that was not addressed by families, given the constraints of our fieldwork relations, was that of sexuality, although we know of one male au pair who was pressed to sleep with the single mother who employed him. When he refused he found his workload increased, and so he finally quit this family. This issue was also written up in the

Sunday Times by a journalist who seemed to view her male au pair as a cross between a Greek god and the perfect housewife:

> I didn't set out to choose a male au pair. It was luck – or God, perhaps – that brought Miroslav to me. . . . I e-mailed every single au pair from Bratislava to Uzbekistan, and gave myself earache interviewing Olga and Magda and Fatima as my children created yet more havoc around me. By the time I spoke to Miroslav from Slovakia, I was feeling cynical and totally desperate. He told me he loved children (don't they all, I thought) and that he didn't mind doing housework (I would believe that when I saw it). . . . What I was not prepared for was the Adonis who stepped out of the taxi, crossed the pavement and lifted my baby daughter from my arms. 'I am Miroslav,' he said, squeezing my hand and kissing my cheek. 'I am here to help you.' Then he went to play football in the park with my son, cooked supper for the children and finished the ironing that I had not been able to face for a week. I had stepped out of Angela's Ashes and into my very own private fantasy. . . . I admit that I love it when he comes in from jogging and takes his shirt off, because he has a beautiful body that he doesn't seem to mind me looking at. (http://women.timesonline.co.uk/article/0,,18030-1579657,00.html)

Certainly Slovak male au pairs who take this work largely as an alternative to building and manual labour are expected by their Slovak girlfriends to maintain a physique that puts them in a very different class to the expectations of middle-class males born in London. They may also do this in order to refute the presumed femininity of their role. As such they certainly have the attributes that could turn them, as a stock figure of disruptive sexuality within the British home, into the complement of the female Swedish au pair. The mothers we interviewed would have certainly denied any such direct analogy, but the enthusiasm with which they talked about these men certainly implied a pleasure in their presence. That said, we did mention the newspaper stories about lustful housewives and male au pairs to a mother who hadn't tried one. She replied: 'Oh my God, if I could only get someone to do the garden – I could get the sex elsewhere!'

In conclusion, men are in an ambiguous position with respect to the au pair's experience – in some ways central to their concerns, yet somehow also peripheral to the dominant relationships with other au pairs. Much wider structures such as immigration rules have a major role in determining the nature of and with whom au pairs have relationships, and yet each is, of course, a highly personal and contingent story. Closer to home, the rules and norms of living in someone else's house also create constraints and ambiguities that make this a strange and difficult circumstance for the conduct of relationships. The specifics of the media in long-distance relationships can also be important. Overall the discourses wildly exaggerate the actual circumstances. Host fathers are rarely a problem, and au pairs are often seeking quite ordinary relationships. But the evidence is clear that this shift in context does make a difference, and there can be promiscuity and a range of what would otherwise be seen as transgressive relationships. But then au pairs are of an age when relationships are, in any case, likely to be central to their sense of the world, and one would hardly expect this to be a period of calm waters. They are also exploring a radical shift in the connections between gender and power, an unprecedented sense of freedom and possibility. Ambiguity is a feature of relationships that can diminish as well as grow. The male au pair had been almost an unthinkable proposition until recently but, once countenanced, seems to suddenly fit in with the desires of London families in all sorts of interesting ways that may yet end up as becoming something quite normal, and then perhaps one day the source of new myths and anticipations.

Snippet

Slovak females are well known for their beauty and grace. This, in combination with their ability to look after the household, becomes a dangerous aphrodisiac for the man of the house. Laura from Brezno did not stay for long in a Parisian family: the woman of the house told her to leave on the second day. The reason? She was too beautiful and young. 'One afternoon I was reading a book in my room. I was alone in the house, as the children were out on a trip with their mother. Suddenly the door opened and the man of the house was standing there dressed only in underwear. I shouted and he asked whether he had scared me. I only asked him where his wife was. He laughed and left', said Kristína from Bratislava. (. . .) 'My friend Ľuba got a placement in the family of a widower with three children', Kristína continued.

> She got on very well with them from the beginning, because she had worked as a kindergarten teacher back in Slovakia. Their father realized he could not find a better mother for his children. He started by increasing her salary, then invited her for dinners and to the movies, and once she found a bunch of roses on the table. She immediately knew what that meant. Since she liked him too, and she had become inseparable from his children, she accepted his offer to marry him.

154

Less lucky was eighteen-year-old Petra. She was seduced by a young lover of the woman of the house, who persuaded her that he slept with all au pairs in the house and that his partner did not mind. Apparently she did, because she sacked Petra at the very moment she discovered her in his bed.

(Adapted from Marína Markušová, 'Au pairs down the mines', *Markíza*, no. 38 (2004), 51)

— 7 —

OUT OF TIME

Rite de passage

'Where are all those brilliant girls we played with at kindergarten, where have they all gone today? Where are Majdalenkas, Apolenkas, Veronikas, Zdenkas, Majkas, Lenkas and Monikas?' These were the lyrics of a 1980s socialist pop hit that was played at pretty much every Czechoslovak party held in London – which was quite reasonable given just how many of these girls, by 2005, were probably living in London. And to be honest they were still pretty young. More than 80 per cent were living away from their parental households for the first time. They may bring with them pictures of their boyfriends, but also of their parents and of themselves when they were at kindergarten. Many also had their teddy bears. But they were not schoolchildren, and if we had met them in Slovakia they would have been quite different: why?

As anthropologists, our first aim is to convey the experience of the au pairs as encountered through our ethnography, but then to account for their behaviour. There exists a very well-established anthropological perspective on how people experience time which is conveniently linked to the idea of stages in life. The concept of a *rite de passage* has become part of common parlance. It originally referred to the way people move from one stage of life to another by passing through a liminal period associated with wildness or a reversal of normal civilized behaviour. In some cosmologies, being human is defined as a contrast to the condition of animals. So, for the *rite de passage* of the Kwakiutl of the west coast of Canada, initiates had go out into the world of nature and become the exemplification of animal wildness before being tamed again by the civilizing influence of human society.

156

We want to suggest that much of the au pairs' behaviour as described in this book can be better understood by thinking about this period in London as just such a *rite de passage* which exposes them to a dualism between transient freedoms as opposed to the responsibilities of the longer term that is common to modern life. Au pairs often describe their stays in London as a lesson in growing up and self-development, a period between living with parents and establishing the conditions for becoming parents. For instance, Elena states:

> I worked for three years as a nursery teacher in my home town and simply, you know, everything was cared for. I did not have to care for anything. I was staying with my parents, the nursery was at the corner and I did not have a single problem. So I just decided to become independent and prove to myself that I can live without being dependent on my parents. Sure, I wanted also to improve my English and to know a new country. But the main thing was to prove something to myself.

Being an au pair can turn this transition from something gentle into something quite dramatic. One day they are living with their parents, being treated, and seeing themselves, as children. The next day, not only are they separated from their parents, but they themselves suddenly have children to look after. In fact they seem to spend more time with these children than their real mothers do. Although they may have been socialized into doing more housework in Slovakia than their contemporaries in London, it is still a shock to have almost sole responsibility for cleaning an entire house. So they are stuck in a strange state. While they are dealing with an exaggeration of the chores associated with adult life, they are in a situation without many of the rights and powers of adulthood, sometimes still being told not only when they have to get up, but even what time they are expected to go to bed.

The fact that au pairs interpret their stay as a trial or as a *rite de passage* on the path to becoming an adult is one of the main reasons that they remain in these situations, however oppressive: they feel it is a test that they are grown up, a test they would fail if they were even to mention their unhappiness to their parents. Eighteen-year-old Silvia found herself in an exploitative and distant host family, who hardly spoke to her, made her work very long hours without pay, and restricted her access to food. She was even expected to use a hair comb to straighten the stripes on the carpet. Though she regularly exchanged letters with her parents, she never wrote anything about how unhappy she was, but focused on her visits to museums or how her English was improving. She explained that it would have been 'childish to complain to my parents'. Being deeply religious, she said: 'Lord Jesus suffered for us all and he suffered incredible pain. And I did not suffer that much. So I had to take it, do it for him. And so become a better person.' Silvia stayed with this family for a year. Zdenka was the au pair who was living on a council estate and sharing her bed with the three-year-old boy she was looking after. She had only one day off a fortnight, worked dreadfully long hours, was forbidden from going out, and was pressured to attend Pentecostal services. She recalled: 'I was crying every single night as I wanted to go home so badly. But I did not return. I could not. My parents knew I was not too happy there and told me to come back, but I did not want to. I simply could not go home like a small child. I had to resist something. I am not that weak.'

The experience of this period as one of pain and trial is common to the *rites de passage* observed by anthropologists. But, in addition, initiates are often expected to regress to a less civilized state of being, often by travelling to an area marginal to their normal social setting. The situation here is more complex, in some ways even inverted, since Slovaks have been designated as marginal, and are subsequently looking to spend periods of time in what they regard as a metropolitan city. Slovakia lacks the size or internationally recognized historical traditions of neighbours such as Hungary or Poland. But even compared with the Czechs, Slovaks have found themselves defined as the more rural and less naturally civilized aspect of Eastern Europe. Over the last two decades, Slovakia has extricated itself from being seen as a satellite of the Soviet sphere, only to be relocated as marginal to the Western sphere. Socialism is now seen as having taken the wrong path to modernity, while places such as the UK, which took the right path, are imagined as being ahead. On the other hand, while London is economically rich, Slovak au pairs often see it as socially poor, standing in striking contrast to economically poor but socially and ritually rich Slovakia. Slovaks go to (now uncivilized and wild) London to become better social persons – fathers, women, mothers or workers – and to fulfil their roles back in Slovakia, which for them is indeed a social centre. So London has the capacity to appear wild in comparison with civilized Slovakia and Slovakia the capacity to appear rural in contrast to London's metropolitanism. The important point is that both can be defined by opposition.

In our first chapter we described a combination of what could be called 'push' and 'pull' factors. The reasons au pairs as particular individuals come to London often have more to do with specific personal issues, such as breaking up with their boyfriends or being fed up with parents. The decision to leave can be quite spontaneous. But the sheer quantity of Slovaks that end up as au pairs in London reflect its significance relative to the self-identity of contemporary Slovakia. Jarmila claimed that those who never spent a period abroad were condemned for their lack of initiative and ambition. Certainly she wanted the money that would allow her to set up home and her hair-dressing salon. But also she felt that anyone with brains or gumption would seize the opportunity to educate themselves in the latest forms of modernity. At the same time they would bring to London qualities they have heard are being lost – the common sense and knowledge of Slovaks to care for houses or for children and to do such things as mend fuses, but also the beauty of their women. On the one hand it is an adventure in the wild. Civilized and beautiful Slovaks will brave the weirdness of Camden Town and uncivilized men in pubs who ask for sex before they have even told you their name. But then they will return with the expertise and graces of advanced consumer culture and the latest styles.

Experiencing wildness

So being an au pair in London is defined as a transient state, a kind of gap year in between high school and university, which will also allow young people time to consider what they want to do in their subsequent lives. As such it is not just a *rite de passage*; it also makes explicit the larger dualism of modern temporality. On the one hand there is the exhilarating promise of freedom from family, tradition and responsibility, and on the other hand it is a stage towards estab-lishing one's own home and family. Jarmila regarded her cousin as a failure because she had already become a wife and mother without having given herself the appropriate period of transitional wild-ness. For Jarmila this was like a mistake, a short cut that would fail because, without having had these wider experiences, one couldn't really settle within such a parochial local environment. There would always be regrets for what one hadn't done.

This is the context that helps explain the au pairs' behaviour once in London – a temporary transformation in the behaviour of the initiates most evident in the ways they treated each other. In chapter 5, it became apparent that behaviour could regress to something more akin to that of the school playground. For instance, Natália decided she would not go to a local Czechoslovak party organized in

Beddlingham for two reasons. One was that the DJ was English and was unlikely to play many Slovak songs. But the main reason was the other au pairs:

> You know, there is a large group of au pairs going there [to the party], whom I really hate. They are a bit simple. And it is the group around Nasťa. And Nasťa, you know, Nasťa came here half a year ago, and she came to work for the family her sister was leaving. And it went without saying Nasťa would be with the group of her sister's friends. But they did not accept her. Basically, they threw her out. So we took her into our group. We called on her when we went to Tesco or somewhere out. So we basically helped her. But then, then she started to avoid us and gossip, even backbite, about us. And once, when we were going to Tesco, we called her up to come along. But she said she had a cleaning job, was tired and just wanted to take a shower and go to bed. And then we met her in Tesco. And another time she said she didn't want to go out. But then next day we met her in the library, and you have to sign up for internet a day in advance, so she was basically lying, she must have gone out. So now I don't feel comfortable in her company and I don't want to go to the party.

In such circumstances the fragility of relationships is exposed and sometimes things can fall apart. Nineteen-year-old Ľubica decided to spend a weekend with Tatiana, her high-school friend, who was working as an au pair in North Finchley. Tatiana's host family allowed her to have good female friends to stay overnight on weekends. For Ľubica that meant at last there was a possibility of discovering Central London properly. They decided that this time they would go clubbing in Camden. Mostly they went either to Czechoslovak events or to live music in local pubs and clubs in either Ľubica's or Tatiana's neighbourhood. A couple of their au pair friends, Majka and Dáša, who were, as they called it, 'into black music', mocked them for their conservative choices in both clubs and style of music. So on this occasion both sets of au pairs decided to spend the evening at the Electric Ballroom in Camden. The clubbing went well, and after a while Majka and Dáša went their own way to another club. But, after what Ľubica felt was a minor argument, Tatiana just left and went home without telling her. Ľubica was shocked. Not only was she frightened by the fact she was alone in a club somewhere in Central London, she didn't know how to get to Tatiana's place. Furthermore, Tatiana, apparently deliberately, did not pick up her mobile phone, so she couldn't actually get to her place for the night, as had been agreed. Neither could she find Majka and Dáša. Finally she managed to contact a male friend who hadn't turned his phone off for the night, and he helped direct her back to safety.

One group of friends, although knowing they had temporary care of some crucial possessions, including the phone of another au pair, simply didn't bother to make arrangements for her things to be collected, although it meant the au pair in question was effectively stranded. Sometimes competition develops over men – au pairs taking advantage of friend's lovers with a casualness or playfulness that shows little consideration of the pain created by their actions. For example, one au pair not only had an affair with the husband of her friend but casually flirted and flaunted her attachment essentially for her own amusement. These more significant acts occur within a context of countless small acts of carelessness or casual lack of concern, such as virtually forcing an au pair to drink alcohol, knowing this to be incompatible with her course of antibiotics. Tereza, after finishing her year as an au pair, managed to find work as a secretary for a company distributing organic agricultural products. Although she was now staying only half an hour's travel from Beddlingham, she simply cut off all contact with Renata, who had been her best friend. She never phoned her and only met once, when she couldn't find an excuse to say no. Tereza confessed that now she was no longer an au pair she was bored by Renata and saw their relationship as temporary and expedient, even though they had spent almost all their leisure time together. Renata couldn't believe such coldness and indifference.

Of course people quarrel, end friendships and mistreat each other in many circumstances. But it was this casual disregard, as well as the sheer frequency of such incidents and the associated rudeness, that particularly differentiates everyday life in London from normative behaviour in Slovakia. The point is that such stories would be exceptional among this same age group in Slovakia, so it is not some character flaw but rather an effect of the very particular circumstances in which they find themselves. Being an au pair is simply a very limited and defined chapter of their life where they experiment, enjoy themselves, become independent, but, somehow without any conscious intent, find that they do not really emotionally invest as much as in the relationships they have had previously back home

One aspect of this more 'animalistic' or less than human state may be seen in various examples of transgressive behaviour. In several instances Zuzana spent time with these same au pairs both before and after she worked with them in London. In London they were more likely to swear openly, using stronger expletives, and they drank much more heavily – not just 'women's' drinks but what would be regarded

161

as serious drinking. We met several au pairs who shoplifted clothes, always lingerie – something they swore they would never have done back in Slovakia. Some, though by no means the majority, become much more promiscuous. They would talk explicitly of experimenting – trying out a whole menu of sexual acts – and be drawn to illicit forms of sex – especially with black men (the category includes men of Middle Eastern and not just Afro-Caribbean origin) – because of the stereotypical warning from their relatives that this is exactly what they should never do. However, things might not amount to anything more than the occasion, for example, when three very young au pairs were trying to find the courage to ask an attractive black man on Brighton beach to pose with them for a photo. Given the discourse about black men that circulates in Slovakia, even this had the frisson of flirting with something forbidden, though we also knew of two au pairs who attempted suicide after becoming pregnant by black men.

An important difference was that in Slovakia women rarely enter intentionally into a temporary relationship with a man or deliberately seek out men viewed as unsuitable or inappropriate. By contrast, in London au pairs might experiment with relationships with different kinds of men, knowing that there is no prospect of these lasting. There was a palpable sense of freedom that it was not necessary to bother with things such as a man's family or education, or how well he would fit with one's circle of friends in the longer term. Such relationships could also feel more authentic, being based entirely on personal attraction, without worrying about that fact that the person concerned shared none of your cultural milieux. Also, au pairs can have more relationships, because in a city such as London people feel anonymous. They will not be condemned as 'whores' if they change their boyfriends too often. As such the evidence for sexual transgression among au pairs does not seem to indicate a more radical questioning of conventional ideas about sexuality or the nature of gender more generally. Rather these lapses are those that are already posed as transgressive according to quite conventional and traditional models of proper sexuality and behaviour. Equally we saw little evidence that this was a period in which au pairs moved away from traditional views on femininity and heterosexuality; rather these were reinforced, though there was certainly the impact of a more general feminism as it applies to the rights and self-respect of women.

The idea of transgressive experimentation applied to a much wider range of experiences than sex. It could include au pairs' relationship with themselves rather than with others. Most au pairs feel positive about the sudden freedom with which they can experiment with their own appearance, sometimes in quite a radical fashion. They might grow their hair, get a piercing, take drugs or wear clothes that would leave people in Slovakia aghast. One very conservative Catholic could not bring herself to wear provocative outerwear but did start to wear erotic lingerie. Another might buy what had seemed like an outrageously expensive perfume. Au pairs going on shopping expeditions as a group encourage each other to experiment and comment on each other's choices. Darinka suddenly went for ethnic items such as Afghan skirts; another au pair bought extremely tight stretch Lycra tops. Some start with unusual tops but then gain the confidence to try piercing, strange jewellery and fancy shoes. These new freedoms may also be expressed in the sheer number of purchases, such as five pairs of Nike trainers or seven pairs of new summer shoes.

What starts out as freedom and experimentation can also imply a general loss of control, clearest in the relationship with the body itself. The original intention is for au pairs to use their time in London positively for such things as growing their hair long. But almost inevitably they are faced instead with what becomes their most obsessive topic of conversation: putting on weight. Only around five of the fifty au pairs seemed immune to what they genuinely saw as an awful condition. While they could point to factors ranging from the change in the daily structure of meals, or trying new and exotic foods generally available for free in their homes, they realized there was something more profound in this. They find that the wildness or absence of conventional constraint expressed in trying out more experimental clothes and identities also leads to a loss of self-control and discipline of the body.

What appeared at first as unlimited freedom could after a while also become debilitating. Without clear structure and direction, they simply could not take decisions or even know what it was they now wanted for themselves. This could result in an extreme passivity accompanied by a kind of hopelessness. This trajectory from freedom to 'anomie', particularly within urban settings, has been a common observation in social science studies of modern life since Durkheim and Simmel. For the au pairs, it was experienced as a general loss of self-confidence in the face of what seemed like an excess of choice and possibility.

It was often au pairs previously characterized as rather quiet who become more outgoing in London, while the most striking cases of indecision and passivity were of women who had been unusually sociable and confident before they came to the UK. Such passivity could be linked with a feeling of subordination relative to a host family, never saying no to anything they were asked, or simply standing and looking dumb. But it was equally manifest in their use of leisure time and the possibilities of London. When work was over, or they had a day off and it would have been simple enough to catch up with that English homework or to go out and meet people, such au pairs seemed unable to find the necessary initiative. It was very common that those who had previously engaged in sports and other activities simply stopped doing so. Similarly, those who had been active academically and used to read widely became lethargic with respect to both – all of which exacerbated the tendency to put on weight. Au pairs felt that it reflected a combination of lack of structure and their distance from the people for whom their choices really mattered – family and true friends.

Coming back

To understand this deeper ambivalence we need to go beyond the idea of a *rite de passage* with its associated animalistic and transgressive behaviour. As noted, for au pairs a *rite de passage* implies that the period in London be experienced as a transition between two states. In itself a period of wildness and transgression, it should then give way to the next stage of life, which is that of settled respectability and long-term commitment. The complication is that, in practice, some au pairs seem to oscillate between these two conditions, while others come to occupy one or other end of this spectrum. This is perhaps clearest in the way au pairs relate to their earnings. Slovak au pairs do not send back remittances, and are not expected to support their families back home. But there is still a deep ambivalence about money. On the one hand it is 'pocket money' – that is, money to be spent ideally on fashion and on having a great time. On the other hand it is 'wages' that could be saved, as it would go a long way to helping establish a house and home after their return.

Au pairs come with an expectation that they should save some money towards their own future. One day Lucia would need to buy a property, and everyone knew how hard it was to save enough money. This follows a historic pattern in peasant households, when young women commonly went into domestic service in order to put aside money for their dowry. No one today talked about a dowry. It was just money in order to settle down. Such talk had another effect, though, on Lucia. It made her appreciate that perhaps her time in London was the only period when she would not have any

164

responsibilities. It may be that, for Lucia and others, spending much of this money on clothing was a kind of unconscious compromise – something fun to do while in London, but also a nod to the tradition of a dowry, much of which consisted of women making their own clothing.

For Ivana this was the first time she felt the freedom and had the resources and opportunity to spend – and not only to spend, but to spend without any control from her parents. She soon became an expert on Beddlingham shops, some of which she might visit every afternoon. On one occasion she purchased a new Barbie doll for her younger sister Soňa's birthday. Soňa loved Barbie dolls and already had two. But for their parents this had been a significant purchase in terms of the cost of such dolls relative to their wages. Ivana, however, could muse about a blonde Barbie with sportswear as against a black Barbie dressed for a ball, aware that the price differentials were of little consequence. Over coffee she noted that the best thing about au pairing is that you can spend your pocket money on whatever silly thing you want. Since she had a room and food, she could have spent the whole lot on Barbies. She said: 'Even as a "servant" I can spend more than my mother can.' In 2005 it was probable that Ivana's pocket money, even without her earnings from subsidiary work, came to more than her mother's wages in Slovakia. Yet the money her mother earned had to be used for such things as housing and food, which were particularly expensive relative to salary. When saying these things, Ivana was also well aware that once she returned she too would take on the self-sacrificial role of wife and mother, with earnings directed to the common good of the household rather than the individual. This was another reason some au pairs returned with several suitcases of clothes for themselves.

So a shopping trip can be accompanied by the feeling that this is going to be the only time in life one can spend carelessly for oneself and treat one's loved ones, but without really forgetting the imperatives of thrift and the need to save for the future. The result may either be buying lots of clothing, but at prices such that au pairs can emphasize how much they saved rather than how much they spent, or oscillating between extremely inexpensive purchases and the occasional extravagance, for example the au pair who bought those Dior sunglasses for £150 at Selfridges – but this was exceptional. The small sums with which au pairs are dealing often seem too paltry to establish serious savings and are therefore better spent on clothes.

Similarly while au pairs might fantasize about or actually experiment with sex, more generally there is ambivalence in their attitude to men that is analogous to this relationship with money, an oscillation between the desire to experience 'wildness' and their goal of settling down with a good-hearted, appropriate and, hopefully, Slovak husband. Actually, given the Slovak discourse about the promiscuity of Slovak women living abroad, Zuzana was surprised that most of the research participants were in practice mainly, during their time in London, looking simply for a positive long-term relationship. But, for some au pairs, the experience of transgressive relationships was a prerequisite for this longer-term settlement back into domesticity. Some reasoned that they needed to experience (both sexually and as potential partners) more men in order to recognize who ultimately would suit them best. For others, experiments with parties, flirting, dating and perhaps sexual promiscuity was a means of getting this wildness 'out of their system', which would ensure that, when they did so, they would settle down without any regrets for their lack of such experiences. Others, sometimes successfully, sometimes not, basically used adventurous sex to 'catch' a man for the long term – feeling that good sex, enhanced by erotically explicit clothing and dancing, or even flirting with other men, could attract the person they really desired. In practice, of course, relationships do not simply follow from deep contradictions of cosmology. Other considerations are pragmatic. For example, an au pair desires a stable long-term relationship but, in the absence of any such promising relationship, may feel the need in the meantime for at least the comfort and caress (or pocket) of some partner.

This dualism with respect to time sets out the frame for the envisaged return to Slovakia: the experience of London, to be followed by a settled life with husband, work and children. In practice, however, there are all sorts of reasons why this may not actually happen. In general, female au pairs probably have less incentive to return to Slovakia than male migrant labourers. Men will usually have earned a great deal more money than au pairs, who will rarely have saved enough to set up businesses for themselves. Their employment prospects are generally less secure than those for men, and in occupations regarded as more demeaning. They have also had more opportunities to form relationships, including relationships with other men who are likely in the future to attract higher incomes than men in Slovakia. Even if relationships were first entered into as transient or transgressive, any of these may develop into genuine, affectionate and successful relationships based on long-term commitment. In such cases, rather than migrate to the country of origin of their partner, they tend to compromise and settle in the UK, which is the ideal place to avoid the issues raised by a mixed couple with different customs and expectations. Finally au pairs may also be reluctant to relinquish what they regard as greater freedoms and equality for women than they anticipate on their return, most obviously in the case of one lesbian couple.

Most au pairs and ex au pairs in London still assume that eventually they will return to Slovakia. We have to bear in mind that many previous migrants to the UK, such as those from South Asia, maintained 'the myth of return' even when it became apparent that they would not go back. That said, theirs was an entirely different structure of migration. It is probably too early in the history of Slovak migration to the UK for us to state with any confidence what the future will be and the extent to which such migration will prove to be permanent. Most of the au pairs with whom we worked simply did not know themselves whether taking up another job, such as waitressing, is simply a move to earn more money before returning or ultimately a stage towards settling in London itself. Often, just as with the reasons why they come, the reasons whether they return will be based on unpredictable and personal factors such as whether they form a relationship with a partner, whether they find their work satisfying and how much they miss their families. Furthermore, with the rise of much cheaper transport and communication systems, opportunities may arise to develop more transnational lives shared between Slovakia and London. As yet, few au pairs or ex-au pairs are having children, so we cannot tell what the consequences will be if they do. At present statistics seem to suggest that the au pairs' assumption that they will mostly return at some point was right.

Once they do return to Slovakia au pairs have to deal with one of the discourses that has arisen about women who have spent time working in London. As we have mentioned, Slovaks believe and constantly assert that their women possess an outstanding beauty and femininity, of which everyone is proud. But just as Slovakia is forced to export all its best-quality products from industry and agriculture, somehow this had led also to their losing the most important product of all, in a kind of political economy of beauty – that ever afterwards these women would be somehow spoilt or corrupted by their experiences with men abroad. This poses a problem also because of the association of women with the reproduction of the nation through its domestic idyll.

Potentially, however, there is an alternative discourse based around the growing idea of au pairing as a colloquial version of what we are calling a *rite de passage*: that people can now respect

167

the experience and opportunity for growing up and achieving a greater degree of autonomy; that learning English and improving one's employment potential are positive; that, after passing through this period, au pairs can fit back into the normative expectations and lives of Slovak women and need not be regarded as significantly different from others except that they have now seen the world. Today these discourses co-exist. Most often people put a positive gloss on the experience of individual women they know and welcome them back into Slovak society. But, when it comes to discussion about au pairs as a generic phenomenon, there is often a fear about their promiscuity and behaviour and a resentment of this ongoing loss to the nation, represented by 'their' women sleeping with other men.

In this book we have mainly eschewed the use of explicit anthropological theory that we would assume of a volume targeted mainly at other academics. But we would hope that in this chapter a great deal is gained by understanding this process as both ritual and comparative to analogous practices of many other peoples. While au pairs themselves would not have any reason to use such a term as *rite de passage*, we have given many examples in this chapter that suggest that they too can come to an understanding of being an au pair that is close to this conception – that they both excuse and explain their behaviour while in London as a stage rather than as an ordinary or normal part of their life and that, for some, what they appear to be in London is more or less the precise opposite of what they expect to be when they return. A *rite de passage* is not then some archaic rite practised by tribal peoples and lost to the industrialized world. It is a logical structure and evident cosmology that can be readily invented and refined as a way of exploiting new circumstances, even for people who did not previously have such a stage in life.

Snippet

Many girls are attracted by the work of an au pair. It offers them an opportunity to know a new country and its culture, to learn a foreign language and, not least, to earn some money. Then, too, the fact that one can sleep around in an environment where no one knows who you are may be an irresistible turn on. Sure, we women are a diverse lot, and do not all respond in the same way to temptation. We form a spectrum all the way from the chaste zombie to the nymphomaniac.

168

1. **Zombie**

   The zombie gets little from her foreign trip. If you ask her about her experience, she will describe in detail the furniture in the house she was living in and the regime for the children she was looking after. They are scared by change; they barely left their dorms at college. Their families are delighted with them, as they spend all day long at home, cleaning, tidying, cooking, looking after children. . . . that's why they so are often exploited. . . . their sexual lives are impoverished. Zombies don't speak to male strangers. But if a man with a nice smile and sweet tongue approaches our poor inexperienced zombie, she is lost.

2. **Intellectual**

   This au pair is the only one immune to flirting men. She is honestly interested in the culture of the country and the possibility of broadening her knowledge. They actually go to museums and galleries to look at art rather than to meet men. They hate men whistling at them in streets. They prefer men who are of at least the same intellectual level as they are. Good looks are merely a plus. If he is educated and experienced, and she feels she can learn something from him, then she takes her opportunities. But in the end she values her certificate from the language school more than the phone list of men who would like to take her out for dinner.

3. **Parasite**

   This group of au pairs is special. They stay with their family only as long as they can see some advantage to it. They never accept overtime and exploitation. They don't mind the attentions of the host father if this adds a little something to their pocket money. Parasites love men. At least she can accept a dinner invitation and use his phone to chat to all her friends. She is happy to be his trophy girlfriend and dresses the part. She will stick with whoever can afford her. If he is rich enough they can form the functional couple; he buys her love and she gets her comfortable life.

4. **Veil-dancer**

   Veil-dancer knows very well why she wants to leave her home. She wants to get married! There was no one at home who wanted to marry her, so she will try her luck elsewhere. She has heard that Western men are more available and really like girls from Eastern Europe. They also come with a better lifestyle and citizenship. They may not be that good looking, but in London that's not so important. Foreign men will be bound to find them beautiful. The motto is 'marry quick'. Having a single father as the host family may provide an excellent opportunity. Every day they can show

169

off their art of cooking, care and cleanliness, as well as personally inspect the value of the property they are (for now) only working in.

(Adapted from Zuzana Gregorová, 'If you want to lose your virginity become an au pair', in the Slovak women's magazine *Es Passion*, no. 4 (2003), 28–31)

CONCLUSION: STRUCTURE, BEHAVIOUR AND CONSEQUENCE

The au pair as an institution

In the last chapter we considered various models that represent au pairing as a particular experience of time, both as a *rite de passage* and as an oscillation between short-term and long-term concerns. In this concluding chapter we suggest that this experience of time derives from an underlying structure. It is the institutional foundation of au pairing that accounts for much of the behaviour of both the au pairs and the host families. We will consider three aspects of this structure and its legal foundations. The first defines the au pair as a temporary state, the second establishes its informality and the third is the concept of 'foreign'.

While the law is normally thought of as that which establishes order, in each of these cases it is the law itself whose consequence has actually been ambiguity and disorder. Now that most of the countries that supply au pairs to the UK are in the EU there is no reason for au pairs to register, nor do they require any formal permit. As a result, our study is bereft of statistics. There is no way of determining how many au pairs there are in the UK or where they are from. During the research it was often said that Slovaks may form the largest single group relative to that country's population. But this claim can be supported only by figures on applications to become au pairs; we simply don't know about final numbers. Until Slovakia joined the EU in May 2004, Slovaks needed visas to enter the UK and the Home Office kept the relevant statistics of holders of special au pair visas. Now all EU citizens are free to live and work in the UK. This also makes it increasingly unclear to whom the legal framework of being an au pair actually applies. Several of our participants fell outside the specified age limit, may not be learning English, and stay for a longer period than is suggested by legislation. But clearly they call themselves au pairs, as do the families and as do we.

Not only are their numbers unclear. Neither the au pairs' scheme nor their work and living conditions are controlled – whether with respect to immigration policy, by a governmental body or even by an NGO. Commercial agencies that are mainly responsible for mediating contacts between the au pairs and host families seem to be strikingly unsatisfactory in this regard. Most agencies supply au pairs (or families) with neither precise information as to the law nor a realistic representation of the conditions. The au pairs with whom we worked did not even know that there was a law regulating their rights and duties. Not only they did not get sufficient information, but they generally reported a complete lack of any support by the agencies mediating their stay. It is usual that such agencies provide au pairs with contact details of other au pairs in the neighbourhood and/or call newly arrived au pairs and host families a couple of weeks after their arrival to check whether everything is all right, but that is usually the sum total of their involvement. No agency ever visited the host families, either before or after the au pair's arrival, to check on the conditions of their accommodation. Indeed, three of the au pairs in our study were, contrary to the law, expected to share a room or even a bed with a child they were supposed to look after. Some of the agencies specify in their contracts that the au pairs could claim their right to change a host family for free if they complain during first two months of their stay, but not later.

There were several cases when the agencies were requested, but totally failed, to help mediate conflicts or to provide help for an au pair who had some issue with their host families. Some of these au pairs were themselves blamed for being confrontational or problematic, or their problems were dismissed as irrelevant. For example, Kristína was sexually harassed by the single father for whom she was working. She immediately contacted the British agency which mediated her stay, but her complaint was dismissed on the grounds that her English was not good enough for her to recognize such sexual harassment. Later, when Kristína refused to have sex with her employer, he told her to leave his household immediately. She phoned the agency again, but they were not prepared to be flexible in helping her to find another host family, to help her with her living conditions or even to facilitate her return home. There were cases of au pairs whose host families terminated their contract of employment without notice, but the agencies did not help them find new accommodation or host families within the previously specified two weeks, or advise them on what to do next. One reason for this neglect of the au pairs' rights can be a possible conflict of interests. The agencies in London receive their fees from the host families and work in collaboration with agencies in the au pairs' country of origin. The au pairs are usually clients of the agencies in their home country, who either cannot provide them with any relevant help from such a distance or suggest that they contact their British counterparts, whom they hope will assist them, but who are really more beholden to the host family. It is only fair to note that, even under present conditions, au pairs recruited through these agencies generally suffer less exploitation and abuse and get more help than those recruited through the internet or adverts posted in newsagents. There are also a very few exceptional agencies providing generous help to au pairs in need – there were even cases of au pairs who, having been sacked by their host families, ended up staying in the homes of the agencies' owners. Outside of the agencies there is essentially no effective institutional support for au pairs whose families have broken the legal rules for their employment. Consequently, the au pairs' practice has generally been to assume that they cannot rely on institutions, but only on personal networks, mostly with other Czech and Slovak au pairs.

As we mentioned in chapter 2, the institution of au pairing is covered by the *European Agreement on 'Au Pair' Placement* (Council of Europe 1969). This specifies that 'the person placed "au pair" is to share the life of the receiving family, while at the same time enjoying a certain degree of independence.' There are subsidiary conditions agreed in Home Office immigration directorates. Since the completion of our research this legal structure has been terminated and replaced by the Youth Mobility Scheme we discuss in the Appendix. On a less formal basis, the conditions for au pairs are also laid down by the British Au Pair Agency Association and by individual au pair agencies.

The legal framework, such as it is, for au pairing as an institution seems to be based on certain assumptions that require further discussion. The first is that of time. Though it is no longer illegal for Slovak au pairs to be in the UK for more than two years, au pairs are, by definition, temporary. The ideology of the institution is that it is a cultural exchange of benefit to young adults, who thereby gain knowledge of both culture and language within the protective environment of a family – an ideology which presumes that being an au pair is a specific and temporary stage in life. Although this is not specified by legislation, au pairs also coincide with a particular life stage for families who are bringing up children. The knowledge that hosting an au pair is just a temporary state is taken as the protection and insurance for an English family that is otherwise extremely dubious about a stranger taking part in the intimate life of their home. Furthermore, few families have merely a single au pair, so each individual is just one of several that pass through the house. In retrospect the au pair is expected to lose their individuality and become simply the backdrop to the central story of how the children grow up. All they typically leave behind are a few anecdotes. This is hugely important to mothers who fear that an au pair might challenge their role as a primary carer, something that becomes evident to au pairs the day they arrive: the family is apparently welcoming, but often in a rather cold mechanical way. The material evidence is present in that white melamine IKEA furniture that makes clear both their anonymity and their replaceability, something to which the au pairs respond with their increasing concern not to leave even the slightest impression of themselves, whether by finishing food or marking a carpet.

No Slovak goes to London thinking they will be an au pair in the long term. Knowing that this is a temporary state of affairs explains why a person with good educational qualifications can take on a period of domestic labour, why they will accept boring work, unpaid overtime, or dehumanizing treatment by the host family. A major reason they may not bother to change host family or complain about working hours or that their room is too dark, damp and cold is that they can bear it 'for now'. In other words, being an au pair is never an identity; it is always a period out from the rest of life. Several au pairs felt offended when their host families offered them the opportunity of staying for a longer period than originally contracted. The families meant this as a compliment, demonstrating how positive they felt about their work and personality. But the au pairs were affronted that the family could imagine that they would want to spend more than a relatively short time in such a relationship. Barbora in particular felt this was a denial of her university education.

In practice the au pairs came to realize that things could be even more temporary and therefore fragile. Agencies could leave them on hold for months and then tell them to be in London within a week. Once they had arrived, the rules seem unclear as to when exactly they may expect to be babysitting, or when they are free to take their leisure. Au pairs may not be informed in advance about the families' holiday plans, which means that it is difficult for them to make any plans for themselves. Then the family might be capricious with respect to how long an au pair is required. Zuzana met an ex au

174

pair who came to London expecting she would spend a year with the host family, and found out that the family had lied to her and needed her for only three weeks, after which they left for a holiday. After unexpectedly being given notice by two families in a row, Paula said that she learnt not to plan anything and would just wait to see what life would bring. In many cases this sheer powerlessness and lack of control over one's own time led to a marked passivity and general acquiescence. This also made it hard to think clearly about the future. Alternatively, au pairs may quickly become quite opportunistic: a job offer might appear suddenly, and they decide on the spot to quit their family. Both families and au pairs feel less constraint about ill-treating the other, because they know the situation is temporary. This becomes much clearer when a date has been set for the au pair to leave, and behaviour often deteriorates on both sides.

This increasing feeling of alienation has one positive effect. At least this period could become one liberated from any close association with work. For example, Ol'ga had just completed her employment as a senior hospital nurse. Her over-identification with her work and her deep concern for the effects of inadequate care on patients had meant a life never free of stress. By comparison, she spoke of how much more relaxed and positive she felt in a situation where ultimately she couldn't give a damn about cleaning toilets or pleasing families. Several chapters of this book have placed emphasis on one consequence of this transience; that the orientation of au pairs is increasingly to a time spent in London rather than a time spent in domestic work.

The second trait that is institutionalized in law is that of informality. This is what makes the conditions of employment of an au pair entirely different from those of a normal job. An illegal migrant doing domestic work may find a certain informality arising as a side effect of their place in the home without any legal infrastructure, but with au pairs this informality is effectively prescribed. The reason au pairs don't pay taxes is because they are supposed to be integrated as a member of the family rather than as an employee. However, as we revealed, families almost invariably employ au pairs as the least bad option for childcare, not because they actually want to instigate a pseudo-family relationship. While au pairs view this as a relatively secure mode for spending time in London, they more often come with an eye to escaping family life rather than joining it.

Nevertheless, Slovaks become au pairs assuming that there will actually be a genuine attempt to treat them within a pseudo-family setting. But, as we demonstrated, they commonly find that they are

175

betrayed by the very ambiguity of this phrasing. The concept of pseudo-family was appealed to when families were asking the au pair to work beyond their agreed hours, or the parents were coming home unexpectedly late. But the opposite was the case when it came to an au pair asking for any kind of special consideration or time off. So the abstraction of the pseudo-family is seen as evidence for the hypocrisy of host families rather than as something positive, facilitated by law. The families themselves are highly ambivalent about the idea of incorporating a stranger into their private lives and would have been as much prone to the *embarrassment of co-presence* as the au pair. They are saved from this by the asymmetry of power, which allows them to dictate the basic house rules and in various ways keep the au pair at a distance.

The third legal precondition for becoming an au pair is that one is, by definition, foreign. The fact that au pairs are both foreign and temporary helps protect the host family, who feel secure that the au pair will not be mixing in the same social milieu as themselves, and that stories about their quarrels and the way they treat each other will only be exported to some other country. This foreignness may also help alleviate the acute sensitivity concerning class in contemporary Britain, a place where it would be equally problematic to admit to inequality by employing someone from a distinctly lower echelon as it would be to employ someone of one's own class in the role of domestic labourer. All of this can be avoided when an au pair is first viewed as foreign. This may have a positive aspect where some families subscribe to the idea of a cultural exchange and feel their children gain from such exposure to differences in customs.

What is entirely ignored in the single term *foreign* is the variety of places au pairs may come from and their motivations for coming. This may not have mattered very much previously. To some degree the institution of the au pair was relatively protected from abuse by the particular circumstances from which it arose – the relative equality between countries such as France, Scandinavia and England. Danny found that several of his au pairs from Scandinavia had been encouraged to come by their mothers, who had themselves previously been au pairs in London and had had very positive experiences. But this history disguises a new trend towards greater inequality. As the image of the generic au pair migrates from that of a Scandinavian to that of an Eastern European, it is very likely that the initial presumption of equality will be lost. This new inequality reflects the increasing difference in economic conditions. Slovak au pairs, who can find their pocket money in London is more remunerative than a wage in

Slovakia, have additional grounds for migration, while English host families who think of Eastern Europeans as a kind of peripheral peasantry largely ignored the fact that thirteen of our participants had university degrees and five had worked on PhDs. As a result we believe that the particular period when our fieldwork took place may represent a crucial transformation in the au pair as an institution, which makes this the appropriate time for suggesting some changes.

If many of the problems that characterize the contemporary au pair experience are directly consequential upon the nature and structure of the institution, then it should be possible to alleviate some of those problems through such changes. Our starting position, however, is that we would retain the au pair scheme. We can envisage many ideal worlds: where all families take responsibility for their own childcare and cleaning, where the state provides full childcare for working parents, where staying at home to look after children is gender equal and is as fully valorized as paid work. However, it would be naïve to assume that any of these would follow if the institution were abolished or that any additional burden would fall equally on both sexes. On the whole it is women who would suffer. Under conditions that are unfortunately likely to remain static for quite some time, families, whether in Britain or Slovakia, who wish to have children at an older age are effectively punished by the labour market. Women (or indeed men) suffer considerable disadvantages if they try and take time off from their careers. We also do not assume that it is 'natural' or even psychologically preferable for children to be looked after only by their biological parents. Anthropologists and historians have documented many societies where childcare is almost entirely in the hands of older siblings, other kin or even non-kin. The au pair institution allows qualified parents to continue to develop their careers while giving over childcare to younger persons, more like those older siblings.

For these reasons we prefer to concentrate on how to reform the actual situation of au pairs rather than gesture to an ideal world within which the institution would disappear. In accepting its continuation we are also strongly influenced by our evidence that most Slovak au pairs themselves informed us that, even under present exploitative conditions, they would still have opted to come to London. Given the universalization of English as a global language, many young people wish to spend time in London to improve their English. Furthermore, many feel that it is better initially to stay with a family, at least while they are getting to know this huge and bewildering metropolitan city. Whatever the problems we have documented for au pairs within families, the alternative is often living in a dilapidated bedsit, which is all they might otherwise be able to afford. Here they are potentially much more exposed to other forms of exploitation and abuse. It seems sensible to judge the au pair institution only in the light of the likely alternatives. We also recognize that au pairing is considerably more benign that other forms of paid domestic work. For example, Danny is currently working with Filipino domestics, where even to find a period to talk with them is difficult given the paucity of the free time they are allocated by the families that employ them. So our attitude to the au pair institution is not generalized to other forms of domestic labour. Finally, in acknowledgement of our documentation of the negative results of the current situation, our judgement is that the au pair institution should adopt changes. We certainly would not wish to support an unreformed institution that creates inequality and exploitation.

Recommendations

The current legislation assumes a balance between inclusion of the au pair within a family and relative autonomy. This has to remain central to the definition of the institution. It is the ideal that in some way the au pair joins a family to ensure that they are not subject to the normal forms of taxation and control of labour. It may seem odd to support this necessarily ambiguous relationship when we have clearly shown how it is subject to abuse. But, without this informality and subsequent lack of taxation, it is likely that both sides would increasingly opt instead for illegal arrangements, to the detriment of employees. Although both sides take advantage of this provision, at present au pairs and families are equally unaware even of those regulations that already exist. We believe that, if there were changes in the legislation, and if far more was done to make sure that both sides were made aware of the legal framework, and finally if there were clear avenues for redress when problems arose, then the situation could be considerably improved. We end this volume with some brief recommendations with respect to each of these three concerns.

1 *Changes in legislation*
The primary problem currently is that the specified maximum of twenty-five hours a week that au pairs are supposed to work is not respected. This should be clarified by making sure that the au pair has the right (but not the duty) not to be present in the home when the designated hours of work have been completed. An alternative

childcarer must be present, so that au pairs are not childminding by default. It should also be stated that there is a maximum of two sessions of babysitting in any given week. We feel that the ambiguity represented by the concept of 'au pair plus' should be eliminated. Au pairs employed beyond the standard twenty-five hours plus two sessions of babysitting should be paid (and taxed) according to at least the minimum wage. We note that the specification of women as au pairs has been abolished. But much more could be done to encourage gender equality in the recruitment of au pairs.

There should be more specificity given to the concept of light cleaning. The listing provided by the British Au Pair Agencies Association (BAPAA) (see below) seems satisfactory, but it is virtually unknown to either au pairs or families, even those who use formal agencies. There should surely be a clear paid holiday entitlement of ten days within each six-month period of employment, though the precise time this is taken will probably need to be left to negotiation. Another change that we feel would make a major difference to this relationship is that host families should be expected to pay half the cost of a return ticket from the au pair's home. This would ensure that both sides have an initial commitment to the relationship, while at present the families have nothing at stake. But the money should be handed over only when au pairs have completed their agreed period of placement (or a lower amount, proportional to the time completed) to avoid the situation of their simply using the period to take advantage of a subsidized trip to London. It seems to us that au pairs have a right to accommodation and food throughout the period of their stay, irrespective of the presence or absence of children or when the family leaves for holidays. But on the other hand we can see that families have a right to ban foods or other substances, such as cigarettes or alcohol, that are incompatible with their cultural preferences. They can also expect to have genuine security measures respected, including forbidding the presence of other people in their homes. We should expect, however, that this would be declared prior to the au pair's arrival.

We have also been shocked by the lack of responsibility taken by some au pair agencies. All agencies should be registered and regulated, as they are often the only institutions mediating in the relationships between au pairs and host families. We think that the ideals of BAPAA and the International Au Pair Association (IAPA) are good and might become the inspiration for further registration. However, membership in BAPAA or IAPA is not sufficient to ensure the fair treatment of au pairs and to secure appropriate intervention in the conditions of their employment by an agency: some of the problematic cases we mentioned above concerned au pairs who actually used agencies registered with BAPAA or IAPA!

We think that phone interviews of the host family are not sufficient and that the agency should both interview the host family in person and see for themselves the home and the room they are intending to use before agreeing to find them an au pair. The agencies should also contact both au pairs and host families on a regular basis, checking whether they are keeping to the agreed contract. Further, they should do much more to mediate in conflicts or misunderstandings between the au pair and the host family and should be held responsible for any failures to disseminate the information referred to in the next section.

We have no expertise in law, but we see no reason why such additional clarification could not quite easily be incorporated into the basic legal framework within which the system operates.

2 Dissemination of information

Merely to amend the legislation is clearly insufficient to reform the present institution, since at present most au pairs and their host families are unaware of the legislation that already exists. So equally important are changes with regard to the dissemination of information. The EU (and the non-EU states allowing au pair exchange) should ensure that information packs are available to all au pairs and families in the own languages. These should include the following:

a) basic information about rights and duties, including human rights issues such as the right to privacy (e.g. that families cannot confiscate passports, etc.) and protection from sexual harassment;
b) details of the specific rights of au pairs as specified in the last section, as well as those in current regulations, such as the right to a separate bedroom (with a lock, especially when the room is still used for family storage), the requirement for two weeks' notice, etc.;
c) basic information on those facilities discussed below, such as an ombudsman for au pairs seeking adjudication or redress.

We suggest that this information should also be available on well-publicized websites and so accessible to those who are not presenting themselves at immigration as au pairs and who do not come through agencies. As part of this general dissemination the EU should require that each country has its own office with information for prospective, current and ex-au pairs that deals with issues particular to the institution. This should hold the information referred to above. It should also provide general information on facilities such as medical care. Such offices should be places where au pairs can disseminate information on their return for future au pairs and should offer retrospective advice or redress for returning au pairs. A further useful addition would be information intended to prevent cultural misunderstanding, such as normative expectations with regard to meals and similar matters. For example, we have published in a Slovak British magazine and its website, often used by Slovak au pairs, some notes about au pairs' rights and duties and basic information on what they might expect when staying with Orthodox Jewish families.

3 Routes to complaint, adjudication and redress
Again and again a problem arose in that au pairs who found themselves in difficulties simply had no idea what to do. There seemed nowhere to go, either to make a complaint or to find out what was a reasonable expectation against which they could judge the way they were being treated. So, as well as changes in the law and the dissemination of information, we suggest a third intervention, which is equally essential. This is the creation of the institution of ombudsman at both the EU and national level. This should be a well-publicized office where au pairs or families can take their grievances in the hope of finding adjudication and redress. Similarly the EU should ensure at a national level that there are 'safe houses' where people suffering abuse can find protection. Money should be available for those suffering from distress to enable them to return home. This can be done through extending services which are currently provided partly by religious or national institutions such as the Czechoslovak Roman Catholic hostel Velehrad.

Finally

One might have hoped that the au pair institution would already be secure, simply because the best way of ensuring that one's children are treated well by the person given responsibility for looking after them is when that person is also treated with respect. This is the central contradiction that exists in any ill-treatment of au pairs. Our evidence does not suggest that this can be relied upon, so regulations are essential to protect families as well as au pairs. Regulation protects families from themselves: it gives them boundaries, clarity and the acknowledgement of equal and mutual rights. We believe most families would prefer to use the au pair relationship as an opportunity to show that they can be generous, kind and sensitive rather than cold, exploitative and insensitive.

Unfortunately, even if this is true of most families, it can never be presumed of all. The primary concern is therefore not with the protection of families but with the welfare of the au pair. We have a clear responsibility to ensure that, before young vulnerable persons, often leaving their own family homes for the first time, are guided into the homes of strangers in a strange land, they are free from any danger that they will be betrayed by the very regulations that are supposed to protect them.

Snippet

The following is a list of duties accepted as light housework by the British Au Pair Agencies Association (www.bapaa.org.uk/displaypage.asp?page=41):

* Washing dishes, including loading and unloading dishwasher
  Preparing simple meals for children
  Keeping kitchen tidy and clean, including sweeping and mopping floors
  Loading and unloading laundry into washing machine
  Ironing for children
  Putting washed clothes away
  Vacuuming
  Dusting
  Making and changing children's beds
  Cleaning children's bathroom
  Everything to do with keeping their own room/bathroom clean and tidy
  Light shopping (not the household shopping)
  Walking and feeding pets
  Emptying bins

The following is a list of duties considered unsuitable for an au pair:

* Gardening
  Window cleaning
  Spring cleaning
  Cleaning the oven, other than simple wiping out
  Washing carpets

Washing the car
Weekly shopping
Pet training
Clearing up after untrained pets
Making parents' bed*
Ironing for parents*
Cleaning parents' en-suite bathroom*
Polishing silver and brassware*
Cooking the family meal, unless the au pair enjoys cooking and has chosen to do this for the family

*These duties can be included where there is less childcare and the children are out of the house for most of the day, if this is agreed in advance.

APPENDIX: ACADEMIC STUDIES OF DOMESTIC LABOUR

There are now quite a few books and papers on the topic of paid domestic labour, but more of these are devoted to hired cleaners, nannies and care for the elderly than to au pairs. Given the importance of au pairing, especially in the UK, the literature is relatively sparse; furthermore, because it appears largely as a subset of the wider literature, its aims and methods are sometimes quite different from our own. The primary concern tends to be debates about migration and forms of exploitation, especially with reference to gender, ethnicity and the international division of labour.

Some of the prior academic research is scholarship of the highest order that provides an essential macro-view of the larger patterns as well as insightful qualitative engagement. We have opted, however, to keep our main text shorn of direct engagement with this literature in order to concentrate on conveying clearly, to the widest possible audience, the insights we believe emerge from our study. But we obviously owe a huge debt to the considerable number of debates and studies that precede our own. At this point, therefore, we wish to make this debt clear and acknowledge how much is gained by seeing our particular study within the wider context of comparative studies.

A large body of feminist research has confirmed that, following economic growth in countries such as the UK, the USA or Hong Kong, the increase in the number of middle-class women working full-time, outside the home, has not been followed by any commensurate change in the labour division within households or matched by state support for accessible pre-school childcare (Anderson 1999, 2000, 2001; Ehrenreich and Hochschild 2003; Gregson and Lowe 1994; Kofman et al. 2000). The ideology that mother or mother-like care taking place in the child's home is best has retained its dominance (Gregson and Lowe 1994; Hondagneu-Sotelo 2001). Simultaneously, routine domestic tasks such as cleaning and ironing have become incompatible with concepts of 'leisure' and 'quality time' and middle-class consumption patterns emerging through the 1980s (Gregson and Lowe 1994). Consequently, the demand for private domestic services has increased in the UK, and throughout the world, largely supplied by migrant women working as nannies, cleaners and housekeepers (Anthias and Lazaridis 2000; Chaney and Castro 1989; Chin 1998; Colen 1995; Constable 1997; Henshall Momsen 1999; Hondagneu-Sotelo 2001; Parreñas 2001; Rollins 1985; Romero 1992; Salzinger 1991). The growing international trade in childcare, in particular, has been variously analysed in terms of global care chains and the global trade in emotional labour – for example, where a Filipino mother comes to work for a European family and sends money back to the Philippines to employ a fellow Filipino to look after her own children. However, the idea that this means that care is now something that can be transnationally traded, much as any other commodity, has been subject to some criticisms (e.g. Hochschild 2000; Isaksen, Devi and Hochschild 2008; McKay 2007; Yeates 2004).

A popular source of childcare and domestic labour in the UK is constituted by au pairs (Anderson 2001, 2007; Cox 1999, 2000, 2006). Despite this being both a frequent route of migration for (not only Eastern European) women and a popular source of childcare, researchers have not paid as much attention to au pairs as to other forms of domestic labour. The localization of au pairs' work in private homes and their immigration status defining them as non-workers does not make them an obvious object of research on labour migration. Furthermore, as mostly white and often middle class, they neither conform to the characterization of migrants as 'poor' or 'uneducated' (Anderson 2007: 250; King 2002) nor belong to any transnational elites. Only in the last decade have researchers focused on au pairs as labour migrants and part of the domestic work industry (Anderson 2007; Anderson et al. 2006; Bahna 2005, 2006; Búriková 2006a, 2006b; Cox 1999, 2006, 2007; Cox and Narula 2004; Hess 2000, 2000–1, 2003; Hess and Puckhaber 2004; Macdonald 1998; Mellini, Yodanis and Godenzi 2007; Williams and Baláž 2004; Yodanis and Lauer 2005). Studies by Bahna, Búriková, Hess, and Williams and Baláž focus on Slovak au pairs in particular.

Au pairs as migrants

Before Slovakia entered the EU, au pairing was one of few possibilities open to young Slovaks hoping to gain British visas for a longer stay in the UK. Researchers recognized that this was already the main destination for Slovak au pairs because of its high cultural capital and the means for gaining knowledge of the English language (Bahna 2005: 457–8; Williams and Baláž 2004). Officially, 4,460 Slovak citizens entered the UK as au pairs in 1996 (out of a total number of 13,400 au pair visas issued in the UK for citizens outside the European Economic Area); figures were 4,850 out of 15,300 in 1997, 2,380 out of 12,900 in 2000, 1,800 out of of 12,000 in 2001, and 3,140 out of 12,800 in 2002 (Bahna 2005: 460). However, the real numbers were higher, as many young Slovaks worked in the UK illegally, using student or tourist visas. The au pair scheme was often the initial stage for a longer stay in the country.

Among the earlier EU member states, only Sweden, Ireland and the UK granted A8 (the accession eight) nationals free access to the labour market immediately upon enlargement on 1 May 2004. This meant A8 workers could migrate and take up employment in the UK without restriction (as long as they registered in the 'Worker Registration Scheme'). As, since EU enlargement, Slovak citizens can freely enter the UK and, unlike other employees, au pairs do not have to register with the Home Office, there are no statistics enabling a direct comparison. Miloslav Bahna's (2005) analysis of publicly available data from webpages of on-line au pair agencies indicates that, in relative numbers, Slovaks remain the most numerous group, from any country, of applicants for au pair placement in the UK.

Other changes have followed from revisions made in November 2008 to the UK immigration process. One of the major changes is the introduction of a points-based application system (PBS) for those who wish to come to work to the UK and the redefinition of existing work categories. As a result, the au pair scheme has been closed and au pairs (together with other temporary workers, students on gap years and voluntary workers) fall under the more general Youth Mobility Scheme (YMS) of Tier 5 of the PBS. Tier 5 is designed to allow temporary workers and eighteen- to thirty-year-olds in the YMS to come to the UK to undertake short-term temporary work to satisfy essentially non-financial objectives. Under the new system, foreign citizens applying to live or work in the UK will have to score a certain number of points in a range of categories in order to secure their visa or permit. The number of points and the areas to which they relate will vary depending on the type of visa that is being applied for (e.g. 40 points for Tier 5). Workers in Tier 5 cannot switch to a different immigration category. Applicants have to provide the evidence that they have sufficient funds (currently £1,600), be a national of a country participating in the scheme, be sponsored by their national government, not have any dependant children and not have spent any previous time in the United Kingdom as a working holidaymaker or on the YMS. Whereas, previously, any additional work taken on by au pairs (unless EU nationals) was forbidden, under the YMS visa conditions young people are free to work while in the UK (but should be not self-employed).

The PBS does not in fact apply to Slovaks or to other EEA and Swiss nationals, who are free to stay and take work in the UK without needing to apply for permission. The countries which have so far made arrangements with the UK to be sponsors for the YMS are Australia, Canada, Japan and New Zealand. British overseas citizens, British overseas territories citizens or British nationals overseas can also apply. Non-EU countries which had previously had arrangements with the UK government under the old au pair scheme (i.e. Andorra, Bosnia-Herzegovina, Croatia, the Faroe Islands, Greenland, Macedonia, Monaco, San Marino and Turkey, have either been refused membership or have not yet reapplied under the new system.

Our fieldwork started at the beginning of October 2004 – five months after EU enlargement – when our data revealed that the numbers of Slovak au pairs remained high. This is notwithstanding that these au pairs could now opt instead for much higher remuneration based on the minimum wage and more control over both their working and their living conditions. There are several reasons for this continuing interest. When considering a longer stay abroad, au pairing still appeared to them as one of the least risky strategies – a simple, safe and inexpensive route (Anderson et al. 2006: 39). Given the legal definition reproduced by the agencies, au pairs expect some kind of family-like integration, or at least appreciation for work which was similar to what they were used to carrying out within their parental households (Hess and Puckhaber 2004). Au pairs in our research contrasted this prospect with the insecurity of looking for jobs in a totally new and strange place without host family support. They did not need any particular qualification to become an au pair, and they could utilize the existing framework of recruiting agencies or personal networking, consisting mostly of friends already staying as au pairs in the UK. Without the costs of accommodation it required comparatively little initial capital. It also appeared to provide genuine earning opportunities, with two-thirds of our sample taking on additional employment such as cleaning and babysitting for other families.

The changes consequent upon EU enlargement were not transforming an entirely static institution. As researchers focusing on au pair migration have revealed, since the early 1990s the dynamics of exchange had already changed significantly, with a new generation of au pairs coming from the post-socialist countries of Central and Eastern Europe (Cox 1999; Hess 2000–1, 2003; Williams and Baláž 2004). While Western European au pairs are seen as coming for cultural tourism and leisure, researchers viewed this new wave of recruits largely as an economic strategy by which Eastern European women could cope with the difficulties of post-socialist transformation. In other words, women become au pairs largely because of enhanced opportunities for income generation compared with work or unemployment in Slovakia. For example, Sabine Hess claims that 'The au pair migration is therefore to be seen as an individual and family based qualification strategy to enhance one's own chances after the return. In regard of the other possibilities at hand it is a highly functional practice of young women to cope with the social risks of the transformations. Temporary migration is in this sense a transformation strategy' (Hess 2003: 3). Even the aspect of au pairing as cultural exchange is often seen in instrumental terms, with learning English being seen as part of a strategy for economic advance in the long term (Cox 2006; Hess 2000–1, 2003; Williams and Baláž 2004).

These interpretations rightly bring out the structural conditions of paid domestic work based on regional economic inequality. In the words of Hondagneu-Sotelo:

> the inequality of nations is a key factor in the globalization of contemporary au pair domestic work. This inequality has three results. First, around the globe, paid domestic work is increasingly performed by women who leave their own nations, their communities and often their families of origin to do it. Second, the occupation draws not only women from the poor socioeconomic classes but also women of relatively high status in their own countries . . . Third, the development of service-based economies in postindustrial nations favors the international migration of women laborers. Unlike in earlier industrial eras, today the demand for gendered labor favours migrant women's services. (Hondagneu-Sotelo 2001: 19)

About au pairs in particular, Hess and Puckhaber (2004) argue that socio-economic differences between Western post-industrial societies and Eastern and Southern parts of the world changed also the character of the au pair institution, making au pairs' work and living conditions much more similar to those of other migrant domestic workers. Based on a study of on-line au pair agencies, Miloslav Bahna (2006) found out that demand for this form of domestic work expands with a country's GDP. These studies are especially valuable in recognizing that the au pair is also to be understood as a particular and important variant within studies of inequality and migration.

However, the material we have presented in this book (especially in chapters 1 and 7) suggests that we should adopt an even more radical approach, one that allows the example of au pairs to challenge what we conventionally understand as the reasons for migration. In our study the boundaries between cultural exchange, the trajectory of personal relationships and issues of labour are quite permeable. Others, such as Anderson (2000: 30), also recognize that domestic workers have personal reasons for migration. It is possible to find Slovaks that would fit into an alternative model of au pairing as a kind of gap year in between high school and university analogous to that taken by many middle-class students in Western Europe (Clarke 2005; King and Ruiz-Gelices 2003). Some may be using this more as time out while they hope to come to a more concrete decision about the direction of their future lives. Others may indeed fit comfortably within the model of economic migration. It is also evident that, just as Clarke notes of the British taking holiday work, many au pairs fail to fall within either high-skilled or low-skilled categories of economic migrants. More often they are 'people in the middle, often motivated to cross borders by non-economic concerns' (Clarke 2005: 308). A structural condition of economic inequality between regions doesn't necessarily mean that au pair migration is only economically motivated.

This volume has emphasized the degree to which many females regard au pairing as a specific life-cycle experience. A similar argument was made by Williams and Baláž (2004: 1818; for an account on migration as *rite de passage*, see, for example, Osella and Osella 2000). Numerous interviewees view this as an appropriate age to 'go out' (the word 'out' was also used during socialism to mean abroad, especially to hardly accessible Western European countries). The notion of a more 'exciting life', 'experience' or 'adventure' repeatedly appeared in interviews with female au pairs (see also Jenčová 2007). Our informants commonly considered au pairing as a lesson in growing up and self-development, analogous to the military service of Slovak men.

To conclude, King remarks that intimate personal relationships have been largely overlooked by migration studies, being seen as individual or personal, and therefore insignificant on a societal level (King 2002: 99). We are not trying to offset the personal against larger macro-economic causes. Rather, as our first chapter demonstrates, such economic concerns are most commonly subsumed within such personal relationships with parents, partners and friends involved in an au pair's decision to leave or stay. Furthermore, it is much more convenient to state that one came in order to earn money or learn the language than that one left in order to escape a tense personal relationship, boring work or a restricted lifestyle. It is not surprising, therefore, that our ethnography produces quite different answers than those emerging from interviews and other research techniques. In our study we often find economic and instrumental causes of migration are most important because of the way in which they provide leigitimation or cover for more complex and less legitimate motivation.

Au pairs as paid domestic workers

Dominant research questions in the literature on paid domestic work are more generally directed at which particular groups perform this kind of poorly regarded work, and why, focusing upon how the relationships between employers and employees are structured. Numerous researchers have emphasized the intersection of gender, class, immigration status and ethnicity as central to the asymmetric power relations within households, demonstrating the role of these social parameters in the exploitation of cheap labour. Generally, lower-class (frequently migrant) women of colour are employed as waged domestic workers, since they are both easily exploitable and fit well with employers' ideas about who should undertake this kind of low-status work (e.g. Anderson 2000; Cock 1980; Ehrenreich and Hochschild 2003; Henshall Momsen 1999; Parreñas 2001; Rollins 1985; Romero 1992). These works have been expanded by researchers identifying other factors structuring the relationship between employers and employees, such as the live-in or live-out status of domestic workers (Anderson 2000).

We hoped that an examination of au pair employment would shed even more light on these questions, since, unlike many other domestic workers, au pairs are generally white (at least that is how they are coded; see Cox 2006, 2007), often middle class and, according to legal definitions, supposed to be treated as equal. We have found Slovak au pairs to occupy a possible point of transition in this regard.

Since they come from an economically less-developed country, they appear as relatively unequal to their hosts, compared with the previous generation of au pairs from Western European countries.

Pseudo-family relationships

Paid domestic work has often been characterized in the literature as different from other kinds of work – as a 'labour of care' rather than as employment, based on the concept of pseudo-familial or false kin relationships. These are supposed to include interaction and treatment (e.g. reciprocity, care, intimacy and mutual help) that are characteristic more of kin relationships than of those between employer and employee (Anderson 2000; Gregson and Lowe 1994). Within the pseudo-family, au pairs are often treated as children. Analysing promotional literature of the au pair agencies, Hess and Puckhaber (2004) notice that they use the image of au pairs as 'bigger sisters'; Cox and Narula (2004) argue that host families very often want their au pairs to obey similar household rules to those to which the children are exposed. Defining the au pair as an institution reinforces this idiom of pseudo-family relations as a means to create a sufficient and affordable market for childcare, especially in European countries, where the norm is a nuclear rather than an extended family and a stronger tradition of fictive kin (Yodanis and Lauer 2005).

It has been recognized that employers often encourage the development of such pseudo-family relations in order to extract more labour from their domestic workers (Anderson 2000; Constable 1997; Cox and Narula 2004; Rollins 1985). Anderson notes how employers take advantage of slippage between the public and private domains, treating workers on some occasions as part of the family governed by customary law and on other occasions as workers governed by civic relations (Anderson 2000: 5). Rollins, in particular, speaks of 'maternalism' – the employers' use of mother-like forms of care and control (e.g. giving gifts, trying to know details of the employee's private life, loaning money or helping to explain legislation) in order to extract from both physical labour and deference (Rollins 1985: 155–203). Anderson argues that becoming 'part of the family' is not only a means of maximizing labour extracted from the worker. It is an attempt to manage contradictions. For the employer it helps manage the contradictions of intimacy and status that attach to the domestic worker, who is at once privy to many of the intimate details of family life yet also their status giver, their myth maker (Anderson

2000: 124). Furthermore, according to Anderson, the pseudo-family relationship helps both employers and domestic workers to negotiate contradictions inherent in the commodification of domestic work and care. For a thoughtful and more theoretical consideration of this ambiguous relationship between money and care, see Zelizer's recent discussion in *The Purchase of Intimacy* (2005). Also Gregson and Lowe argue that 'false kinship relations' emerge because nannies inevitably get emotionally attached to children and mothers see their nannies as mother-substitutes and feel indebted to them (Gregson and Lowe 1994: 201–6).

There are the exceptions to this preference for pseudo-family relationships from the employers' side. As both Hondagneu-Sotelo (2001) and Cox and Narula (2004) found, employers often try to create distance from, rather than intimacy with, their domestic workers. For au pairs, in particular, Cox and Narula (2004) claim that employers could take either a strict 'parenting' approach or more of a negotiated 'personalizing' approach. Host families did not treat their au pairs as children in order to integrate them into the family, but to create distance. Exploring what it means to delegate a mother's work to nannies and au pairs, Macdonald shows that both mothers and paid childcare providers share dominant beliefs in intensive mothering. This ideology assumes that a child needs one primary caregiver – a mother – who should create a psychological bond with her child through a series of practices such as feeding, holding, disciplining and age appropriate stimulation and interaction: 'Because of these tensions, the mothers I interviewed wanted a "shadow mother": an extension of themselves who would stay home as if she were the mother, but who would vanish upon the *real* mother's return, leaving no trace of her presence in the lives of children they shared' (Macdonald 1998: 34). Macdonald argues that this was a problem especially for au pairs, who, as young and far from home, 'wanted to be considered part of the family, but instead found that at the end of the workday they were expected to perform the extra work of vanishing to help create "family time"' (ibid.: 36).

From another perspective, Bakan and Stasiulis (1997: 11) claim that many domestic workers reject the pseudo-family relationship with their employers because it masks their actual subordination. On the other hand, Hondagneu-Sotelo (2001) argues that domestic workers prefer personalized (but not maternalistic) relationships with their employers, as, unlike exploitative, dehumanizing or purely market-like relationships, they would acknowledge their humanity and dignity. Our evidence in chapter 2 confirms both this ambivalence and the contradictions inherent in the idiom, as well as the ways in which it can of itself contribute to exploitation. Our study of material culture also reveals the subtle ways in which families and au pairs try to achieve distance from each other (see also Búriková 2006a).

Ethnicity

Numerous studies confirm that ethnicity and ethnic stereotypes in particular figure as an important factor in shaping employment relationships in paid domestic work. Such work tends to be carried out by women of other ethnic groups, often seen as inferior (e.g. Cock 1980). In her book *Doing the Dirty Work?*, Anderson found that, though domestic workers do similar tasks as wives and mothers, they are differently constructed. Their role is to reproduce the status of their female employer, who can therefore be seen as middle class, a non-labourer, white and clean, in contrast to her domestic, who is doomed to be a worker, coloured, dirty and degraded (Anderson 2000: 15–21). Additionally, the fact that it is not the worker's labour power but her personhood that is commodified results in the paid domestic worker being dishonoured and exploited (ibid.: 113–14). Anderson believes that this is important for understanding why domestic work is often undertaken by racialized groups. Employers, being afraid of pollution, transfer this onto another group of women: 'the relationship between hatred of women (misogyny), hatred of body (somatophobia) and hatred of racialised groups (racism) is played out in the use of racialised female labour to do the work of servicing the body, and in the treatment of domestic workers by their employers' (ibid.: 142).

Rollins (1985) argues that a labour market structured around race, class and gender limits employment opportunities for women of colour, who most often end up as domestic workers. Examining Chicanas working as domestic helpers in the United States, Romero suggests that it is racism that underpins relations of domestic labour employment (Romero 1992). Anderson sums up these arguments: 'Racist stereotypes intersect with issues of citizenship, and result in a racist hierarchy which uses skin colour, religion and nationality to construct some women as being more suitable for domestic work than others' (Anderson 2000: 2). However, several different social differentiations may be employed. For example, in the case they examined, Gregson and Lowe (1994) found that, typically in the UK outside London, it was lower-class English women rather than foreigners who worked as cleaners and nannies. Since in terms of ethnic origin au pairs are mostly white Europeans, Williams and Baláž (2004) argue that they are not the object of such systemic racialized abuse as noted for other forms of domestic work.

Other writings (Anderson 2007; Pratt 1997) reveal how both employers and agencies stereotype particular ethnic groups as appropriate to work as au pairs, nannies or cleaners. This stereotyping often leads to exploitation. For example, examining the agents' representations of European and Filipino nannies, Pratt (1997) revealed that, while European nannies are constructed as educated tourists, Filipino nannies appear as uncivilized and childlike, but as loving, hard-working and gentle servants. Consequently, starting salaries of Filipino nannies are much lower than those of British nannies doing the very same work. Pratt's nuanced analysis shows how racial stereotyping works in relation to anxieties about mothering but also the other way around. Pratt found out that agents generally identified abusive employers as ethnic minorities – i.e. not 'normal' Canadian (ibid.: 167). Also Hondagneu-Sotelo notes that Latina domestic workers consider employers of particular ethnicity (e.g. Iranians or Israeli Jews) as bad employers and are highly selective when identifying categories of abusive employers, largely following established stereotypes (2001: 58–9, 100–1). A similar argument about ethnic stereotyping was central to chapter 4 in this volume.

Immigration status

Domestic work globally tends to be undertaken by migrants. Anderson argues that low wages are not the only reason for the proliferation of migrants in this sector. She believes that migrants are attractive because of their flexibility: they do not leave their employers' household to look after their own families (as these are far away), and they do not have many relationships which would interfere with their role as domestic workers and therefore it is easier to see them in terms of pseudo-family relationship (Anderson 2000: 151). As non-citizens, paid domestic workers are in a particular relation to the state. Their position is dependent on the specific regulatory framework for entering the country (Williams and Baláž 2004: 1817). National regulatory frameworks for au pairs use as their base the *European Agreement on Au Pair Placement* (Council of Europe 1969). Examining au pair policies in the USA, Australia and the UK, Yodanis and Lauer (2005) argue that, even in liberal states not providing childcare, social policy sets rules and indeed creates markets in childcare. Au pairs do not need workers' visas or permits (i.e. they can enter the country more easily than other labour migrants), but their nationality, age, gender, class and educational background, as well as their length of stay, are restricted and they do not earn the minimum wage.

Generally, the presence of migrant domestic workers is tolerated by the state as long as they are needed by their employers. The fact that employers are predominantly citizens formalizes an unequal distribution of power: examining the status of migrant domestic workers in the 1990s in five European cities – Athens, Barcelona, Bologna, Berlin and Paris – Anderson (2000: 177) argues that whether they live in the employer household or not is a key variable in determining their working conditions. Furthermore, she revealed that immigration status and live-in or live-out work are interdependent, as many domestic workers live in because they remain undocumented (ibid.: 84–5).

Our work confirms these findings. We found out that before Slovakia's entry into the EU employers sometimes tended to use the threat of visa withdrawal to extract more labour or deference from their Slovak au pairs: three individuals reported that their host families explicitly claimed that they had to accept working or living conditions they did not like, because otherwise they would have to leave the country. Zuzana also met au pairs and former au pairs (who were not our interviewees) whose host families expected them (and told them) to accept a higher workload or not to attend language school because of their immigration status or Eastern European origin (implying that all Eastern European au pairs were economic migrants).

A consequence of EU enlargement is that Slovak au pairs neither have to register with the Home Office nor require a visa. Thus the research participants include people who would not have met the earlier definition of an au pair. Four were above the age limit and four others had exceeded the two-year limit of stay. Au pairs can now shift to other occupations more easily, as noted by some host families, who prefer au pairs with poor English as security that they are less likely to migrate to other jobs (see also Anderson et al. 2006: 85). The ending of visas has shifted power relations more generally, making it easier for au pairs to negotiate the arrangements or leave the family when they want to. Au pairs themselves can also exploit families, using them as a comfortable conduit to other employment and leaving them without notice when they find a more suitable occupation. Thus EU enlargement has in a sense democratized the au pair institution and shifted the power distribution somewhat, but has also created new possibilities for exploitation in both directions.

Power and exploitation

In chapter 3 we noted that in eighty-two out of eighty-six cases families expected their au pairs to work beyond the hours specified by law, or in other respects did not obey the legal rules. But, if we consider major issues such as the withdrawal of passports, starvation, limitation of free movement (being locked in the house), violence or serious sexual abuse, then these turned out to be, if anything, rather less prevalent than anticipated, and certainly not on a par with the situation that is described in the literature on other forms of paid domestic work (e.g. Anderson 2000; Constable 1997; Chaney and Castro 1989; Chin 1998) or starting to emerge in Danny's current fieldwork on Filipino domestic workers. This confirms Williams and Baláž's (2004) argument that au pairs, as mostly white, European and working within a specific legal framework, are distinct from other migrant domestic workers and their conditions are comparatively benign in relation to those of domestic work in general.

On the other hand our evidence supports that of Mellini, Yodanis and Godenzi (2007) in emphasizing less formal and institutional and more personal and intimate issues of au pair treatment, such as reciprocity in doing favours, sharing information and engaging in family activities. We hope these subtle asymmetries of power are most clearly illustrated through our emphasis on material culture analysis. As has been demonstrated by previous research (Bourdieu 1977, 1999; Buchli 2002; Keane 1997; Kuechler 2002; Miller 1998, 2001; Tilley 1999; Tilley et al. 2006), close attention to the material world gives us access to actual practices that complement research focused more on language and on interviews. Possessions have increasingly been recognized as an important source of information in migration studies (see Basu and Coleman 2008; Burrell 2008; Mehta and Belk 1991; Parkin 1999; and several of the portraits in Miller 2008). In chapter 2 we showed how the physical nature of the home sets a precondition for au pair placement. For example, the au pair's room eloquently expresses the basic ambiguity of apparent rather than actual autonomy. Furthermore, an au pair's work itself is intrinsically related to the materiality of the home, which determines much of the daily routine. The subsequent response of au pairs to their conditions is revealed in their difficult relationship with food as well as as with the furnishing provided and the possessions that they initially bring with them (see also Búriková 2006a).

Though researchers focusing on paid domestic labour have acknowledged the physicality of the home as the context for negotiating relationships (e.g. Henshall Momsen 1999: 11–12; Hondagneu-Sotelo 2001; Rollins 1985; Yeoh and Huang 1999), some attention has been paid to the home itself – the spatial arrangements and material culture more generally – as a symptom or sign of domination, oppression, resistance and subversion, or exclusion and inclusion (Constable 1997; Chin 1998; Henshall Momsen 1999; Hondagneu-Sotelo 2001; Rollins 1985). Researchers have recognized that the prospect of having one's own protected space within a private home may facilitate the decision to work abroad (Hess 2000–1; Pappas-DeLuca 1999), but also that this may not, in practice, provide for either privacy or independence or protection from control over both working and living conditions (Chin 1998; Constable 1997). In some cases spatial distance within a large home may facilitate emotional distance (Hondagneu-Sotelo 2001: 188–9). But spatial order, such as the placement of the TV, can also be used to exclude maids from family social life (Chin 1998).The condition of living in is recognized as having the potential to facilitate exploitation and control, where working hours are not respected and domestic workers are on call twenty-four hours a day (Hondagneu-Sotelo 2001). Enforced isolation is another means of controlling live-in domestic workers (Constable 1997; Hondagneu-Sotelo 2001: 146–7).

In addition, Anderson (2000: 140), Hondagneu-Sotelo (2001: 33–5), Cox and Narula (2004: 341–2) and Hess and Puckhaber (2004: 74–5) have considered the significance of food – the ways it is distributed, restricted or wasted in employers' households – for live-in domestic workers. In some cases workers are often not given satisfactory amounts of food or food of decent quality, or they experience food as excluding or including them in the lives of their employers. Food is central even to determining the extent to which they are recognized as human beings.

The best accounts of the role of materiality are offered by researchers focusing on household rules and relations (Constable 1997, 2003; Cox and Narula 2004). In particular, Nicole Constable (1997: 83–111, 2003) examines the ways employers discipline Filipino maids in Hong Kong through control over their bodies and the use of space – even to the extent of locking them in their rooms during their absence (as portrayed in the Filipino film *Anak*). Domestic workers' physical appearance and personal hygiene may also be controlled, as they may be ordered to shorten their hair, not to use nail polish, wear clothes of particular kind, or take a shower or bath at prescribed times. The work of Cox and Narula focuses on au pairs in particular. They examine the way employers may restrict au pairs' access to certain spaces within the home or prevent them from having visitors. They stress that 'rules that control space and behaviour within the home are an important way in which power relations are expressed and reinforced' (Cox and Narula 2004: 343). Finally, material representations of au pairs have consequences for their working and living conditions. In her most recent work, Cox (2007) illustrates how the media in Britain depict au pairs as sexually available or promiscuous, while agencies portray them as desexualized happy childcarers. Cox argues that both representations deny the fact that au pairs are actually workers doing physically demanding labour.

Our research extends these studies, revealing how the ambivalences of the pseudo-family relationship unfold through the medium of material culture – the ways families furnish and au pairs decorate or refuse to decorate their rooms, as well as how both organize food consumption and usage of space. This is not an artificial focus that comes just from our choice of analytical approach. It was very clear during the ethnography that the au pairs themselves were particularly sensitive to asymmetries of power that emerge in the 'little things'. These are often young people lacking in confidence, leaving their parental home for the first time, and finding themselves strangers without the means to engage properly with their host family. This is why so much of our account is about such things as whether they are served a piece of cake, whether someone bothers to say good morning, notices that a surface has been cleaned, or thinks to ask them if they also need to go out.

We examine this within the larger context of asymmetries of age, authority, language, property, income and control, as well as the institutional conditions that mean host families do not pay transportation fares and have less at stake in the selection of any particular au pair who has no obvious point of redress if poorly treated. Under such conditions, we can see how people who might never have wanted to exploit others are tempted by the pressures of their own work and the stress of parenting. The institution makes it simply too easy to want a little more from this 'help' that one is supposed to be taking. We certainly have no desire to condone or limit our exposure of the exploitation of au pairs. But under the circumstance we also can't pretend to be surprised by it.

To conclude, the academic literature properly identifies a wide range of structural and institutional factors that underlie domestic labour, as well as the central role of economic inequality. We hope that our ethnography adds to this the importance of appreciating the au pairs' own personal relationships, the subtleties of material culture and the wider context of this period out of time. We also hope we have demonstrated the considerable number of institutional contradictions, cultural ambiguities and individual differences that make these relationships so complex even within a single case study and that, in combination with the available literature, our work will help ground such academic issues within the empathetic perspective on au pairs' own experience that we have tried to convey in this volume.

REFERENCES

Anderson, B. (1999) Overseas domestic workers in the European Union, in J. Henshall Momsen (ed.), *Gender, Migration and Domestic Service*. London and New York: Routledge, pp. 117–33.

Anderson, B. (2000) *Doing the Dirty Work? The Global Politics of Domestic Labour*. London: Zed Books.

Anderson, B. (2001) Reproductive labour and migration. Paper given at the Sixth Metropolis Conference, Rotterdam, www.transcomm.ox.ac.uk/working%20papers/WPTC-0201%20Anderson.doc.pdf.

Anderson, B. (2007) A very private business: exploring the demand for paid domestic workers, *European Journal of Women's Studies*, 14(3): 246–64.

Anderson, B., Ruhs, M., Regaly, B., and Spencer, S. (2006) *Fair Enough? Central and East European Migrants in Low-wage Employment in the UK*, www.compas.ox.ac.uk/changingstatus.

Anthias, F., and Lazaridis, G. (eds) (2000) *Gender and Migration in Southern Europe: Women on the Move*. Oxford and New York: Berg.

Bahna, M. (2005) Latentná ekonomika kultúrnej výmeny au pair, *Sociológia*, 37(5): 449–74.

Bahna, M. (2006) The au pair employers: who are they, whom do they search for and what do they await, *Slovak Sociological Review*, 38(3): 245–66.

Bakan, A. B., and Stasiulis, D. (1997) Introduction, in A. B. Bakan and D. Stasiulis (eds), *Not One of the Family: Foreign Domestic Workers in Canada*. Toronto: University of Toronto Press, pp. 3–27.

Basu, P., and Coleman, S. (2008) Migrant worlds, material cultures, *Mobilities*, 3(3): 313–30.

Bourdieu, P. (1977) *Outline of a Theory of Practice*. Cambridge: Cambridge University Press.

Bourdieu, P. (1999) *Distinction: A Social Critique of the Judgement of Taste*. London: Routledge.

Buchli, V. A. (2002) *The Material Culture Reader*. Oxford and New York: Berg.

Búriková, Z. (2006a) The embarrassment of co-presence: au pairs and their rooms, *Home Cultures*, 3(2): 1–24.

Búriková, Z. (2006b) Prečo majú britské matky au pair a čo sa na tom slovenským au pair nepáči, *Slovenský národopis*, 54(4): 341–56.

Burrell, K. (2008) Managing, learning and sending: the material lives and journeys of Polish women in Britain, *Journal of Material Culture*, 13(1): 63–83.

Chaney, E. M., and Castro, M. G. (eds) (1989) *Muchachas No More: Household Workers in Latin America and the Caribbean*. Philadelphia: Temple University Press.

Chin, C. B. N. (1998) *In Service and Servitude: Foreign Female Domestic Workers and the Malaysian 'Modernity' Project*. New York: Columbia University Press.

Clarke, N. (2005) Detailing transnational lives of the middle: British working holiday makers in Australia, *Journal of Ethnic and Migration Studies*, 31(2): 307–22.

Cock, J. (1980) *Maids and Madams: Domestic Workers under Apartheid*. London: Women's Press.

Colen, S. (1995) 'Like a mother to them': stratified reproduction and West Indian childcare workers and employers in New York, in F. D. Ginsburg and R. Rapp (eds), *Conceiving the New World Order: the Global Politics of Reproduction*. Berkeley and London: University of California Press.

Constable, N. (1997) *Maid to Order in Hong Kong: Stories of Filipina Workers*. Ithaca, NY, and London: Cornell University Press.

Constable, N. (2003) Filipina workers in Hong Kong homes: household rules and relations, in B. Ehrenreich and A. R. Hochschild (eds), *Global Woman: Nannies, Maids and Sex Workers in the New Economy*. London: Granta, pp. 115–41.

Council of Europe (1969) *European Agreement on Au Pair Placement*, Strasbourg, http://conventions.coe.int/treaty/en/Treaties/Html/068.htm.

Cox, R. (1999) The role of ethnicity in shaping the domestic employment sector in Britain, in J. Henshall Momsen (ed.), *Gender, Migration and Domestic Service*. London and New York: Routledge, pp. 134–47.

Cox, R. (2000) Exploring the growth of paid domestic labour: a case study of London, *Geography*, 85(3): 241–51.

Cox, R. (2006) *Servant Problem: Domestic Employment in a Global Economy*. London: I. B. Tauris.

Cox, R. (2007) The au pair body: sex object, sister or student? *European Journal of Women's Studies*, 14(3): 281–96.

Cox, R., and Narula, R. (2004) Playing happy families: rules and relationships in au pair employing households in London, England, *Gender, Place and Culture*, 10(4): 333–44.

Ehrenreich, B., and Hochschild, A. R. (eds) (2003) *Global Woman: Nannies, Maids and Sex Workers in the New Economy*. London: Granta.

Gregson, N., and Lowe, M., (1994), *Servicing the Middle Classes: Class, Gender and Waged Domestic Labour in Contemporary Britain*. London: Routledge.

Henshall Momsen, J. (ed.) (1999) Gender *Migration and Domestic Service*. London and New York: Routledge.

Hess, S. (2000) Au Pairs als informalisierte Hausarbeiterinnen: Flexibilisierung und Ethnisierung der Versorgungsarbeiten, in C. Gather et al. (eds), *Privathaushalt: bezahlte Haushaltsarbeit im globalen Wandel*. Münster: Westfälisches Dampfboot.

Hess, S. (2000–1) Au-pairstvo: migračná stratégia mladých žien zo Slovenska, *Aspekt*: 265–71.

Hess, S. (2003) *Transmigration of Eastern European Women as Transformation Strategy*, www.illegalisiert.at/migration/women_transmigration260403.htm.

Hess, S., and Puckhaber, A. (2004) 'Big sisters' are better domestic servants?! Comments on booming au pair as business, *Feminist Review*, 77: 65–78.

Hochschild, A. (2000) Global care chains and emotional surplus value, in W. Hutton and A. Giddens (eds), *On the Edge: Living with Global Capitalism*, London: Jonathan Cape, pp. 130–46.

Home Office (2009) *Points Based System Tier 5 (Youth Mobility Scheme) (INF 28)*, www.ukvisas.gov.uk/en/howtoapply/infs/inf28pbsyouthmobility.

Hondagneu-Sotelo, P. (2001) *Doméstica: Immigrant Workers Cleaning and Caring in the Shadows of Affluence*. Berkeley and London: University of California Press.

Isaksen, L., Devi, S., and Hochschild, A. (2008) Global care crisis: a problem of capital, care chain, or commons? *American Behavioral Scientist*, 52(3): 405–25.

Jenčová, I. (2007) Migrácia ako dobrodružstvo, *Slovenský Národopis*, 55(4): 457–63.

Keane, W. (1997) *Signs of Recognition: Powers and Hazards of Representation in an Indonesian Society*, Berkeley: University of California Press.

King, R. (2002) Towards a new map of European migration, *International Journal of Population Geography*, 8: 89–106.

King, R., and Ruiz-Gelices, E. (2003) International student migration and a European 'year abroad': effects on European identity and subsequent migration behavior, *International Journal of Population Geography*, 9: 229–52.

Kofman, E., Phizacklea, A., Raghuram, P., and Slaes, R. (2000) *Gender and International Migration in Europe: Employment, Welfare and Politics*, London and New York: Routledge.

Kuechler, S. (2002) *Malanggan: Art, Memory and Sacrifice*. Oxford: Berg.

Macdonald, C. L. (1998) Manufacturing motherhood: shadow work of nannies and au pairs, *Qualitative Sociology*, 21(1): 25–53.

McKay, D. (2007) 'Sending dollars shows feeling': emotions and economies in Filipino migration, *Mobilities* 2(2): 175–94.

Mehta, R., and Belk, R. W. (1991) Artefacts, identity and transition: favourite possessions of Indians and Indian immigrants to the United States, *Journal of Consumer Research*, 17, March: 398–411.

Mellini, L., Yodanis, C., and Godenzi, A. (2007) 'On par'? The role of the au pair in Switzerland and France, *European Societies*, 9(1): 45–64.

Miller, D. (ed.) (1998) *Material Cultures: Why Some Things Matter*. London: UCL Press.

Miller, D. (ed.) (2001) *Home Possessions: Material Culture behind Closed Doors*. Oxford and New York: Berg.

Miller, D. (2008) *The Comfort of Things*. Cambridge: Polity.

Osella, F., and Osella, C. (2000) Migration, money and masculinity in Kerala. *Journal of the Royal Anthropological Institute*, 6(1): 117–33.

Pappas-DeLuca, K. (1999) Transcending gendered boundaries: migration for domestic labour in Chile, in J. Henshall Momsen (ed.), *Gender, Migration and Domestic Service*. London and New York: Routledge, pp. 98–113.

Parkin, D. (1999) Mementoes as transitional objects in human displacement, *Journal of Material Culture*, 4(3): 303–20.

Parreñas, S. R. (2001) *Servants of Globalization: Women, Migration and domestic Work*. Stanford, CA: Stanford University Press.

Pratt, G. (1997) Stereotypes and ambivalence: the construction of domestic workers in Vancouver, British Columbia, *Gender, Place and Culture: A Journal of Feminist Geography*, 4(2): 159–78.

Rollins, J. (1985) *Between Women: Domestics and their Employers*. Philadelphia: Temple University Press.

Romero, M. (1992) *Maid in the U.S.A.* New York: Routledge.

Salzinger, L. (1991) A maid by any other name: the transformation of 'dirty work' by Central American immigrants, in M. Burawoy (ed.), *Ethnography Unbound: Power and Resistance in the Modern Metropolis*. Berkeley: University of California Press, pp. 139–60

Tilley, C. (1999) *Metaphor and Material Culture*. Oxford: Blackwell.

Tilley, C., Kuechler-Fogden, S., Keane, W., Rowlands, M., and Spyer, P. (eds) (2006) *Handbook of Material Culture*. London: Sage.

Williams, A. M., and Baláž, V. (2004) From private to public sphere: the commodification of the au pair experience? Returned migrants from Slovakia to the UK, *Environment and Planning A*, 36: 1813–33.

Yeates, N. (2004) Global care chains, *International Feminist Journal of Politics*, 6(3): 269–91.

Yeoh, B. S. A., and Huang, S. (1999) Singapore women and foreign domestic workers: negotiating domestic work and motherhood, in J. Henshall Momsen (ed.), *Gender, Migration and Domestic Service*. London and New York: Routledge, pp. 277–300.

Yodanis, C., and Lauer, S. R. (2005) Foreign visitor, exchange student or family member? A study of au pair policies in the United States, United Kingdom and Australia, *International Journal of Sociology and Social Policy*, 25(9): 41–64.

Zelizer, V. A. (2005) *The Purchase of Intimacy*. Princeton, NJ,: Princeton University Press.

INDEX